I first met Nicky at a place called something like the Plush Pup in a part of a corner lot in the San Fernando Valley. He was twenty years old then, frying hot dogs and hamburgers and dreaming big dreams, my friend Ed Taylor and I were 19 and in our sophomore years at Pomona College and also dreaming big dreams. We soon adopted one another. Nick came out to Pomona College and promptly snagged the most beautiful and gifted girl there and we shared wild and good times for the next three years. Now it's a mere sixty years later, Eddie has died as has the beautiful girl Nan, but Nicky and I are still sharing dreams. Nicky has written a memoir, much of it experienced before we met. It's been unique reading a stunning memoir by someone who had lived such a rich and varied life, which in many ways we shared years before we met...It's been a unique experience to read an unexpectedly gifted retelling of that life with memories of times and places which we had unknowingly shared.

Robert Towne,
Academy Award-Winning Screenwriter

Another Whole Afternoon

A Memoir by Nicolas Coster

First Edition Design Publishing
Sarasota, Florida USA

Another Whole Afternoon, A Memoir
Copyright ©2021 Nicolas Coster

ISBN 978-1506-910-23-9 HCJ
ISBN 978-1506-910-24-6 PBK
ISBN 978-1506-910-25-3 EBK

LCCN 2021900858

March 2021

Published and Distributed by
First Edition Design Publishing, Inc.
P.O. Box 17646, Sarasota, FL 34276-3217
www.firsteditiondesignpublishing.com

Cover Photo by Dinneen Photography

Introduction

To Ian

My son was a sun, now a somber memory of a mysterious moon lingering till dawn while puzzling a sleepless father.

My beloved Ian was all; bright, melancholy or wickedly humorous; very attentive, most supportive to friends and family. A mix of RuPaul and Oscar Wilde, with a splash of Florence Nightingale.

Nah, I can't write much about this gift right now. Too recent - his passing, three and some years ago. So close and far too much love of him still evident in everyday thoughts.

I must live with those warm and loving sentiments and try to get through the nights of waking up in near despair at the loss of the body which contained that wonderful soul.

Some of those sleepless nights have been spent writing *Another Whole Afternoon*.

I was nervous looking down the barrel of the writing gun. The formidable task ahead, the hours to be spent searching sometimes tattered memories, always with the knowledge that any semi-literate reader already had in their memory bank scores of historically valuable, trenchant, illuminating and quite often amusing biographies. Would I compare? SHOULD I compare? My father, the London film critic and columnist, Ian Coster was a fine writer, my mother, Martha Harris, though not published later in life, was a fine practitioner of the writing craft with a massive vocabulary at her disposal.

So much for all of that. I myself said early on, in a different context but equally apt here, "If you're gonna be an artist nothing will stop you. If you ain't, almost anything will." With that youthfully arrogant admonition scorchingly remembered, and with the pushing, nudging and indulgent encouragement from my wives, past and present, plus the most supportive members of my psychological group therapy gang a few years ago, who advised, "Just tell the story, Nicolas. You do it all the time!"...I finally took the plunge.

My witty father started his book, *Friends In Aspic* with the contrite plea, "Forgive me my friends, I had to pay the rent." I start mine with the simple hope that it retains interest, amuses from time to time and sheds some light on that worth seeing during my eight plus decades of experiences - the result of several crossings of great and smaller oceans and, of course, more than a few other whole afternoons.

Dear son, Ian, dear son, 1990-2016

CHAPTER 1

First Crossing

I have an image in my mind that is slightly over eighty years old.

The image is of an English harbor in the late afternoon, the end of summer, 1939. The very small cargo vessel glides past a rusty freighter lying at anchor in the outer harbor. One hears the gong of a buoy rocking in the slight swell. As we pass the cargo ship, a few of the crew wave to a small boy standing at the rail of the smaller ship below. I was that small boy, soon - in December - to be six years old, leaving his home and country, taken by his American mother, along with his older brother and younger sister, to the supposed safety of an American shore.

The ship I was on was the THYRA S. I never asked what the "S' stood for. It was, as I say, very small for a trans-Atlantic voyage, apparently the only passage available in that time of hurried exodus from Europe and England by all sorts of people who feared what was coming.

A small boy is not told a great deal about things like impending wars, or if he is told, he weaves the tale into a game, a fantasy, perhaps more to the most recent fairy tale read, or maybe, as in my case, to the story in a children's pantomime play in the London theatre - those familiar fairy tales like Peter Pan and Puss and Boots put to the stage - not really the same as grown up fears. One notices the worried looks, the hushed conversations between parents just before sailing.

Ian Coster, 38-year-old critic and journalist, did not come with us. Long after that I learned that he joined the Royal Marines and went off to war. We were told at the time that he had things to do, but would join us later. Never happened. He stayed on the dock. Did he wave or did he just stand on it fading from view as the ship pulled out? I don't remember.

Convenient thing, a child's memory. The sound of that deep clanging gong, the smell of diesel oil, the faces of the crew on that rusty ship waving as if the world was not about to come to an end for most cargo ships in the North Atlantic.

Just before embarking, an incident of kindness which I had almost forgotten. My brother, two years older than I, reminded me not long ago of this singular act: I had a stuffed animal, a monkey named "Ponkey", my security blanket, my best chum and practically the only personal belonging allowed to travel with me across the vast Atlantic. I was clutching Ponkey lightly whilst standing at the rail, and suddenly poor Ponkey slipped from my grasp! He spiraled down past the several decks into the black waters of the Liverpool harbor. Between the ship and dock, there he bobbed, kept afloat by his inner lifejacket of cotton and horsehair. My brother and others called out in protective dismay, and the Danish crew, rising to the call of duty, interrupted their docking procedures just long enough to rush with grappling hooks and sweep Ponkey from his watery peril and presented the soaking stuffed monkey - dear Ponkey - to this crying, grateful five-and-a-half-year-old. For years afterwards, the unique odor of Liverpool harbor clung to the then tattered but ever loved Ponkey.

My mother put upper body harnesses on my siblings and me. The harnesses were then attached to a piece of line that was tied to something fixed on deck. The reason we were told for this elaborate precaution was that on a previous voyage a child had been lost overboard, apparently having fallen through the space in the rails where the lifeboats were hanging.

Martha Harris Coster was going to have none of that. The length of movement from the tether point was limited to about six feet as I remember. Frustrating for a child who'd had the length of a lovely garden in Highgate in North London in which to wander, or Hampstead Heath with Nanny; my brother, sister and I rolling sideways down the green grass of the slopes on the Heath.

So there we children were: Confined by the leash and yet gazing out onto an endless sea.

The THYRA S. was a Danish ship with very few passengers and a small streamlined smoke stack or funnel as the English call it. A pretty and modern ship. Decades later, I was to travel in the same direction as the only passenger on another Scandinavian ship, a tanker the R.M.S. SUNNAAS. A story for another afternoon.

I have never been able to find out whether it was true or simply part of a childhood extension of the whole troublesome memory of war - the rumor or fact that the THYRA S. was torpedoed on the way back from our Canadian destination, war having started by that time.

In the drawing room of Hampton Lodge (even in-town houses in England sometimes have names), my mother and father entertained regularly. 'Salons', I later found they were called. The difference I gathered between a Salon and just plain old entertaining, was the intellectual level of the conversation, or the quality of music being played and or poetry spouted. Later, when living in a small house in California, "broke but not poor" as the legendary film producer Mike Todd called it, my mother would regale us with tales of those long-gone Salons.

Mother had gone from being a brash American newspaper woman to editing, in England, a highbrow magazine called *Nash's*, where she then hired the recently arrived New Zealander, Ian Coster, who went on to become a leading film critic and columnist in England.

In that modest house in California where we started the Western adventure part of this sort-of-biography, our mother would tell us of the stimulating talks she had with the likes of Robert Graves and others from the zippy literary, political, and social scene of thirties London, Paris and Berlin. Years later, when the freshness of the California landscape had, for her, lost all bloom and become a life so lonely and quietly desperate that just in saying, whispering the names of Lytton Strachey, Gertrude Stein and all the others she had known in the 20s and 30s, they then became symbols of us having survived. They, those people, had ACTUALLY existed in that exciting, stimulating world between the Wars, and my mother's sanity in what had by then become a ghastly and dreary routine of sixty-hour work weeks, depended on the validity of those memories.

Which leads to a bit of confusion in childhood-then-grownup memory: How much again is fact and how much is the memory of my mother's vivid retelling of incidents?

I do remember this...In England, we children used to slide down the side stairs on our eiderdowns (from the feathers of an "eider"? or whatever that bird was!), quilts as they are called now, from our third-floor bedroom to just beside the second-floor drawing room. Sometimes nanny would catch us, sometimes not.

Some of the overheard talk: Particularly vivid is the memory of a German guy, a friend of my parents, telling them of his being a machine gunner in the Great War and seeing the Americans throw wave after wave of inexperienced young men against the impossible odds of his and others' rapid-fire weapons. The first widespread use of this awful "machine gun". He told of how his gun barrel would get red hot and warped under the heavy use. He had to turn and scream for a replacement weapon before being overrun by this naïve horde.

In 1982, while in London, acting in *The Little Foxes*, a play by Lillian Hellman, I returned to Hampton Lodge with Elizabeth Taylor, our star. Elizabeth and I had both gone to the same prep school, Byron House, (formerly Lord Byron's) which was next door to our Hampton Lodge house in Highgate, North London.

We first made a stop at Byron House, which by then had been returned to private ownership, and had tea with a delightful American woman whose son had written the movie *Elephant Man*. My former house was next. An elegant, tall, blonde young man with an aristocratic accent said when confronted by us, "Oh, I'll get Mummy." He got Mummy. Mummy was also tall and blonde and without blinking said, "Oh, do come in." I told her that I had lived in the house until almost six. We looked around a bit and after entering the dining room, I looked behind the door to the kitchen and exclaimed, "Oh, the stairs aren't there anymore!" On seeing the quizzical look on the face of Madame D'elegance, I explained how they were the very stairs upon which we slid on our blankets and eiderdowns to overhear the goings-on in the drawing room, and from there on down to the kitchen where cook could sneak us a treat. The superbly preserved blonde, without a trace of astonishment said, "Oh, you really did live here." To which I replied, with the best of my remembered British wryness, "Didn't you believe me?" She answered with a sly, discreet smile whilst glancing toward Elizabeth, "It didn't really matter, did it?"

I think the first time one starts to become glib in one's life is when one has to deal with too many people, to seek approval from too many people at too young an age. In my case it was my attempts to sway at least three remembered nannies by the time I was five. Strange relationship, nannies, and children.

My two favorites were Rosa, an Austrian and Sarah, an Irish woman. Rosa played the flute to us when it was bedtime. What a treat. She had dark hair and an enveloping kindness about her.

Then there was a German woman who was also nice to us. We heard she was fired because mother found maps of London in her room and suspected her of being a German spy. True? I dunno. Mummy had witnessed the Storm Troopers in Berlin in the early thirties on many trips there and told us how she had been pushed off the sidewalk by the Brown-Shirts. She also had an active imagination, but when there are rumors of the Nazis being capable of anything, one cannot be too careful. can one? Or was it the fact that my mother believed this woman would, for convenience, put us to sleep, even when we were not tired, by getting us to breathe a little natural gas! Yes! I don't know if that was true or not. I vaguely remember the smell of gas from that period. I don't think it was a leaky stove.

The next was the Irish, ginger haired, Sarah. She used to give us tea and tell lovely Irish horror stories to us. One of these stories was about an old fisherman who takes a young girl to the river, loves her desperately, and with no return of that declared affection, drowns her and then uses her hair for strings and her bones for the lute-like instrument upon which he then plays doleful songs that echo down the river valley.

I think it was the giving us tea that got her fired. Even then in the late thirties among the savvy set, it was known that caffeine was harmful to children. Only later did mummy find out about the dreadful stories. My brother, sister and I loved the flute and loved the stories. We, at least I, became perhaps too fond of both Rosa and Sarah.

My brother, Ian, is two years older and my Sister Georgiana, two and a half years younger than I. Both have age-perspective and of course gene-leaning memories of the same incidents.

Except for Mrs. Woods.

My sister does not remember and my brother was not there at the presentation of evidence of Mrs. Woods boxing my ears! Yes. The clenching of fists and then the pounding with those fists around and on the ears of the (in this case) child. Corporal punishment was widespread among even the well informed in that day. My mother being no exception. A slap upside the head, as it came to be known, was quite acceptable. However, mummy did not believe me when I regaled her, quite dramatically, with the tale of Mrs. Woods' primitive punishment.

One of the summer places we all loved was La Touquet on the French Coast. My first soda pop was served me in the bar at the small hotel. It was Grenadine and soda water. The rich and bright red hue of the Grenadine syrup was a gorgeous color with which to compete with our parent's deep red and mysterious smelling wine. A wonderful French taste for a small boy. I loved sitting at the bar and being sophisticated, but it was on the dunes of this lovely French resort I got my revenge on dear old Mrs. Woods.

The scene was Mrs. Woods and I alone on the dunes. I am sure I did something provocative, I shall give Mrs. W. that much, but she did, in fact, box my ears. Very painful. My mother, who had followed behind, but not far enough behind for Mrs. Woods' sake, witnessed the incident. From her reaction I knew at that moment what a seething, protective lion a mother is capable of becoming, especially when the guilt of not having believed her darling and now proven innocent son adds to the adrenaline. Ah, the sight of my not very tall Mother running, if one can call a short-legged raging woman plowing through the up-to-the-knee sand dunes, running, then landing atop Mrs. Woods and bashing her.

Mrs. Woods was then, in mummy's most imperious terms, fired, sent-a-packing back to England.

I don't wear sandals because of another summer incident when I was about three or four.

A different summer. We were in a Sea Coast town on the English side of the channel, Frinton. We were roaming in a beautiful pasture crawling with dairy cows. Whilst skipping along in this pasture I plunged my sandaled foot into the largest, moist cow-pie I had ever seen. It is still, of course, the largest. Up to the ankle oozed the bovine detritus, through every separation of toe and toe. encasing my entire foot. I have never worn sandals since.

Later, in 1939, I had no idea as to why, I got to sit on Gene Autry's horse, Champion, in the lobby of the Savoy Hotel with flash bulbs popping all around. Not fiction. Gene Autry, the most famous cowboy star in the world! In the pictures my sister saved, there it is! I recently showed that photo to an acquaintance of mine, Arnold Schwartzman, O.B.E, whose father was head waiter at the Savoy at the time. He was astonished. It is fun to see on another's face the tracings of long-gone-by memories coming so alive again!

There are no pics, however, of our celebrity newspaperman father taking us to the London Fire Brigade, with all the giant red machines of mercy and the pictorial history on the walls of the Great Fire of London. Now THAT was a treat. Dad knew everybody, which again seemed quite natural. Why wouldn't such a man as he knows everybody from grizzled Captains of museum-like sailing ships anchored in the Thames to engine drivers on the fastest train of its day, The Royal Scot. Privileged kids? NO! Not possible. The thought never occurred. I did notice that not all the kids down Highgate Hill had on silk shirts and velvet trousers. But so what?

On one occasion, the beginning of many attempts to run away from home over the next decade or so - until ultimately successful - I was stopped almost at the beginning of my odyssey by a very large London bobby who courteously suggested he take my hand and lead me home. That British wanderlust was in my bones as surely as Francis Drake's and Captain Cook's. (One does enlarge the scope of a three city-block adventure when one is five years old.) Was it parental abandonment (so many nannies!) or just simply British blood that compelled me to leave whatever little island I was in or on and strike out for faraway lands.

In my mind and by observation, things were happening out there that were worlds beyond the limited adventures of Byron House School and Hampton Lodge. The bobby fed me an ice cream and extracted from me the promise that I would not repeat the touring event. I kept that promise until three years later in America.

On the deck of the THYRA S. I thought of England and of all these things, but I was not yet actually missing anything. We had all been told that even if there were to be a war, (it was to start in two weeks), it would be over very quickly; nothing like the Great War.

I don't remember missing my father at first, but then both mother and father had been away in Europe and elsewhere so much, it was not unusual to have one or both gone for short lengths of time. I did miss Veronica; my first great love. I remembered this beautiful blonde girl with ringlets shoulder length at a birthday party of mine, and also remembered thinking something prematurely romantic for a five-year-old. Recently my sister found some old pictures from that period and there she was: Veronica, lovely, with golden ringlets, just as recalled.

Why? Why, you well might well ask, am I so absorbed in such infinite details from a life from so long ago? Perhaps to trace the formation of what became a lifestyle both corrupted and honorable? The stunted, then only periodic growth of moral importance. The plaguing temptation towards "corruption", perhaps began back in that house in Highgate when, on one of my "listening times" on that staircase to the rear of the drawing room, I overheard my mother and father discussing me.

I cannot remember the context, but I do remember the shock at hearing them blithely condemn me with the phrase - agreed to by both, "well, he doesn't have a good character, does he?" Can you imagine a child hearing such a sentence? The stab-wound-hurt of that notion? I remember being puzzled as to how they had arrived at such a diagnosis. Did I, in fact, for years to come, in defiance, set out to prove they were right? Possibly. Probably.

At sea on our way to America, the small ship tossed and rolled. More than once I looked at that gap between the rails by the lifeboats and got frightfully sad thinking of the poor child who had fallen, perhaps with a similar roll of the ship, over to the froth and dark cold depths below.

I have loved diesel smell ever since that voyage. I got very attached to the THYRA S. and her crew. Most tough guys seem to be nice to little kids. I grew to love the sea and the men who were responsible for my safe journey.

Some people find diesel smell disgusting. I associate it with all that is good about reliability, conjoined with adventure. Diesel smoke represented fairly quiet propulsion, which one could be almost sure would get one across that vast ocean. Coal smoke is another matter. Well into the twentieth century, ships ran on coal fired steam. I smelled such smoke at the railway stations.

Lots of people found that smell romantic; whether it was an English worker seeing mum off to the North, or in my case, later on, when a newly-American country boy sat on a Chatsworth hillside in California and listened to the drawn-out sound of the freight train whistle from the valley below; a sound less gleeful than the European trains; a different pitch, a deeper and more mournful extended vowel. Seeing and smelling the long trail of smoke from a steam engine roaring across the vast American countryside became more appealing to me eventually.

Other than that, the smell of coal I recall and associate very vividly with the great fogs in the early fifties in which so many died in London. I recalled it because I got bronchial pneumonia when I returned to England and might have joined the rest of those poor dead souls - there were thousands - had it not been for the benefits of excellent, by then socialized medicine and, of course, the gifts of youthful body, blood, and spirit.

CHAPTER 2

Finding Dad

As I have said, we left dad at the dock in Liverpool in September, 1939. I was not to see him again until the fall of 1950, when I returned to England. I shall skip the intervening years for a moment or two.

When one does not see one's father for eleven years, from five to almost seventeen, one has no idea what to make of him upon re-meeting him. During the war, while in America, I had made up substitute fathers, from movie stars like Joel McRae to Bob Stephens, the ranch manager of the Kentucky Ranch in Paso Robles, California, owned by the American director Tay Garnett, another pre-war buddy of my dad's, where I visited as a small boy and worked as a ranch hand when I was a teenager.

Joel McRae was on celluloid, so he didn't quite fit the bill, but WHAT an image! A man of character (in most films) and substance. The ranch manager, Bob Stephens, even looked like McCrae, and was a man of apparent strength and a patient teacher of riding, cutting cattle (one separates them by riding in between and steering them along), side-arms, hunting rifle, digging fence-post-holes, and harvesting grain. He had also served as a Naval pilot off the first ever aircraft carrier the Langley, just after WW-1. What a model man!

Huge clouds of barley dust blew from the giant harvester, then came lifting heavy sacks of grain from the newly shorn field and heaving them onto a two-and-a-half-ton truck. The sacks weighed almost as much as my thin but strengthening frame...the life of a cowboy.

In the summer of 1950, we would sometimes take a break from the eighteen-hour days; drive 40 miles over the rolling, summer bleached hills to pry abalones off the rocks at low tide in Morro Bay on what was then a clean and almost deserted California Coast. Abalone, a shellfish, larger than most, varies in length from 4 to 9 inches; the inner shell becomes the decorative, "mother of pearl" found in costume jewelry. Fresh from its Pacific Ocean home, it is to me, the single, most glorious flavor imaginable; delicate, thinly sliced, lightly cooked in just butter and lemon juice, certainly the finest fragment in the mosaic of my seafood memories.

Manly days they were. Incredibly necessary for a boy with no consistent male pilot on the journey to manhood.

I remember…In the early dawn mist appeared the "6 point buck" (a superb rack of antlers with six prongs on them). He loomed on a slight rise not 100 feet away, clear and inviting, from my hushed path. I had learned to track silently from my mentor who seemed to know everything of the woods and cattle. He had taught me to use the 30.06 rifle with a scope sight. I raised the sleek dark wood and metal machine for the kill, placing the left side of the deer just behind the shoulder in the cross hairs of the sight, and then paused, paused too long. The magnificent animal turned his head and saw a reflection or smelled my scent, the scent of adrenaline and anticipation perhaps, and in one enormous leap - for an instant defiantly towards me - he was in the air. He then veered and vanished into the protective woods.

My pause was not from fear, but shamefully, or fortuitously, I saw before me a momentary vision of the great father deer in the film, *Bambi*. One simply did not kill Bambi's father. I walked slowly back to my jeep, loaded the rifle aboard and never killed another mammal…until years later. Ah, but that is another afternoon, an entire evening perhaps and then some.

When I later returned to England in the fall of 1950, I got very ill and needed medicine. I managed to make it to a pharmacy and when presented with my father's check for the prescription, the chemist looked at the check and then at me and said," Is this IAN Coster, the newspaperman?" And I said "Yes it is."

The chemist then handed the check back to me and said, with an emotion filled voice, "This man, your father, in the late thirties wrote a piece about religions. He didn't do it like some professor, He interviewed workers and small merchants, the regular people. I'm Jewish and I can tell you he did more for a better understanding of my religion than anybody ever had in an English periodical. Please convey to him, my fondest regards and thank him…"

I stood there, as a sixteen-year-old and choked up, watching, and hearing this mild little guy speak of Ian Coster. There was a lot more to find out about this man who had become a stranger to me during those eleven years.

My mother loved the sun and the ocean. She had a cute figure and on deck of the THYRA S. wore a bathing suit of the period which was a sort of light brown and cream tiger-striped two-piece get-up of short-shorts and a halter top. She would lie there on the deck in the sun with the very few other passengers passing by.

Who was this woman, the protective mother, escaping the war, returning to America with her brood? I do not know to this day many details of her mysterious life. I say mysterious because despite knowing certain elements of her earlier life, others remain unknown to me and my siblings to this day.

We DO know she was the first young woman of her Southern family to be sent away to school since the civil war. The reconstruction period was, as replayed in *Gone With The Wind*, difficult and indeed threadbare.

There were five Pierce sisters in the mid 1800's. Their father was a doctor who died just after the end of the civil war, "The war between the States", as my family preferred to call it. My grandmother, Ethel, was the eldest. It was said that towards the end of that war, the Union Cavalry rode up to the house and were going to burn it, but my great grandfather, Dr. Pierce, met the Union commander out front and it is said that each found the other to be a 32nd degree Mason. After secret communications apparently known only to Masons at the time, perhaps still, the cavalry officer saluted and with his troop, turned and left. Dr. Pierce died soon after.

My grandmother and her sisters somehow survived. Probably because she was the eldest, she ran things for the family and married late for that period. My mother was born when Ethel Harris was 33, in 1898 and I was born in late 1933. In two generations, we go back to 1865!

Eppy, we called my grandmother, started serious air travel at 90 years of age. Before that, the rails bore her West to visit. When asked why she had switched to the then riskier mode of travel in gasoline driven airplanes, she said with quiet glee, "Oh, those adorable, dear stewardesses took such good care of me and, of course, one does not have to navigate to the dining car commencing through those perilous steel doors and the drafty spaces in between!"

Probably my greatest influence toward the theatre was Eppy regaling me stories in her soft Southern accent of seeing the great actor Joseph Jefferson, who had played Rip Van Winkle for over thirty years, apparently never tiring. I cannot remember whether Eppy actually saw Edwin Booth, but her stories about him were inspiring, so perhaps she did or perhaps her sisters did, or perhaps she just read about him, having lived during his greatest years.

The point is, she impressed this young kid in the Chatsworth hills. I started "hankerin", as the cowboys called it, to go to the Royal Academy of Dramatic Art (RADA) in London.

The THYRA S. was, as I have said, very small for a cargo ship. I was once told that the difference between a boat and a ship is that a boat goes on a ship, the opposite being impossible. Seemed simple enough. We were on a ship, small as it was. Fortunately, that fateful September in 1939 was, for us at least, full of fairly calm seas and lots of sun. If there were periscopes jutting through the ocean surface waiting for the time to kill, we were oblivious. The time had not yet come.

When we awoke in Halifax Nova Scotia, on the Bay of Fundy, the boat was almost on its side. The only things keeping it fairly upright were the great thick dock lines. stronger than the lines at Liverpool, in faraway England. The Bay of Fundy has the largest tidal drop in the world; some fifty feet of change every twelve hours; what had been the sea was now only mud. Only mud for miles. The tide was out.

My first glimpse of North America. Astonishing.

From there we were quickly hustled to a silver fox farm in the country outside of Halifax. Like diesel, the smell of apple cider and the taste of fresh water out of a rain barrel will always be with me. The farm had both. It also supplied the faraway well-to-do with fox coats and oh, the stoles, replete with implanted glass eyes encircling the necks and shoulders of those who could afford them. We spent two weeks in Canada. As we left for California via New York, the Second World War exploded into being.

CHAPTER 3

Country Life and Country Matters

Eagle Mountain Road, Chatsworth, California is in a little cul-de-sac hemmed by sandstone hills. Those hills have been used as a backdrop for countless Western movies, mostly low budget, over the decades since movies began. They, the hills, are dry, dusty and most of the year a golden wheat-like plant seems to dominate the hillsides. A dry wind blows most days, broken in the winter by rains which form rushing brown streams, which then find their way down the canyons, and then quite often into the houses that stand in the paths.

Around the end of the War (WW-2), Ma bought a little house on Eagle Mountain Road. The sandrock hills hovered over the narrow canyon road which, when visited just some few months ago, was still only partially paved. Deep rain-caused furrows plague the journey in a modern low-slung car. I imagine that must have been the reason for the Model T Ford being so high off the ground...unpaved roads.

From Eagle Mountain Road, it was a four-mile trek to school. They had school buses, but if you missed the bus coming or going, you walked that distance. I missed it often, being on the cross-country team in autumn, and the track team in springtime. It was a pleasant walk, even for a teenage boy, past orange groves, watermelon, and tomato fields, all of which morphed in the late 50s and 60s into rows of look-alike but needed housing.

Until the actual end of the war, Italian and then German Prisoners of War harvested the citrus fruit from the productive trees. The Italians were incredibly friendly to this gangly boy strolling home through the orange groves, whilst usually munching on a juicy California orange; bright oranges could be had except where the POWs were working. The Italians would call out to the kids! "Hey bambinos!" and other stuff we didn't understand and they would laugh. I suppose they had reason to laugh. The war had been over for Italy since before the fall of Mussolini, they were paid for their labor per the Geneva convention rules. Many of them saved the fifty cents a day or whatever it was and came back to the U.S. after the war, blended in and became part of the American tapestry. The Germans were generally more formal than their Italian counterparts and rarely spoke to us.

Not for political reasons, but just because of overcrowding, a few of us from Canoga Park Elementary school were sent by bus to the Eaton Avenue School. Eaton was a Mexican-American school. At that time in the Valley and indeed in our entire city, there was de-facto segregation. The Mexican as well as the African American was treated with less than dignity, to say nothing of the Japanese American. Yes, I too had a friend who was carted off in early 1942 to a Japanese internment camp. Years later we met again at high school. Bitterness had taken its toll on what had been the bright, friendly face of a 7-year-old boy.

From Eaton, I learned about my Latino brethren. I learned every Spanish swear word extant. That was a must. I ate the food and dreamed about the girls. I also relished the stories of Zapata and Pancho Villa. When we got to Canoga Park High School, we defended each other, mostly with fists, but occasionally with the mind and the gift of gab, a quality which was to lift me eventually from what at one time promised to be a shady life of petty crime.

I was, I know, influenced by my Brit-in-America experiences as a small boy. The feelings of being different and alone in a flood of tongues of Americana, not Britannia. I felt a kinship with my brown skinned brothers who spoke Spanish at home with their parents and grandparents, but at that time were so intimidated that they would not even refer to themselves as Mexican; they would say, "I'm Spanish". Was this then, the beginnings of my socially aware character? I suspect so.

My mother, I realized much later, was a fantastic teacher. Her apparent ambivalence about religion had no influence on her widely flung opinions. The dialogue around the table was always a debate. Some of that influence was not good. The patronizing element I developed, which has taken me years of therapy to get rid of, included a certain competitiveness which often spoiled the genuine enjoyment of exchanging ideas. Years later, I had a girlfriend in Washington D.C., a brilliant young lawyer, who, when only in her twenties, had argued before the Supreme Court. She said, in the midst of what became a heated debate instead of a conversation, "Do you always have to do that?" "What?" I asked. "Win?" It was asked quietly but tellingly.

Ma, as we called her, trying to be American (the British "Mummy" was unacceptable at Carpenter Avenue grammar school in Studio City California, my second school in America, my first being in Tampa Florida with grandparents), taught us everything, from ironing one's own trousers to sewing on a button. We had seen a movie, *The Yearling*, a movie with Gregory Peck and Claude Jarman, Jr. as his young son. The Jarman character called his mother "Ma" and it was amusing enough to my mother to be referred to forever after in that 19th century rural twang as "Ma".

Our English accents, too, disappeared and morphed into the then California accent, which was a combination of Arkansas and West Texas, with a touch of Kansas, begot from all the depression era migrants who ended up as far West as their broken-down jalopies would take them. These dialects blended with those others formed since the gold rush of the 1850s.

One more bitter-sweet memory is of walking home from Carpenter Avenue school and being attacked by an older boy for, being a "little Limey fucking bastard" (obviously his parents were either German or Irish). I was really getting the shit kicked outta me when my brother with whom, at that age, I had little in common, raced up unexpectedly, grabbed the guy, tore him off me and pounded him enough for a lesson to be learned: Never beat up a younger kid without first looking around for an older brother.

California in the early 1940s, before an even greater migration in search of defense jobs, was rural in both dialect and attitude. The traveled rich who lived in the citadels of Hancock Park and Pasadena, spoke, for the most part, with a western equivalent of the "Lahhchmont" Eastern dialect, but the rest were more working class, what is now called middle class. The middle class now, when politicians talk of it, are those who owe money on their houses, drive SUVs with chrome wheels and have a boat in the driveway. To me, they are now the untalked of working class who got a few things they had always wanted.

During the Second World War, I saw the defense workers gradually acquire "things". After the war, quite understandably, the hands that had made the B-17 bombers, Flying Fortresses, along with the few brave souls left who had flown them, demanded better conditions. The unions grew stronger. Returning vets would not stand for pre-war working conditions. Still, some of these conditions existed in factories well into the 50s.

In my house, led by a mother who worked endless hours as a story analyst at Republic Studios in the 40s, 50s and into the 60s, there was always stimulating conversation.

In late 1940, she got that job at Republic Studios in what is now CBS Studios in the San Fernando Valley, where we rented a house next to the Los Angeles River. There were no sterile cement banks as there are now, but swim-deep pools and sandy banks strewn with knee deep patches of watercress, which my brother and I harvested. The biggest thrill was chasing down the scurrying crayfish, a fresh water shrimp like shellfish, which then made their way to our dinner table. A delight not lost on Ma, who had grown up in the South eating crawdaddies, as they called them.

The river was fresh and vital and scenic, except when it flooded; and when it flooded, as it did the winters of 1939 and 1940, great chunks of river banks broke off, sometimes taking riverfront houses with the mass of mud and rocks that became part of the destruction, the erosion. This led eventually to the huge cement banks/walls being built. Now, decades later, groups of dedicated nature lovers are restoring the long-time polluted river. Lovely green patches are cropping up again, beginning to cover the angular bunker-like cement walls and everybody gains.

The beginnings of my juvenile delinquency - "JDs", that's what they used to quaintly call naughty, misbehaving boys - all probably started in the days when my brother and I would wade across the L.A. River and sneak up the opposite bank into the backlot at Republic Studios. No fence, no regular "security" as everybody now has. The Curtis P40 airplane life-size mockups, which had been used in the John Wayne movie *Flying Tigers*, were there for small boys to climb in and sit with imaginations roaring into flight in search of the dreaded "Japs", who threatened our shores.

There was that, and then also exploring the vast array of cardboard and paper mâché tunnels used primarily for the Saturday afternoon cowboy serials so popular in the days before TV. There was no fiberglass at the time, so paper mâché ruled as a material for producing false rocks and granite walls. When the occasional studio guard would wander around, we would hide in the ore cars which were used in mine scenes.

The biggest prank executed (not by my brother and me, but a couple of real delinquents) was taking a wooden coffin replete with a life size doll, which they laboriously hauled down to the river banks and watched in anticipation as it floated down the river, a mysterious lost, false corpse to be found by whom? A child swimmer? A worried mom who would shriek with terror? We never knew.

The job Ma had at Republic was a sizable fall from the prominence of her pre-war success as a London publisher and display artist, the latter of which professions took her from designing the windows of Selfridges, Simpsons, Harrods and Jaegers, all the way to a Bronze Medal for design of the British Pavilion at the Paris Exposition of 1937. We still have that bronze medal. A German named Albert Speer won the gold.

Yes, all that to the lowly position of "Reader" as they called Story Analysts before there was a guild, all because my father, the film critic, had been nice to Gene Autry back in the day when he was under contract to Republic Studios. The job for my mother was not all frustrating despite the long hours. The big boss, a strange and distant man, Herbert Yates, had, as many Hollywood moguls of the time, worked himself up from selling newspapers or something to be the head of a studio. He prized good minds including Ma's. People loved reading and then discussing her synopses of screenplays. Wonderful writers like Daniel Tarradash and Orson Welles, along with directors such as Fritz Lang, Alan Dwann and John Ford all wandered through Republic at the time, but left, unfortunately, for greater fame. They used to say "you start at Republic, but don't end up there!"

At some point I became a mildly talented musician. I had learned to play the trombone one semester after starting in the band as a drummer. The trombone became my only love for several years. My mother had bought it for me from a used instrument shop. It was an Olds, at that time the premier brass instrument. It was an original Olds, made by the old man himself. It had an enormous bell of gold with a silver rim with a magical tone, which only a boob could destroy. I became known for that tone, if not my technique. Ma provided music lessons (Lord knows with what funding). I went on the red trolley car all the way to South Central L.A to study in an all-black music school, the Hightower School of Music. My mother, when she realized how much I loved the trombone, inquired in the music department of Republic Studios as to where a budding jazz man should study.

The Hightower School Of Music was at 40th and Avalon. I was the only white student. I was a curiosity, but never made to feel uncomfortable. Mrs Hightower, a distinguished, graceful lady of indeterminate older age, was soft spoken in a lilting Southern accent with very clear consonants and melodious vowels. Her favorite admonition was, "You got to learn the chords, honey." I flourished for a while. The "bad" boy would stand practicing on the side of the hill in our cul-de-sac and with the melodies of Tommy Dorsey, and great songs from the twenties and thirties like *Deep Purple*, *Stardust* and *Getting Sentimental*, I would entertain the neighbors with my music floating down the canyon below. Two lesbians who lived down to the right of us, were very cultured (they loved me, so, of course, they were!), would stop, while they were gardening to listen and then applaud.

My mother, still the liberal, adored them. Ma had read Radcliffe Hall's, *Well of Loneliness* in her youth and actually knew Djuna Barnes, so she was not of the closed-minded anti-gay population of the time.

Born into a family of Southern aristocrats, Ma had many of the best qualities of her class, with few of its faults. She was not anti-black. Her cold, thin-lipped father was another sort. A Klansman into at least the 20s? I never found out for sure. He was the descendant of Henry Harris who, it is told, had been granted land in Virginia in 1681. The most famous of grandfather's ancestors was Isham G. Harris, the Governor of Tennessee during the Civil War. He was, I believe, the only Southern leader granted a pardon after that war, subsequently serving as a United States Senator until his death some 25 years later. The Harris coat of arms is a strange assortment of a colorful shield surrounded by wild boars and the like. I had a copy sent to me long ago.

With that aristocratic background being constantly thrown at me as a child, I'm sure it, as well as the pre-war life in London, influenced my subsequent desire to re-create the life which had gone with it. Unfortunately, it also bent one's behavior toward "puttin' on airs" as southerners said of affectation when one had little money or grand property to show for it. Fortunately, that history did not influence my passionate feelings about civil rights.

Ma's family were Baptists and Methodists, anti-Catholic, but no religion imposed on her as a child seemed to have had much influence on her as a teenager...other than turning her into an agnostic, hell raising liberal. However, Adelaide Cormack, widow of dad's chum and well-known pre-war screenwriter, Bartlett Cormack, became my Godmother. She took great care in seeing to our early introduction to the sweet-smelling mysteries of the Episcopal All Saints Church in Beverly Hills. I suspect it was also to remind us that along with religion and its moral teachings, came contacts in the fur draped circles of Beverly Hills society.

One of Ma's great early influences was her regaling my brother and I with her memories of the Cincinnati Symphony Orchestra from her youth.

Radio in the 1940s was full of fine music; Heifetz, Kreisler and Stern were the most well-known violinists of the time. Nights were spent listening to Toscanini conduct the NBC Symphony Orchestra. *Concerti* they used to call them. Symphonies and sonatas filled the small living rooms and large concert halls across the nation. I was almost umbilically attached to all of it.

The Metropolitan Opera was broadcast way back then. Jussi Bjerling, one of the all-time great tenors, was a hugely popular radio singer, known to millions. My brother told me years later when I marveled at his becoming an opera devotee, that I had learned the plots and most of the music from dozens of operas...I had forgotten that affection.

Somewhere during that time, this small, skinny boy took a real interest in the tenor and light baritone sounds of the violin. The sometimes strident but more often smooth and soothing sounds of horsehair bows stroking cat gut strings intrigued me.

The outset of my mother supporting my artistic bent was quickly evident.

Where and how she found Adolf Rabner I'm not sure. He lived in a little apartment off North La Brea in Hollywood, a new guest of a fellow named Steiner, who was a chess columnist for The L.A. Times. He taught their son, Armand, to play the violin. This kindly family had taken in the newly escaped Jewish musician and befriended him. I took the trolley car and red bus down to their very nice two-story Spanish style home and made my way to the guest apartment in the rear.

Adolf Rebner had silver hair, was wiry and gentle. For me, the Nazi atrocities were first heard from his carefully chosen Austrian accented words and sighs. Never self-pitying, but obviously missing the family and life of pre-war Germany and Vienna. He had, in his youth, been a member of the Brahms Quartet in 1898! He knew great composers like Hindemith.

And so, it started. I did learn quickly. He informed my mother that perhaps I could go on to be a concert violinist. I practiced. I played little minuets at home for my family. A budding real violinist was emerging...and then concentration drifted. I'm not sure what happened. Interest in girls at an early age? I was almost 10 years old in 1944. Emotional turmoil at home? The war years, loneliness, over worked and financial stress were all affecting Ma. More than once in a late afternoon, she'd come home and find me NOT in my room practicing the violin, but out playing with pretty Charlene who lived down the street, or reading a comic book in our backyard.

Fed up and frustrated, and of course revealing the sacrifice it took to provide me with Herr Rabner's lessons, she cancelled them. Devastated. I, however, was too proud to admit my juvenile lapse. I was also much too proud to admit that the loss of those lessons was a stomach twisting one which I did not get over,

Some few years later, before my re-emergence in high school onto the musical scene, I developed a nervous "tick"; my neck on the left side would contract involuntarily, causing my chin to drop slightly to the left. That went on for years and actually increased noticeably.

Finally, as even others noticed it, ma, suspecting a vitamin shortage or thyroid condition, took me to the family doctor whose name eludes me now. A very kind and soft-spoken fellow. After examining me, he talked of his newly acquired background in psychology. He asked me what I might be holding in or feeling badly about, perhaps, even guiltily of. I eventually admitted to feeling dreadful about my violin lessons having been stopped, aware of the paradox of understanding my mother's reluctance to continue, but anger at her for stopping them.

And so, it went. Several sessions later, He suddenly asked me how I held the violin. I showed how one prepares the handkerchief on the chin rest or plate and then how one cocks their head to the left, chin down on that plate. Almost together from the good doctor and me came the gasp followed by, "Ah!"

The "tick", the nervous display of the loss of the most creative feelings I had ever had and regret for the misunderstanding, was revealed then and there to both of us. He said, "This is a developed nervous habit. My suggestion is to treat the lingering feelings of guilt with this formula: BE creative. Find another source. Follow it. Work at it and my guess is that this tick will diminish." It did.

I soon took up first drums in the school band. I got pretty good at it, then came the trombone. I absolutely adored the sound of that horn. The gift of playing it also, like the violin, depended on your ear and fingers FINDING the right place to place the slide for pitch. There were no valves or frets like a guitar for pinpointing the notes...only your ear and memory.

A footnote: The tick returned briefly in later years when I was involved too long or had capitulated by joining a mediocre non-artistic venture. I would then, with that alarm quite clearly felt, quickly shift to something more purely creative. The warning alarm disappeared. To this day, I always try to be a part of something creative, occasionally with some degree of satisfaction.

***

My first experience with attempted suicide came during that period. Halfway down the hillside from us was another house, just above the two adoring women fans. I was walking up the dirt road to my house when I heard agonized moaning among the golden wild wheat of the hillside, just above the road. I crawled up the bank and found the writhing body of a neighbor I barely knew. She was of fading looks, henna dyed hair, overdrawn "stop red" lips... a former beauty who led a desperately lonely life.

I was strong even at 15 from my ranch hand work and hauled her up to her house. There, I found an empty iodine bottle on the floor. I then went quickly and made some soapy water in the kitchen and poured it into her mouth. Gasping for breath with much gurgling, she spat up nasty brown liquid. I called the police and they came and took her away.

The depressing end to that story was that when her husband returned home somewhat later, I was cleaning up and the only remark he made was what an idiot I was for leaving the coffee pot to burn up on the stove. Nothing about the well or ill-being of his wife. One did not have to wonder what might have, at least in part, contributed to the attempted suicide.

L.A. in those days was closed to other progressive thought as well. Joseph McCarthy was rampant on the American political scene. Canoga Park, it's faculty and students were heavily influenced by the times.

One of my Mexican American buddies came to me bleeding from the nose and mouth. He said that he had been razzing the student body president, who was a phony; that the student body president had paid another kid five bucks to beat him up. I went marching into the principal's office and demanded that the student body president answer to these charges. I was told by that principal, a known right winger, that I was a "troublemaker" and to get out.

I defended my inquiry, appealing for justice with some degree of articulateness apparently, because listening at the door to the outer office was the public speaking teacher. She called to me as I was leaving and said, "I think we should use that big mouth of yours to do some good."

And with that I joined her class and entered a Lion's Club speech contest. I won the school competition, the Valley region, and went to the Southern California finals. By the time my turn came up, the audience was restless - I could feel it - and having an already acute sense of an audience, I sped up the delivery of my speech. I won. But then I was disqualified for being forty-five seconds under the minimum time! The winner as I remember, went on to win the State competition and a four-year scholarship to Stanford University.

A footnote on that period: two teachers, sponsors of our legendary student government, Ms. Bettington and Ms. Eisenberg, were summarily dismissed without trial for being suspected communists, the only teachers in the United States so treated. Thirty-five years later Eisenberg received an apology and some remuneration. Bettington had long since died. A sad chapter in American history.

In high school we had our cliques, now called gangs. Mostly boys from (oh, the cliche) broken homes, usually without the influence of a solid father figure. Ours was a group of gifted underachievers. We despised those who had their shiny satin jackets with club emblems on the breast trumpeting their presence. We all had a small tattoo of a shamrock on our leg. For us brainy but belligerent kids, that nihilistic view of life seemed to make a kind of odd macabre sense of life in the 50s, with its phony, not-too-far-beneath-the surface white bread, racist values. That was our agreement. Nothing emblematic on any clothing or body part which symbolized anything. None of us were Irish, so the shamrock meant...nothing.

The tattoo had been applied one night out on what was then the construction site of a stretch of Ventura Freeway, which became known as the "101". Agoura, where several of our gang lived, was a trailer-trash haven mixed with a few country homes; a small settlement amid ancient scrub oak trees and golden, wild, wheat filled hills. Now it is full of gated, gilded houses and no visible trailer trash.

We boys had been drinking a mix of Seagram's 7, a rye type whiskey, and Coke. For the tattoo, a needle was inserted partially, into a rubber pencil eraser, then a picture of a shamrock was painted with India ink on the leg to be tattooed. With an enormous chug of whiskey preceding the art work, one braced oneself for the multiple shallow stabs from the slightly protruding end of the needle.

Several years later, my aunt (actually my mother's cousin) Dorothy, who was a woman of astonishingly lasting beauty in an age before rampant plastic surgery, and who lived a life of quiet, social correctness in Pasadena, inquired, when I was her guest at the Valley Hunt Club pool, whether I had "bruised" my lower calf? The tattoo from the Ventura Freeway remains to this day. It was not completed; one corner of it is absent. Mike, the artist for my particular branding, fell on his drunken face in the middle of the freeway just before completing the puncturing picture.

Sex to a country boy, for that is indeed what I had become with my motorcycles, low-slung dirty jeans and well-developed twang of a western dialect, was a fantasy indulged in whilst imagining almost all the girls in school in a state of undress. The back of the school bus became the rhythmic, jolting place in which I experienced my first erection at the age of eleven. I was getting the after-draft of an open window ahead of me and with that breeze wafted the sweet-hair smell of Judy, sitting unknowingly while my jeans rose to her rear....so to speak. I had some trouble using my notebook to conceal my embarrassment as I dove off the yellow bus at my stop.

That initial urge was supplanted by months, perhaps a couple of years of longing. Sitting by the Chatsworth lake at night, sometimes with a neighbor girl who had horses up on the ridge, I would very quietly suggest that we go skinny dippin' in the lake. (Actually, I only suggested that once and with her astonished I shall not call it horrified look, I never brought the idea up again.)

My fantasies were fed by the movies. Gene Tierney was my most well detailed fantasy. I imagined the various scents with which she adorned herself. Scent has always been a biggie with me. But no real satisfaction came to me while masturbating out in the chill night air of the West Valley lakefront. Until high school, that is. Our little gang or clique as we laughingly called it to satisfy Ma's curiosity as to who my companions were and what we did, roamed the hills of Agoura and Calabasas, which were, as I have said, extremely rural,

One night while hanging out with a member of our group in a small, trailer-like house which we now elegantly call "manufactured homes", I got acquainted with the mother of one of our host clique members. She was married to an alcoholic who could not be dragged away from the black and white television set in his bedroom.

That evening she, the platinum blonde mother, was also a bit loaded. As we boys sat sprawled on the couch drinking beer which she allowed (as did no other mother), she started to dance alone. She was about thirty-five and still had the body of the dancer she had once been, lithe and serpentine. She undulated in front of me. Her son was, by that time, passed out on a nearby sofa. She eventually looked down at me and said temptingly, "Wanna dance?"

I, with great nonchalance (I thought), rose to join her, and within a few minutes of slow dancing pressed against this formidable and obviously longing body, rose again within my jeans to meet the challenge. After a few more minutes, she whispered, "Would you like me to pick you up from school tomorrow?" Her nicely dyed blonde hair almost choked me as open mouthed, I tried to summon a sophisticated reply. "To go dancing, right?" was my infinitely dumb-assed reply. "Yes, to go dancing," she murmured with quiet amusement.

She picked me up from Canoga Park High School. I didn't have track practice that day. And I missed a few after that.

The motorcycle hill climbs in Woodland Hills, a few miles away, were just that. Movie stars like Gable and Keenan Wynn used to take their English bikes and go to test their flagging testosterone on the steep vertical trial angles in them thar hills. Below these climbs were the last vestiges of valleys and glens, which in the 60s to follow, were built up with the fancy houses of South of Ventura. In one such glade we had sandwiches, iced tea and disrobed surprisingly quickly. It, the deed, was more than I expected it to be. A sheer delight. I was taught beautifully.

The affair went on for months. I suppose it did spoil me. I didn't have to work for it.

In those days if one did not have a convertible and had very little money, it was not easy to get a date with the really hot girls in the school. The exception being, if you were a football star; in that case you scored on and off the field. I was a minor track star. In those days track was not as fashionable as it became later. I was a member of the first Cross Country team ever formed at Canoga High, placing third in the Valley League and about 126th in the City Finals, my only satisfaction being that I beat the first two Valley League finalists.

Increasingly, our gang activities became more adventurous. We needed money so we rationalized, as rebels do, that the folks in ly country cabins around Malibu Lake near Agoura did not need their Wo War II gun collections. So, we relieved them of their artifacts and, havi contact in the real underworld, transferred them to a Buick station wa which was driven sometimes by us across the border to Mexico. there, the contents were removed from the built-in secret compart under the seats and in door panels, and we were paid. Years later told by some Mexican authorities that had we been stopped at th with a hidden ordinance, we would have been shot on the spot.

The money "earned" from those transactions, as well as from booze we lifted from local shops, were used to buy, among other things, a 1934 Packard Limousine, replete with a side pocket for golf bags; a magnificent vehicle with a long nose of dark blue and a "freewheeling" system, a forerunner of "cruise control". We also purchased a 1937 Harley Davidson VL motorcycle, one of the formidable two-wheel machines of the day. Because of the interruption of the War, when only tanks, military motorcycles and jeeps were made by the auto and motorcycle industry, the post war machines were not much more advanced than those of the pre-war era. Hence, a 1937 Harley was still a hot machine in 1950. The Packard did, of course, raise some eyebrows when we pulled up in it to high school. We also sported overcoats. Looking like the Capone gang, we would attend our classes.

Our life of ill-gotten gains was to come shortly to a halt. I should mention that elaborate planning was always our cornerstone; We bought Salvation Army shoes and poured lead into the toes in order to fool the cops as to how large we were; we used clothes that would never be worn again in the event that we left a thread on a branch or a window sill; we "borrowed" cars from out of the area for the occasions...All that from the minds of boys sixteen and less who, with our cleverness, might, just as easily found a way to use our brains for something more useful than planning these "perfect crimes". I might add, in a semblance of defense, at we never did anything violent. No guns were ever used or muggings mmitted. For us it was more the intrigue of out-witting the adults.

Broken homes, even among the very bright, are breeding grounds for o do more than mischief. Stan, we shall call him, lived nearby the site then most recent job, relieving a country store of a few cases of its quor. The cops regularly questioned all kids who lived in the hood where a crime had been committed. So, they came to school viewed" those kids.

't before, Stan, who lived with his father, stepmother, and their y, had left a jar of aspirin open on the coffee table. The kid had ts of them and died.

orning, Stan had, in his distress, come to school not knowing . We all, in our "gangster movie" code of honor, had agreed each other. If one was caught, he would "take the rap". n was in no condition to remember this code, which was ful, guilty condition, too abstract to obey or even confronted, blurted out not only the previous night's L that we had accomplished in our life of "perfect o years.

While sitting in the Malibu Sheriff's jail those next twenty-four hours, my savvy mother was busy. She had not been what is now called an investigative reporter (for the Brooklyn Eagle) for nothing. In those scant twenty-four hours she managed to find out that the man to whom we sold the weaponry had big time political connections in California state politics. Armed with that information, she approached the authorities with a solution: I would be allowed to return to my father, in England forthwith...on the next plane in fact; all the nasty facts of my delinquency would be buried.

I was on a four engine DC4 airplane that night in the fall of 1950. Did I feel deep remorse for my recent escapades? Not enough. Not nearly enough. Perhaps as a teenager one is more consumed with cutting the cord from a single mother than guilt over misdeeds. I felt regret, especially for Stan and the loss of his baby half-brother, but I looked forward to being on my own; making my own decisions. The unknown future was exciting and appealed to this adventurer.

CHAPTER 4

London via NYC

I landed in New York in October, supposedly there for a short time while awaiting the cheapest available passage to England, and then to be (hopefully) welcomed by my father. He had not been told of my imminent arrival.

Shortly there would be a hurricane. Windows blew out on high floors. Glass came falling like wanton, punitive pieces of ice. Dodging these missiles, I wondered why anybody would live in the East.

With about $40 in my jeans, I went to the Sloane House YMCA, no longer there, and stayed in a tiny, spare cubicle with a bathroom shared by many uninhibited often smelly men. The abundant male noises and whiffs in bathrooms and hallways were sounds and scents to become familiar to me during the years of my comparative poverty, and, of course, during the time I spent in the army.

The YMCA boxing ring, on my first visit, featured a lanky, speedy young fighter who was beating the shit out of a much smaller, pathetically unskilled kid with a waist the size of an-about-to–explode inflated tire. I, ever gallant and with the confidence born of many a school fight on the playground of Canoga Park High school, said to the victor who was still pounding the battered boy, "Wanna go a few rounds with me?" Wiping his victim's sweat off his chin, he said with a quiet confidence of a sadistic bastard, "Sure! Step up."

I did. I made many of my fancy California steps, jabbing the air in preparation for my swift victory, when a flurry of well-trained combinations flattened my nose and left me reeling within a minute in hopeless defeat; the end of my boxing days. I was not to fight again until decades later on the streets of New York when I actually had to defend myself in what turned out to be mortal combat. But that story is, yes, for another afternoon.

I got a job, very briefly, on the New York docks. A guy at the YMCA who was amused at my California humor, "Youse guys from California are different" "You mean by the way we tawk" I said, imitating his "Noo Yawk" accent, "Naw, by the way you wawk...Ya gotta kind of John Wayne lope, ya know?" I accepted that description and more than once tried to observe that "wawk" while passing a shop window. He was leaving to go west, to someplace called Las Vegas. He had some "connections" and worked on the docks...One had to have a "ticket" to do so. He gave me his ticket and instructed me on the dos and don'ts of waterfront stevedore life.

You went to the "shape up" in the morning, at which time the head longshoreman would pick out the men required for that day. No automated loading in those days; muscle was needed. In the evening, there, waiting at the end of the pay line, were the guys who without speaking were handed a chunk of that pay. I provided the muscle and the "commission" for my one day of very hard labor. I did notice that they looked at me somewhat strangely at me.

Perhaps because I looked and "tawked" differently, I did not get picked from the shape up the following day or the next after that. Perhaps I looked like a Federal agent? I'm sure it was not because of my work. I did self-observe that, as with the ranch life, I didn't shy away from hard physical labor.

Almost immediately thereafter, with help from my perennially caring ma, I got my waited-for ticket from Boston to England.

CHAPTER 5

Rahdahh

I arrived in London after shipping over on a small ocean liner from Boston. The crossing in early November was rough. A forward hatch cover blew off and the ship tossed mightily in 15 to 40 foot seas. Watching the rain soaked crew struggle to re-fasten that hatch in the huge breaking seas was my first lesson in the more dangerous sides of merchant seamanship.

During all that 10 day journey, I was invited to the First Class quarters by the playwright Mark Reed whose most famous play was *Yes, My Darling Daughter*. He and his lovely wife took me in as a son. A very normal, bright, and sharing couple, they taught me, and we played canasta night after night. I observed their abundantly courteous life. Sometimes the cards came flying off the table as the ship rolled and groaned.

In between those visits with the Reeds, I thought lots about my recent adventures in New York; very little of my near disastrous juvenile crimes in California. I did however, take time to marvel at my mother's uncanny ability to get me out of that tight spot and whisk me off to New York in a middle–of–the–night legal escape. "Cutting the cord" did not stop me from those short but telling recollections of her sacrifices.

My passage was of course in what used to be called, "steerage", meaning way down below, near the rudder. Not a pleasant ride. The crossing was, as said, very rough. Standing and looking forward in the First-Class Lounge, one could see the great 30- and 40-foot waves crashing over the bow, eventually tearing off at least one hatch cover. Adrenaline rushing, I would return to the Reeds cabin and resume civilized games of canasta. The Reeds traveled often, but even they exhibited some degree of anxiety, hidden mostly by very good New England manners.

Arriving in Liverpool some 12 days later, I didn't quite know how to inform my father that his son had arrived unexpectedly from America. Nor could I imagine the man I would meet. What had the war done to him? Was there grey at the temples, paunch at the middle? Was there remembered fondness to be repeated? I grew nervous. I can't remember how I got his phone number, but perhaps I called his newspaper. He, upon answering in his much-surprised voice, told me he was living in Lansing by the Sea, and

would of cour... ush to London to meet me. That apparent enthusiasm
comforted m... e agreed to meet firstly at one of his favorite clubs, not a
staid, leath... d paneled wood, stuffy club, but a jazzy place called The
Albany n ...he famous, sedate Brown's Hotel close by the Ritz and
Piccadilhy had very good black-market food. Rationing was still on
Th ar as England's sources of beef, Australia, and Argentina, were
fro ng droughts or hoof and mouth disease or both. I was treated to
b calopes de veau Holstein, a veal cutlet sautéed perfectly with a
g on top. I studied, between scrumptious bites, the face of this man
late forties.

...as he going to be the idol I had been parted from? What is, after-all, a
...vly found father to a rebellious 16-year-old who had been raised by a
...rong single mother? He looked essentially like the man I remembered. His voice was smooth and genuine. He said something that has stuck with me to this day. Sitting there, and after several fine brandies, he, studying me said, "You know, after eleven years, blood ties don't mean a helluva lot...It's just a matter of whether you LIKE the person or not...and I think I'm going to like you."

Could a rediscovered father have said anything less mawkish, more emotionally effective? I don't think so. He asked me what I wanted to do. I replied, "Be an actor." He then seized on that and said, "Then we must introduce you to some actors!" And he did.

He never asked me WHY I wanted to be an actor. I've rarely reflected on my motivation, my "calling". I suppose, the moment of realization, struck when I did so well in the speech contest at Canoga Park High School. The absolutely visceral feeling, the blood flowing to the temples, the sounds, the murmurs of understanding from the audience when salient points were made, shaped by sculptured sounds. All, all, left the full-bodied feeling that I might just have a gift for communicating. The profession of politics did not at that point interest me. Interpreting the great writers of the day and those from yesteryears did. I had the gift of delivery, they provided the ideas which at times influenced the thinking of a great many people.

My Dad's enthusiastic welcome from the fine actors of the time was abundant. To a person, everyone knew him, respected him as a critic. One said he was never mean just to turn a phrase at the expense of the actor.

First came Michael Redgrave. Lunch at The Ivy. He brought his two teenage daughters, Vanessa and Lynn. Very pleasant, but I can't remember what help came from it. However, that next summer I went to Stratford and saw his intense and poetic *Richard II*. Knowing someone, however briefly, and then seeing them play a character, helps one distinguish the

choices actors make in their interpretation of character. Y
I met, by chance, the brilliantly talented Vanessa on a fli* *later, when*
somewhere, I asked if she'd recalled our luncheon. Sa*to or from*
sensitivity, she said she hadn't.   *ut with*

The next on my dad's list was Lord Attenborough, then kno
old man as Dickie, who was starring in the West End at the Savoy *my*
He was immensely helpful and when I asked if I was perhaps a
young for the Royal Academy of Art (RADA, as it was called, or RAHi
as it was pronounced exaggeratedly by the students, the humorous, or
critical) he replied, "Hell no. I'm still the youngest who ever went there!

I applied. I got an audition date. I chose, as my modern piece, a
monologue from O'Neil's, *Ah, Wilderness,* and for classical, a prose speech
from *Hamlet*, delivered to Rosenkranz and Guildenstern, which begins, "I
have of late, lost all my mirth…" I had been warned not to do *Hamlet*, but I
ignored those instructions. I simply didn't know anything else and there
had been little time to prepare.

For years I assumed that it was my alarmingly obvious talent that got
me in, forgetting completely that my father. as still a member of the critic's
circle was pulling strings.

I was a cheeky 16-year-old boy when I arrived at 62 Gower street to
begin my adventures at "RADAHH". The façade of the building hid from
sight, the destruction barely inside: A German bomb had made a direct hit
in the middle of the building which stretched from one street to the next.
The main theatre was gone. Only a lab theatre remained which every class
had to share. Classes were held on both sides of the bomb crater. One
crossed the chasm on scaffolds of wood and metal.

All of London had these skeletal remains of charred brick and mortar
as reminders, even in 1950, of the terrible devastation to civilian life as
well as military. I had tinges of guilt when seeing these poignant ruins. I
smelled the burnt timbers, and felt badly that I had not stayed and "done
my bit". I was five when the war started, eleven when it ended. Ridiculous
guilt, but real.

This institute randomly singled out for a direct hit was shortly to be
gifted with a re-build by none other than George Bernard Shaw, who died
during my beginnings there. His other gift was to further the use of his very
sensible new alphabet for the English language…I'm not terribly sure what
happened to that idea, but the Vanbrugh Memorial Theatre of the RADA
still stands today. It is named after Irene and Violet Vanbrugh, sisters of Sir
Kenneth Barnes one of the founders of The Royal Academy of Dramatic Art.

Sir Kenneth looked like a classic English old-man professor, balding
with uncut wandering sides of grey-white hair, the requisite spectacles,
gold rimmed circles of magnified glass almost shielding the ever-curious

eyes. He spoke in measured cadences, always correct grammar, no slang, reflecting a career in theatrical education which had gone back to the days of the great Sir Henry Irving (the first actor ever knighted) and John Forbes Robertson, along with Sir Kenneth's sisters, the aforementioned Violet and Irene Van Braugh, who were well known actresses of the Edwardian era.

He, just talking, sometimes reminiscing, took one back to that magical era, the era of the young George Bernard Shaw, the great composer, Edward Elgar, Picasso and all the others who preceded the Great War to end all wars.

An example of his formal but never boring rhythms: I had done my first play on stage there, *Midsummer Night's Dream* in which I played Lysander, the lover boy. We all gathered in Sir Kenneth's office to hear his criticism of the production. To me he said, after a slight pause to recollect, "Mr. Coster, in your performance today, you seemed to exhibit a maximum of personality and only a modicum of characterization." THAT was the impression I left on dear old Sir Kenneth not unkind, his reaction, but certainly only a "modicum" of admiration.

His next critique of my acting came the following semester after a performance of *All's Well That Ends Well*. I was an old man, Lafew, in that one. Sir Kenneth's criticism of my Lafew was, "Mr. Coster, you seem to be totally unaware that there is some metric consideration in the delivery of Shakespearian blank verse." Ah, once again, the admiration was hugely apparent!

I learned from this and much more scathing criticism. We all do, or at least we should. My diction improved, my voice too, albeit only slightly. I recall the registrar asking in a flutey upper middle-class accent, "You ARE English, are you not Mr. Coster?" I said, "Yes I was born here," in my Western twang. The registrar then with her overlapping upper teeth glistening beyond her pale skin asked, "Then where on earth did you contract that American accent? To which I, in deadpan manner replied, "Along with the influenza in 1918..."

She, not amused and ignoring my reply, said, "Then since you are British, you should relearn English, proper English" " Then I shall," says I....and I did. Within weeks I got my old accent back into usage. I learned quickly. My authentic English eventually got me many jobs in America on Broadway with the likes of Olivier and Pinter as well as lots of TV and other stage work.

But it was to be the teaching years later at the Neighborhood Playhouse in New York of Robert Williams, who went on to become the first Chair of Voice at Juilliard, that made a real difference; he and a singing teacher, Sylas Engum, who changed, vastly, my voice production. I developed the capable voice which eventually inspired the great director, Sir Tyrone

Guthrie, to compliment me simply. "Nicolas, you have one of the finest voices in the American theatre..." He had no idea how much time, money and agony preceded that marvelous moment.

For the entire time I was in England, my father always saw to it that I ate well. I learned after my first semester at RADA that he was very short of money at the time and that it was a great sacrifice of which my new step mother, Kate, never complained...at least not to me.

In a taxi following a dinner a short time later, my father, slightly plastered but making sense to his more than slightly plastered son, did confess that he had felt badly about not coming to see his American family at all during the war. He had been an officer in the Royal Marines, had gone off to India after serving with Lord Mountbatten raiding France as a Commando. He admitted having fallen for Kate after returning from one of those raids. She was a Woman's Air Force officer who, when I asked how they met, said, "Your dad returned from one of those raids on France with black chalk all over his face, and, well, somebody had to wipe it off, didn't they?" I accepted her candid and witty explanation of his infidelity and we moved on. Or did we? That was one of my glib adjustments to sometimes very traumatic events. One does learn to bury things that hurt.

They had a son, Johnny, my half-brother, who at four, was adorable. He was to become a headmaster and adopted three super children as well as marrying the fine Jane, who recently passed on. To this day we are still very tight friends, including all their children and grand ones.

On the very first day at RADA, I met and fell instantly in love with one Elizabeth Wallace. Porcelain light skin, jet black and most compelling hair, and a scent which appealed to this easily aroused kid the entire time I knew her. We took to each other it seemed, for indeed we stayed very close friends through our last meeting in 1982.

Thelma Holt was another very attractive gal who became Elizabeth's and my pal. She also became a very successful producer of, among other things, Japanese theatre in London. She survives as of this writing today. I keep in loose touch through her ex-husband, a fine actor, Larry Pressman whom I see often.

David Airy, was another upper-class buddy. It was he who politely suggested upon sniffing my unwashed body odors, that I "attend to my toilet!" I did. Quickly...fearing that polite young women of the time would never mention such a thing. David was tall, a fine square jaw and a voice deep and melodious, which needed no repair from the teachers at RADA.

A moment of reflection preceding the next stories:

When I returned to England as a teenager, I must admit now that unconsciously or not, a great deal of time was spent trying to create what I imagined might be my dress, attitude and behavior signaling the evolution into a grown-up gentleman - a continuation of my Hampton Lodge beginnings. Longing for those days, I tried, on meagre funds, to have the clothes, including a gentleman's tightly rolled umbrella, and a black Homburg hat. It wasn't just an acting job. I was, sadly enough, trying to re-create a life gone but not forgotten.

The coming stories will illustrate some of that pathos.

Alexander Revides, a Greek, older than I (as were all but one of the other students), had been in the Greek Army during the war and spoke with great pride of his skirt-wearing regiment in the failing cause of defending Greece from the Nazi paratroopers. Alex was a close buddy. He too was in love with the oft adored Elizabeth Wallace and he too did not succeed in swaying her affections. Alexander loved to party. He was a bit taller than me, with a nose like John Barrymore; more alike than mine which was referred to as, "That aquiline nose one associates with the bridge of a British destroyer". I will admit his looks and mine made quite a stir when we frequented the pubs with our share of pretty maids.

A young woman who became a pal was Rosemary Harris. She was already in "Finals", the last class before graduating. I can't remember why this wonderful actress (she deservedly won the highest honor at the RADA, the Bancroft Gold Medal) liked me. But she was ever such a friend. Rosemary went on to fame on Broadway and London's West End. What was the attraction mutually? I don't know. Slightly older, ever curious eyes and much more mature, she remained a most attractive mystery.

I had other American friends there: Amanda Steel, Rosemary Harris's best friend whom I adored, and who died in a terrible accident on a motor scooter shortly after I left. Rosemary, then established the American scholarship to RADA in Amanda's name.

Jerry Hardin, a fine, fine actor, became one of my closest friends. Later, he kindly shared his walk-up apartment in Hell's Kitchen in New York City...and it was indeed HELL's Kitchen. 4 floors up, no elevator. When rats gathered in the garbage cans of the ground floor hallway, we would - with a broom handle - quickly open the tops if there were tops and, with super athletic jabs, spear the rats at the bottom of the bins! Primitive sanitation!

The apartment was furnished with a mad assortment of relics found on streets or "liberated" from apartments vacant but many times left with unwanted belongings. The empty buildings were awaiting demolition to make way for what became Lincoln Center, a square consisting of theatres and concert halls. The greatest prizes were several huge bevelled glass mirrors, beautifully framed, one of which hangs in my ex-wife Candace's apartment in West Hollywood. The most bizarre and baroque of our scavenged items was a huge throne-like gold painted chair which Jerry had torn the seat out of and then placed over an ancient pull-chain-toilet, creating indeed, a throne! The finishing touch was a long, flat golden cloth cord with, of course, a silken tassel at the end. A less imaginative spell was when we were ALL terribly broke and eating out of the same huge kettle of lentil soup for a week! It took me 40 years to face lentil soup again.

We both worked at the Barter Theatre in Virginia and then at Arena Stage in Washington D.C. Jerry had a close buddy at RADA, Donald Merk, who made a living, believe it or not, as an Elizabethan minstrel! He had a lute and everything, which accompanied his singing of old English songs, and made honey-mead wine which he carried in a flagon. His Elizabethan handle was Seraphym. He walked everywhere singing songs and passing out a few sips of mead to his listeners on the road. Ironically, he was killed by a car on a modern highway.

Our other roommate, Del Close went on to found the Second City troupe in Chicago, from which so many fine talents have emerged, including a favorite actor and friend, Alan Alda. A quick story about Del Close: He, and Jerry Hardin, had been founders of the first major improvisational group, The Compass in St. Louis, along with Mike Nichols and Elaine May and Shelley Berman. Years later as said, Del founded the Second City in Chicago. He was brilliant and weird! I adored Del. However, when I left that fourth floor walkup apartment in Hell's Kitchen to go on tour for a couple of months, I came back to discover that my beautiful, blonde, scratchy voiced Dutch girlfriend had found succor from missing me, in Del's hospitable arms and loins. Admittedly my hurt was more manifested in astonishment than injured anger.

"But he doesn't even wash!" I exclaimed. "I washed him" was her simple, slightly apologetic reply.

Other friends from RADA with whom I've sadly lost touch include Ingrid Wyndham, who became a Baroness twice, firstly by marrying John Guinness, who was soon to become Lord Moyne, heir to the Guinness beer fortune.

Ah, now that was a wedding! Talk about Brideshead Revisited! My being asked to and attending that fabulous event, was everything my fantasies of returning to a grand life had ached for. I BELONGED! A shallow conceit? An unnecessary voyage to a life no longer there? Perhaps, but by god it was terrific!!

They hired a train for the party to come from London to Buckinghamshire. We men dressed in the (still appropriate) "morning suits" - black swallow tail coats, striped trousers and grey or other colored waistcoats with grey top hats for the country, as opposed to black for in-town. I was very lucky to have been given a morning suit by a pal of my dad's, Jimmy Walker who was well known for something in London, I have no idea what. He gladly handed me the Savile Row made suit which no longer fit him and with a grand slap on the back, wished me good times. It fit my figure as it had his in his youth, perfectly. I looked in the mirror and saw the young aristocrat my mother had always told me I was ....part of the Southern hubris of "puttin' on airs" which kept other fallen families' illusions alive after the devastating Civil War.

The train was met by a bevy of classic cars: 1936 Bentley Touring, Lagondas and Rolls Royces. The wedding was held at the Guinness estate in Buckinghamshire. They served gallons and gallons of "Black Velvet", half Champagne and half Guinness. I danced, chatted, drank, and indulged my fantasies of really belonging to these people. forgetting completely that aristocratic living was a result of immense wealth earned or stolen or by conquering.

Ingrid in some ways had become my really best friend at RADA. She was thin, blonde, graceful, what they used to call "fined boned", very British and an absolute dear. She seemed to adore me. Indeed, I think I was one of very few from RADA to be asked to the wedding. I lost touch and then in my haste to leave England after a year, never saw her again. I looked her up recently on Google and found that she had divorced Guinness and then married yet another Baron. The "double Baroness" died not too long ago. A real regret that we did not meet again.

At RADA I did excel in at least one class; mime. Mary Phillips taught it. You had a choice of doing it to music or without, what they subsequently called improvising, but without speech. One fashioned a story and then performed it with or without a partner. My fondest recollection of that class was the creation by an American, Ted Flicker, who went on to be a film producer. His mime consisted of a man constrained in some sort of bondage, but standing, looking about in an obviously anxious state and as the music (possibly Ravel's *Bolero* or some such relentless piece) played. As the music swelled and the man's fear increased, we became aware that his feet were locked into position and he was on a beach with the ocean rising. Ah, the terror. Yes, he was a victim of gangster revenge in what was called, "a cement foot-bath" and placed where the rising tide would eventually engulf him! A lesson well learned and appreciated in what the imagination and a body could do without uttering a word.

My father had gotten me a room in South Kensington which was then, if not war ravaged, not exactly the posh side of town. My room had the requisite "geezer", a small box into which one pushed a shilling, and when fed with the coin, would turn on the gas for heating and boiling water on a little one burner stove.

In the room, I welcomed a chap I had met in a pub. Young but older than I by a couple of years and very well educated in either Harrow or Eton, a fine university, and then drafted for National Service into the army. I quickly understood that he was a deserter. There was no war on at the time, so I found his reasons for escaping to the comfort of the pub rather than "doing his duty", compelling if not excusable. However, after providing him tea in my room, I left to go to the "loo" down the hall and when I returned saw that he had broken into the geezer, taken the few shillings, and escaped into the night.

The landlord called my father the next morning and kicked me out!

I was most embarrassed and shortly thereafter found a hostel in which to stay; five pounds a week including breakfast and dinner! The breakfast was porridge cooked forever, the dinner was dull codfish or beef stew with loads of tasteless greasy gravy and bread that was thick and wet cardboard-like in looks and taste.

I did, at the hostel, learn about the wars of forty years past from the point of view of a seaman in the Royal Navy, for indeed, my bunkmate on the lower bunk was such a veteran of steep waves and cannon blasts. He also snored mightily. I slept little. I also quickly recalled what it was like back at the YMCA, living close to older, paunchy men and their specific smells and sounds.

I stayed at that hostel my first couple of months in London and then my new found friends, David Conville, who went on to produce the Regents Park Shakespeare Festival, and Anthony Livesay, an actor, invited me to stay with them with a much-reduced share of the rent. They had both served as officers in fine regiments and had a flat in Belgravia, a very POSH two-story flat, in what was called a maisonette in those days. It had once belonged to Noel Coward and still had pictures in the dining room of Noel and his pals. I had my own room. It was grand and near to the library, which quickly became my favorite place.

I, in my ignorance, knew little of English or any other poetry. I feasted on the books in that library. I learned of and became utterly fascinated with the First World War poets, Wilfred Owen, Rupert Brooke and others. Brooke, and his poem "The Soldier" especially caught my fancy. To this day if there is such a thing as reincarnation, I truly believe I was a Canadian soldier who died at the second battle of the Ypres where the Germans first used poison gas.

I had, as a kid, been walking down Ventura Boulevard in Studio City California, and after buying, for 25 cents, a First World War helmet at a thrift shop on the way, I wandered into a radio shop near my mother's studio. The owner saw my flat tin helmet and seemed interested as to where and why I had acquired it. I asked him if he had been in The Great War, to which he replied "Yes, as a Canadian. I was wounded at the 2nd battle of the Ypres in 1915..."

For reasons unknown to me to this day, I described to him the scene of battle, the sights, the gas used by the Germans (the first use of gas, in that case chlorine, in warfare). After my unprompted description, the man freaked! He could not get over my highly detailed re-telling of place and events. As said, it is the only reason I even entertain thoughts of reincarnation. Did I die there...the first time?

I was, thus, obviously taken to Rupert Brooke's stuff. I read many other books and poems by English and other writers trying in somewhat patchy fashion to fill in gaps from my San Fernando Valley playboy-pseudo-intellectual shortcomings.

David and Anthony were both most kind. David, during the worst of rationing, brought eggs and other lovely treats from his farm in Dorset and we had wonderful parties! At one I remember, we, in our "cups", as in being fucking drunk was politely called, invited the entire chorus line from the Empire Leicester Square (a large movie palace like Radio City Musical Hall replete with lovely-legged chorus girls.)

They came, all of them, or so it seemed. The fine knees and ankles and bottoms adorning every square foot of our grand home. Did it turn into the hoped for orgy? Nah. I don't remember David's or Tony's luck, but mine fizzled in conversation.

I was luckier with my dad's secretary at the RADA ball. My father, who in his youth had been much the same size, gave me his Savile Row made elegant white tie and tails outfit which he had kept in mothballs all those years. Again, as in the morning suit from Jimmy Walker, I was lucky. With cuffs let out on the trousers, it fit nearly perfectly. I invited Joan, my dad's secretary to the ball. Joan had red hair that fell luxuriously over an Helenic white evening gown, which draped in most complimentary fashion over an equally Grecian figure. She was absolutely stunning. She was the hit of the ball, and by association I was as well.

The only time I can remember my dad giving me any sexual advice was after the dance...a week or so after the dance.

"if you are going to fuck my secretary, have the decency to call her afterwards"

I've never forgotten that remonstration. Youthful males can be most unthoughtful after enjoying a conquest. I felt awful at the realization that physical intimacy could be much more meaningful to one than the other, but that is no excuse for being thoughtless. I gave the same advice, but more gently, to my own son after his first experience with a gal pal for whom it was also a first. He responded well and to the day of his death, even though he had long since gone in other directions sexually, he was always (as far as I know) considerate.

Most British girls were very proper in those days. Elizabeth Wallace, the dark-haired Scot whom I adored passionately, was no exception. We dated, had fun, hugged, kissed, but never did "the deed". Others who lived in North London and who had stayed out past the time the tube closed, slept sometimes in the same bed, but knew they were safe from advances...it just wasn't done.

RADA had a profound influence on this teenager. The actors who came to visit, the very good teachers, Clifford Evens and Leslie Dean, who were of the few who saw SOMETHING in me. I learned to fence well under Herr Froeschlen and years later in a TV special of the Three Musketeers in New York, was actually hired as a fencer! It came in handy at the Guthrie Theatre in Minneapolis much later when I had to fence skillfully as Laertes in Hamlet. I loved epee' and sabre. Foil, not so much.

We had a ballet mistress, Nell Fisher, a woman who had come from what is now the Royal Ballet, then Sadlers Wells. She was astonished by my lack of ballet talent, saying later, "Nicolas, after an entire year of ballet, you still haven't a clue, have you?" I didn't. Not proud of it, but the athleticism of fencing was far more appealing, and I had not yet been introduced to the wonders of dance at the Lester Horton Studio in L.A, in 1952, with Bella Lewitsky and the then unknown, Alvin Ailey and Carmen de Lavelade. At the Neighborhood Playhouse School years later, when my stint in the army had turned me into a coordinated physical treat, the teacher, who had been Martha Graham's assistant, marveled at the height of my leaps and musical ability. She asked, "Why weren't you a dancer?" I explained my late blooming and thanked her for her kindness.

J. Clifford Turner, was head of Voice Production at RADA. Tall, angular, with a carriage-horse jaw consistently held on the side by lengthy fingers perched to catch the vibrations from a fabulous deep baritone voice, his first comment on my then raspy, toneless and with limited range of pitch, if one could call it that, was, "Nicolas, you will be my cross to bear." He was not unkind; he tried. He put a little wooden spacer between my teeth (to keep the mouth open) and really tried with all sorts of exercises, to correct the production of wind through my vocal cords, with little success.

Turner was famous at the time for supposedly having taught King George how to speak. A few years ago, we learned (from the film, The King's Speech) that an Aussie voice teacher, Lionel Logue, was actually responsible for that vocal miracle. They even depicted a teacher resembling, in some ways, J. Clifford, in unkindly fashion. As depicted, he was a bit of a boob who failed with his little wooden inserts. Fortunately, Mr Turner was, by the time of the film's showing, long gone.

I also absorbed the influences of rich and poor. I did become the gentleman I had wanted to be as a grownup without losing awareness of how injurious social injustice can be.

One of our fellow students at RADA held a birthday party at the hotel Streatham Palace. It was then a middle-class place for modest budgets. The girl's father was a dentist, not a successful Londoner, but a sweet, lower middle-class guy from the suburbs. Some of the other students who happened to be from privileged classes, started poking fun at the place and the people hosting.

I, in the great spirit remembered of my mother's Suffragist days, actually got up, went over to these rowdy snobs and audibly dressed them down for insensitivity. I did so in an overly clear upper-class accent. They actually felt sheepish at their indiscretion. A minor victory, but I never forgot the look on that dear girl's face....the hurt. The degradation. Happy Birthday? I think not.

Was this the dormant moral character which might now be emerging? Possibly....

So much for the education at RADA for the almost hopeless Yank. I did learn. I did improve. I got lousy grades (dug up recently by my not unkind, but astonished brother who had excelled at Millfield School while in England). That Euro-Brit experience has influenced my entire life...on stage and off.

Still, at the end of my third term at RADA. I decided it was time to go for two reasons, perhaps three:

1. My mother who had sacrificed so much that I might thrive on opportunities, was not well and beckoned;
2. I was about to be drafted into the British Armed Service, as I was still a Brit by citizenship. No educational deferment. The UK Government did not consider an education in drama as vital for national security; I actually wanted to stay and join up...Imitating Dad? Perhaps.
3. By then I realized that my dear papa, with a new child and no regular job, was nearly broke. After five years of service and the ever-present memories of fallen comrades still fresh, he probably lacked the drive to be successful. It just wasn't important anymore. He never again achieved the star-like success of pre-war days. I observed his dilemma and was aware that he really didn't need another burden.

I arrived in Dundee Scotland just before Christmas, 1951. It was necessary for me to be there, for indeed the R.M.S. SUNNAAS was to leave port on its maiden voyage at any moment.

The richly dark haired lovely, Elizabeth Wallace, whom I was so crazy about all the time at RADA, lived there. She invited me for New Years, called "Hogmanay" (spelled phonetically here). Christmas being a family religious time in those days, I didn't quite know how to be in Scotland without being a bother to Elizabeth BEFORE New Year's, so I quietly got a room in a small rooming house by the water's edge...paneled wooden walls and a lovely "loo" as the Brits call the toilet. It was white porcelain with pale blue pictures of pastures and trees therein. Like a Wedgewood teacup. Amazing, I thought, that people would actually want you to experience art there in the bowl of the loo before darkening it with the shadow of one's arse.

On Christmas morning, I had a rare spiritual experience. I walked through and past the quiet, reverent town, past the slowly swirling smoke drifting into the blue Scottish sky from row upon row of brick and stone chimneys. Up, up, the hill at the top of which one could see the whole Bay of Dundee and beyond, to the sea. Looking the other way, one saw the rolling hills of the Scottish Highlands, chilled, silent, except for the winds, the constant winds.

At the very top, standing in remembrance, or perhaps warning, stood the monument to the Black Watch Regiment. Before WW-1, British regiments were gathered mostly from that town which was their home. "The Ladies From Hell" as the Germans called the Scots in their kilts with bagpipes playing as they advanced though the stinging hell of bullets and barbed wire, were a fearsome sight and sound.

So many brave lads were lost in those terrible battles that Dundee found itself without more than half its young men at the end of that conflict. Thereafter, young men from many towns and cities made up these regiments.

As a sometime student of World War One, I feel akin to these souls, not only because many of my ancestors were Scottish, but just that kinship with the fallen and the wounded I had experienced since my days of visiting wounded veterans during the war, and, of course, having a father who had been a Royal Marine Commando officer, spending over five years in the war, Europe and then Burma.

I stood...the slight winter's wind turning my cheeks and nose to a frosty pinkish-red. And then I felt a call; not a collective call, nor an individual, just a kind of beckoning. I knelt and for one of the few times in my life, I prayed silently for their souls and the souls of others lost.

In the next few days, I did see Elizabeth...often. Her family owned the Wallace bakeries, then, a large chain in Scotland. Her mother reminded me of the wife of then King George VI, who was also Elizabeth, also a Scottish lass, mother of the future Queen.

I got word that the SUNNAAS was to leave port on January 2, 1952.

I was invited on New Year's Eve to attend a really posh dinner-dance on a sailing ship still docked in the harbor. And what an evening it was! Fortunately, I had packed my beautiful white tie and tails outfit (full evening dress they called it); I, in my English Savile Row finery and the Scot lads in their velvet tunics, white lace shirts, family crested kilts and sporrans (a kind of belongings bag which hangs in front of the pocketless kilt) and the lassies in long flowing gowns. The stunning Elizabeth, confident but not haughty, shone across the ballroom of the lovely sailing vessel, a frigate, perhaps larger, from the 18th Century.

We danced into the night. The young gentlemen danced a special Scottish dance, with crossed swords on the floor into which one dare not catch one's patent leather slipper. The sad part for me, was that Elizabeth had a date. Long before my announced arrival in Scotland to catch a ship home, she had been asked by a young Ensign in the Royal Navy for the evening. Robin his name was, I forget the rest. He went on to become an Admiral. To my smug satisfaction, he did not win her hand. She eventually married a Guards Officer, who apparently did not treat her well.

I last saw dear Elizabeth in 1982 when I was performing in London. She had kindly managed to assist in getting my youngest daughter Dinneen, into the American School there - preceding my arrival a couple of weeks later. I was to be in London for months, and had voluntary custody of my kids.

She was living in quiet elegance in Belgravia...very quiet, very posh...very lonely. She, like so many of my RADA comrades, is gone...hopefully to join the seductive, wild scents of the Scottish Highlands from whence she came.

My dad, Ian Coster, circa 1947

Bio of Prince Phillip by my dad, Ian Coster

My first crush, Veronica, 1938

Brother Ian and I with Ma and super sister, Georgiana

*On Gene Autry's horse, Champion, in the
lobby of the Savoy Hotel, London, 1938*

With my beloved Ponkey in 1940

Then unknown cowboy, Roy Rogers,
I on left, bother Ian on right, training for gun control, 1940

With dad, Ian Coster, circa 1935

Brother Ian and I, Republic Studios 1941

High school "tough guys", 1950

My first professional photo, 1949

At the Royal Academy of Dramatic Art (RADA), 1951

CHAPTER 6

Another Rough Crossing

January 2, 1952: With a shocking hangover, barely concealable, I boarded the RMS SUNNAAS, up the gleaming new gangway to meet the Captain.

My father had been at lunch with a pal, an executive at Shell Oil. He jokingly asked that fellow if there might be a tanker on which his son, who had overspent his allowance, might return to America. I was there. The guy said, "Yes. matter of fact we have one, just launched, sailing from Dundee shortly." My father said he had actually been joking in asking. The guy was not.

I too, eagerly took to the idea.

"One small point: Tankers do not carry passengers, only owners and crew. This tanker was chartered with a Norwegian crew. They do take cadets in the Norwegian Merchant Navy. I looked forward to that enlistment.

I greeted the captain. He was a kindly soul who had been at sea since serving as a cabin-boy on sailing ships at the turn of the century. Some of the crew spoke a little English. One of the many times my ear and mind had to attune quickly to another language. Astonishingly, and very civilized I thought, they had hostesses for the crew. Not many but there they were "WOMEN at sea! Wow!" I thought. But, alas, they were only there to provide food and clean sheets, not love interests.

I spent many hours on the bridge learning as much about navigation as I could. I also heard wonderful stories about life at sea from our kindly skipper. He gave me books about Australian settlements, the names of which elude me just now; from the following events you will soon understand I might have wiped clean such memories.

I read and read, for indeed there was little else to do. My cabin was forward in the bridge section. One went aft over a long steel gangway to the crew and general dining quarters. Nothing to it in calm waters.

But then the waters turned angry just outside the Hebrides Islands. We heard our first S.O.S. from ships ahead of us caught in the fury of a storm which stretched to the Bay of Biscay. Some of these ships broke in half and went down with all hands.

SUNNAAS was brand new. We took on ballast (water in the hold in order to make the ship heavy so as not to be caught between two giant waves and therefore have its back broken). There was risk in that. Being heavier meant the ship could be swamped by giant waves surging over the smokestacks and so on. It was a choice the Captain made. He explained that and other choices to me with infinite patience.

For the moment we were alright. And then we heard, as did the world, the S.O.S from Captain Carlson and his foundering ship, Flying Enterprise. He was only two hundred miles south of us, but in these high seas and with our slow speed, we were helpless to do anything but listen to and feel the unfolding drama. Carlson managed, while the world was listening, to get all his crew off the ship to safety and then decided to stay and not abandon his beloved vessel. "He's staying with the ship" came calls from everywhere. Days later he was saved along with his ship and towed to shore.

We were at sea, a sea which was growing worse. A tanker, even a smallish one compared to today's super-duper tankers, was a large vessel. To see, to feel it roll from side to side, waves roaring over the decks with increasing fury, was harrowing.

I was on the bridge with the captain, first officer and helmsman. One could not even think of going aft across the open deck on the slippery gangway, so I didn't. For eighteen hours, wave after wave hit, damaging the newborn craft. And then IT hit; a monster rogue wave of some 85 feet! I looked up, and there, over the masthead, high above the bridge, was the ferocious almost living force! I looked, the captain looked, the first officer looked, the helmsman stayed glued to his compass.

Then, with terrible force, thousands of tons of water hit the ship. The vessel groaned and shuddered. Everything went flying. The bow went up, thank God, and through the wave at probably forty feet of depth. The captain in his early sixties held on, barely. I had a few nips of Norwegian gin in me and didn't really give a damn. I held on. Did I also hold the captain? I don't remember. And eventually, with a whimper, it passed. Somewhere off the coast of Bermuda, days later, we assessed the damage. Much of the gleaming white paint had been stripped from its new steel, 1½ inch steel valves were gone, picked like springtime daffodils, and tossed to an ocean grave. The battle between ocean and new metal had been barely won by RMS Sunaas. I asked the captain whether, in his half century at sea, he had ever experienced such a wave. "No, never," he said simply.

We ended up, after thirty days, in Galveston Texas. The young idiot who had signed on as a cadet in the Norwegian Merchant Navy was thrilled at the journey's end, and then roomed for a month in a tacky boarding house in Galveston.

I was informed upon disembarking that I owed, as an officer candidate, my mess bill. Officers paid for their mess, regular crew did not. Part time jobs in Galveston finally enabled me to pay off that debt.

On a trip with my generous daughter Candace, only a few years ago, I went to the Maritime Museum in Oslo, Norway, and, yes, there they were, the records of the Sunaas. Unfortunately, I did not have time to look for a crew manifest. I wonder if a young, adventurous Yank was listed as cadet?

CHAPTER 7

Back in L.A., God's Gift to Hollywood

I had survived nights of Norwegian gin and 85 foot waves, 30 solid days at sea on a tanker, then a month in Galveston Texas doing temp jobs while finding enough money to get a ride back to California. I was saved by hearing of a gig driving cars across the country, thereby getting a free ride.

I was assigned a Kaiser to drive, a brand-new Kaiser, rather modern in those days. The steel magnate, Henry Kaiser, who had made a fortune in WW-2, had, with a guy named Frazer, started a company, the Kaiser-Frazer Corporation. Frazer was the luxury version. Kaiser was "the peoples' car" just before the smaller VW swept the west in popularity. A couple of other youngish guys and I drove across the vast, weird, and flat countryside of Texas and made it to LA, driving nonstop on the legendary Route 66, in less than 30 hours; a feat in those days before the freeway network.

Upon reaching L.A., I secured a series of jobs in machine shops, starting with a short lived one at a drill press, where one night I forgot to put on a protective apron and therefore soaked my belly and male member in kerosene, producing a painful rash. Okay, enough about that. It did, however, temporarily halt any expectations I might have had of continuing my healthy, vigorous London love life.

The one pleasant aspect of my machine shop time, was getting to know an Englishman, John Robbins, a nearby business owner, who had been an officer in the Grenadier Guards, serving at the terrifying ordeal of the Anzio landings in Sicily in WW-2. It had been the first Allied landing on the continent and the cost in lives was heavy.

I suppose as a lonely Brit in Van Nuys California he found some comfort talking at our meal breaks with the kid who had just returned from London and whose father had served in The Royal Marine Commandos, early in the war raiding the French coast among other things. We talked of the English countryside and Rupert Brooke, Siegfried Sassoon, Wilfred Owen and the lot, the WW-1 poets whom he adored. He enjoyed hearing of my exploits in Mayfair, his home before the war. But most of all, he talked of Ischia, a small island off the coast of Italy, where he had spent some time after fighting up to Rome. He had discovered it whilst on a brief pass from the battlefield, and instantly loved it. Bathing in the clear waters, attempting in brine and sunshine to wash away the stench of battle, he returned after the war. I gathered he'd had a love affair there that had gone south, prompting him to book passage to America and the new, unfortunately dull life in the San Fernando valley. I lost touch with my Grenadier Guards officer buddy; one moves fast as a youth, probably in order not to miss anything and thereby missing so much.

From the machine shop, where we manufactured only a single part, a piping joint for military airplane wing tanks - expendable items...lots of them - I went with my kerosene-soaked groin to a nearby sweat shop called Pacific Mercury where we put together TV sets for Sears Roebuck stores. It was 105 degrees in the shop, no air and a belligerent boss whose motto was "Put up with it or quit". 1952 was not a great year for unskilled labor, but still we went on strike, and I, among others, was most vocal; the first of many labor actions I was to be involved in over the years. We got ventilation.

In my use of American slang, expressions pop up from time to time influenced by army buddies of totally different backgrounds as well as those from people with whom I have worked. The assembly line at Pacific Mercury provided a wealth of such material. Memorable was the phrase from a vastly intelligent, but hard and old beyond-his-years young man who had done time in at least one penitentiary. A loner, who at meal times liked to be in solitude for that short period, he would, upon hearing annoying conversation, simply say, "radio that shit". It was clear from this quietly dangerous man that he thought the subject matter if not the volume was an intrusion. "Radio that shit!" What could be more clear? We quieted down.

He also passed on another memorable if slightly more abstract expression, heard once or twice when somebody on a break was "talkin' shit" as we now say. He, this narrow eyed, handsome, mysterious man, would say quietly to the fool, "You talk like a man with a paper asshole" What does that mean? We all kind of kind of just knew.

We had cowboys, actually many of them there in that factory. Buzz Henry was one of them. A year or so later, when he and I played brothers in a Western called, *The Outcast*, he, for some reason or another, did not wish to acknowledge our time working in the sweat shop at Pacific Mercury TV. He was, in fact, a rodeo cowboy who finally got a job acting as a cowboy, my brother in this movie. My other brother was played by Slim Pickens, who later famously rode the bomb down in Kubrick' s *Doctor Strangelove.* More on him later.

The long, hot hours of boring, repetitive work lost its appeal after the drama of the strike was over and I moved on, or as a cowboy would put it, "movin' on". Most of the real cowboys vanished for other pastures as well.

Wishing to provide myself with a means of living including meals, I applied for and got a job on the soda fountain at Bob's Big Boy, a drive-in restaurant. Everybody started on the soda fountain at Bob's, a company policy so that future managers would know all jobs over which they were to be the bosses. I graduated soon to the "Big Boy corner" where we (not McDonalds) put together what was the first double decker hamburger. McDonalds was still a small joint in San Bernardino. I recently saw the film *The Founder* with the brilliant Michael Keaton as Ray Kroc, who built that burger bar from a roadside café to the giant of giants in fast food. He lifted ideas from everyone apparently.

Bob's Big Boy in 1952 already had nine "stores", as they called them. The original was still in Glendale, California. I started at the drive-in at Toluca Lake, a fashionable suburb of Burbank, where, among others, Bob Hope called home. Ducktail-haircut customers parked their hot rods in slots, were greeted by curvy, ruby lipsticked car hops with "pillbox hats", who took their orders, which were then eaten in the car from trays attached to the open car windows.

I gradually made my way up the ladder to the "Steak side". The top of the heap was the "Egg side". Bob's had the cleanest griddles, floors and refrigerators and counters I have ever seen in any restaurant, with an accompanying motto "Cleanliness, quality of food and service are the keys to success", and indeed it was true to that motto. Bob was a handsome fiftyish man of medium height and slim figure, slightly greying hair and enormous energy, who had started with a 12 stool coffee shop in the mid-thirties.

Whilst at Bob's, a fellow used to come in, sit at the counter and seemed to be casually studying the operation. After a few weeks, he asked the waitress to call me from the grill and talk to him. Larry O'Larry was a thin, balding man of 50 or so with sparkling, very much alive eyes. He was half Jewish, half Irish, but with his high cheekbones, narrow face and full lips I would've bet Spanish. He dressed impeccably in cashmere slacks, expensive shirts, alligator shoes, a Patek Philippe gold watch and Countess DeMarco ties.

"Ya wanna be in the restaurant business?" he asked. "I already am," I countered. "Nah, I mean with me?" He went on to explain that his wife had recently divorced him, had gotten the leading divorce lawyer at the time, Greg Bautzer, which ended up with the judge ordering Larry to get a job and pay his ex or get arrested for vagrancy! He went out and bought a failing cafe called The Poodle Hut, a reference to their specialty hot dogs.

"I bought this little joint that went under. I don't know nuthin' about the restaurant business so you come and run it for me. I been watchin' you and you're good. Okay?"

The salary was twice that at Bobs. So, yes, "okay".

The faded Poodle Hut was on a promontory just south of Ventura Boulevard next to what is now the "405". There was no 405 then, only Sepulveda Boulevard taking one to and from the valley to Brentwood and points south. It also was one of the only routes to Las Vegas from Los Angeles.

With lessons I'd learned from Bob Wian, the Poodle Hut opened to instant success. A pleasant patio faced Sepulveda, the kitchen was close to the counter so that the customers could actually talk to the chef as the cooking went on.

I had a few inventions: A quarter pound hamburger made with ground sirloin of quality. I think only Hamburger Hamlet, a new place at the time, had meat of that quality; not a money maker, but the "lead item" on our menu. I invented a dish called "Plate O'Chicken", which consisted of 3 pieces of deep-fried chicken, french fried potatoes and a wedge of lettuce with Thousand Island dressing, a "borrowed" Bob's concoction of ketchup, mayonnaise, and relish. Other cafes in years to come were to have variations of that concept. A huge hit as well was a steak sandwich made from Spencer steak, what most now call a rib-eye. Served "medium" like Bob's unless otherwise ordered.

The quality of the food was superb, but our food costs for a single location restaurant was more than most fast-food joints at the time, about 32%. My rationale for creating that was the budget was based on providing top notch quality food...it appealed and got us off to a fast start. Most cafes, if successful at all, fail in the first 6 months!

Larry stuck to that for about nine months, but then one day I came in, looked at a tray of Spencer's and saw the glassy, uninteresting look of cheap meat. When I said politely, "What the fuck is this shit?" He sheepishly explained that a "contact" of his had given him meat at a much better price than what we were paying. Which brings me to the whole murky area of "contacts" and "connections".

Larry had indicated to me early on that his business had been based largely on "connections" and timing. At the end of WW-2 there was no chromium to be had. A critical metal, the war machine had used every bit of chrome available for years. Therefore, no cars manufactured from 1942 to 1946 had chrome bumpers and trim. Larry, through his connections, secured a monopoly on chrome, sold it to one of the major car companies - and that company only - at an enormous profit. The car was the first after the war to have chrome bumpers! A great advantage in a market that loved gaudy, post war show-off cars. When asked where all this happened, he replied cryptically, "Yeah, well I was big in Detroit."

He was indeed. Years later, when playing Detroit in *Beckett* with Laurence Olivier and Arthur Kennedy, I took Sir Laurence to The London Chop House wherein my old boss had said he had eaten often when he was "big" in Detroit. When seated with deference - as I was with Laurence Olivier - I asked the maître d' if an old customer, Larry O' Larry, had been "big" in Detroit. With a grim look of suspicion at the odd question from a touring actor, he said quietly, "Yeah, he was big." Olivier got the biggest kick out of my regaling him with stories of conquering Hollywood...at the Poodle Hut!

At the beginning of our partnership, Larry O'Larry, cautiously asked, "Kid, ya wanna be in the rackets?" The "rackets" was a term applying to the involvement in the underworld of gambling, protection, prostitution, and God knows what else. I replied to Larry's invitation to join the "rackets" with a polite "no thanks". Instincts prevailing. He was okay with that, but did spit out the admonition, "Then don't ever listen to a conversation." Agreeing not to, we proceeded with our restaurant experience.

He loved it! He would come into the kitchen and wash dishes with his Patek Philippe watch on, spilling dish water on his incredibly expensive handmade alligator shoes. I would yell at him, saying really instructive things like, "What the fuck Larry, think of how many starving displaced persons could live for a month on the price of those shoes...and give me the fucking watch before it's ruined!" He would hand me the watch, chuckle and go right on. Larry loved socializing. He was a good storyteller and the customers would be fascinated with this obvious millionaire cleaning tables, talking endlessly. And so it went, that year of 1954.

Larry was newly married to Vera, a lanky, attractive, considerably younger woman with a figure like Jane Fonda, or a Barbie Doll. Vera had a firm hand and slightly flirty but careful not-inviting eyes. Larry was always going on about his past life in Detroit with the "bimbos" and other trinkets of a leading gangster's life. He did occasionally go a bit too far: as an older man, he had to assure us that Vera, whom he really adored, had not married him for his money; that he was indeed, still a stallion of considerable capability.

One day, much to even my surprise (who, at twenty-one, had seen a lot and done a little), Larry was talking about the length of his dick and then without hesitation, unzipped his cashmere trousers and flipped the member out on the counter for the few of us present to see...There, even flaccid, was a splendid eight or so inches of available sausage. We laughed and told him how rare his splendid protuberance was and that he should be proud.

Larry would have various visitors who would come and talk in the shade of the umbrellas on the Poodle Hut patio - I would make sure that I was a distance away. Visitors from back East, bookies from L.A., some looking as if they were straight out of *Guys and Dolls*, others looking like accountants from Boise.

One day, Larry was nervous. He said somebody big was stopping by on their way to Vegas. Up rolled a fleet of limousines. Out of the cars stepped the requisite bimbos, bleached blondes with wrap-around chinchilla fur coats, followed by, first, the big and not so big henchmen. Then with quiet majesty, stepped out "The Man"; silver hair, sunglasses, a Miami tan perhaps. Larry was like a suppliant lackey, almost bowing as this mysterious "boss of bosses" sat down in the modest patio of the Poodle Hut.

After a short visit during which I did NOT listen, the fleet left for Vegas, and an exhausted Larry said in a whisper, "Ya know who that was?" "No," I said innocently, but wise at least from newspaper photos over the years, "but he looked vaguely familiar." My ridiculous attempts to cover my inquiring ass failed. He just looked at this boob of a partner and said, "Yeah, that was fuckin' Frank Costello." I said eloquently, "Yeah, of course." Costello was indeed, after Lucky Luciano, the "Boss of Bosses".

The Poodle Hut era was the only year in my life I worked every single day. I left the café only to do a few films, leaving Larry, whom I had taught to cook by that time, to run the joint with the elegant Vera doing the chores. Quite a sight, but she was game and very supportive....I think she actually loved the guy. A year later, the Poodle Hut was gone. Neglect or just the capricious whims of the mercurial Larry O'Larry leading him to seek roads elsewhere.

To their and my continued amusement, my pals from Pomona College would stop by on weekends to talk and laugh at Chef Nicky cooking with a constant dervish-like whirr as taught so well at Bob's Big Boy. The cooking there was voluminous, ergo one had to really move to keep up. I made that speed and effort at the Poodle Hut into a sort of show. The customers seemed to enjoy it. My pals included the rangy Ed Taylor who became a Rhodes Scholar, along with the equally rangy Robert Towne, who became one of the leading screenwriters/directors of all time.

Tall and amiable, Robert, coming from wealth had, as I recall, a fine car. In the fall of 1954, it was a new Ford convertible. With that and other cars which preceded it, he rescued me more than once on the roads to and from Pomona. As said, there were no freeways - hard to imagine now, seeing the tangled web of concrete which envelops L.A. - but there we were in the early 50s, with two lane highways but also the beginnings of steel rod and cement and giant bulldozers left to sleep on furrowed land destined to become the 101, the 60, the 10 and of course the now damned, jammed 405 with its inadequate 10 lanes, optimistically and foolishly planned to handle L.A. traffic in the 2000s .

It was on the under-construction Pomona Freeway in 1954, on one of my many per-week races to see my adored Nancy, that I, coming off another work day at the Poodle Hut, was so tired that my eyelids dropped shut somewhere between Anaheim and Cucamonga. I awoke to the sound of a metal-to-metal crunch and the smell of dust and watermelons as I and my victim pushed like two Panzer tanks over the embankment and into, yes, a watermelon field. There were yells – in Spanish...Okay, not injured yells, more like, if one were to interpret freely, "What the fuck!!" and the slurs of drunkenness were noticeable before actually smelling the wafts of beer and Tequila which joined the aroma of watermelons and dust.

I climbed out of my side-battered old Lincoln and approached, apologetically, my dusty co-wreckers. Before I could open my mouth, in unison, they all started sputtering in Spanish and Spanglish, their abject apologies for falling asleep and bashing my car. They climbed out of their heavily dented but still usable car and all of us pushed-pulled the 1947 Lincoln.

Remarkably, it was still drive-able. I had put into that giant gas guzzler, instead of its original V12 engine, a Cadillac tank engine from WW-2, which I had found in a genius-mechanic's garage. All rebuilt, it was indeed a super monster car. I was clocked at 102 miles an hour coming back from Pomona on the West Covina grade, a long tempting straight road downhill for several miles. The cop who stopped me after a chase, seemed more amazed at the speed accomplished by this car than offended by my attempt to rival Fangio, the leading race car driver of the day. I got a ticket for doing 85, not 102...likely more. Nice guy. Luckily, I had not been drinking, just momentary insanity.

I had started these journeys whilst dating a blonde lovely named Joan. Her father was a wealthy obstetrician. I met Joan upon returning from England in February of 1952. She, 17, was studying piano with Winnefred Byrd, who had been a quite well-respected pianist. My sister Georgie also studied there and introduced us. Instantly, sparks between 19-year-old Nicko and 17-year-old Joan.

We lasted well over a year. She was Roman Catholic and proper...up to a point... penetration, or rather the lack of it prevailed. I started my Pomona association while dating her. Parties, sneaking in on classes at Pomona College (I was still at Bob's, and so had one day off), all while courting the anglo-Joan with her strong gaze and stronger resolve.

One night after a date, I dropped her off at her parents' fine house "South of Ventura" in Sherman Oaks, just North and West of Hollywood, in

"The Valley". I had forgotten something at her house, and went back to get it...and there was Joan kissing another guy on her doorstep.

I felt a rage I had never felt before. Two years my girlfriend, no completed sex out of respect for her and her damn religion! Jesus, I had even studied Catholicism, The Councils of Trent and Nicaea, all that jazz...Went to church any Sunday when I could. All that disappeared with the blond hair draped on another guy's shoulder as his mouth devoured hers.

I swore at the time that if I ever had the reason to be jealous again, I'd "get rid of the reason." An infantile but simple strategy.

I slipped away into the night, but the next day confronted the not-at-all guilty Joan. She made up a story about him being just a friend not realizing how much I had seen.

"Bullshit! The truth! Gimme the truth!"

Truth was, she felt him more promising as a life-partner. A bit methodical I thought in one so young. I went to the wedding reception and wished her "ill"...Joan had a good wit and laughed. She felt this guy was headed for the Presidency of the good ol' USA! Yeah, well, there is some justice. He ended up a lawyer for the EPA in Colorado or something. Years later, I was in Washington, DC doing a good part in something at the Arena Stage and she, visiting as Republican Committee Women from Colorado, came to see me. Afterwards, with brazen charm she commented that she had no idea how good I'd turn out and flirted. Too late babe! Ha!

Of course, the "ha" was actually on me. My acting had improved a great deal since those early days just after The Royal Academy, but I never forgot the immensity of hurt. Rejection, especially after invested faith, 'tis bloody awful.

After Joan, I was most fortunate to start dating Nancy Irvin, also at Pomona. She had the ability to seem perfectly feminine while modestly exhibiting a vast intelligence and comprehension of art, music, and ideas. I would, without a second thought, drive 40 miles to Pomona, sometimes as much as thrice weekly to see her.

Nancy and I lasted until I went into the army in 1955. I'm not sure what happened...young men and women do outgrow each other. I will never really know. She wrote me that she was going to marry a professor at what was then Claremont Men's College. He was older, bright and a very nice man. Who could blame her? But, my god, it did hurt. I held a candle to that fabulous affair for years.

Nancy came to Pomona College reunions. I actually hosted one at my house in West Hollywood. At that party, in the late 1980s, Nancy returned to me, as a gift, a porcelain and doré bronze powder box I had given her in 1953. It was still in the perfectly preserved cardboard box it came in. I was really touched when she said, "I never had a daughter, I would love for one of yours to have it." Her husband told me by telephone not long ago that she had died of a stroke. A sad loss of that gracious and beautiful woman.

When I returned after a few brief absences to do films and TV, I would almost always see changes at the Poodle Hut, first minor, then major. Larry's connections once again began intruding on the purchasing, and that along with Vera's penchant for frugality and an increasing irritation with Larry's constant involvement with this hobby, led to a steady downfall. The quality of the food had diminished and the café was no longer up to standard on cleanliness and customers were waiting way too long for orders.

Lowry's, the famous steak house and seasoning maker, had actually, at one point, offered us the possibility of becoming a chain....I had to make a choice: To become a full time restauranteur or stay an actor. With many considerations weighing on me at the end of 1954, plus the impending draft into service looming in the near future, I decided to continue with my pursuit of acting.

I do wonder from time to time, what would have become of a Poodle Hut chain. Of course, we would have changed the name to what? "Nickos" "Nicky's"? Larry-Nick? Or Larry's Long Dick Cafe!?"

CHAPTER 8

First Movies, Brits to Cowboys

When you're young, I don't know at what age it starts, you make promises to yourself. I am really going to be a pilot, go to China, I am really going to stop burping in the back of the class in grammar school...Later on, it's I am going to finish that history essay two weeks before it is due; in high school, I am going to ask Dixie Nelson, who became Lori Nelson, out on a date. The prettiest girl in the school, (and of 50s movies mild-fame). And later, I am going to see my name in lights above a Broadway marquee...

I never became a pilot nor did I stop burping and I never did ask Dixie out on a date. So far, the closest I got was my name below the lights.

In 1952, I returned from The Royal Academy of Dramatic Art as, in my opinion at the time, god's gift to Hollywood. Unfortunately, the fashion then was guys six feet two inches tall with wide set blue eyes and button noses. I was five ten, with a long nose you could ski-jump off. Between 1952 and 1955, I had a host of jobs from machine shops to Bob's Big Boy restaurants. I did manage to slip in the few films mentioned, mostly at Republic Pictures, thanks to Mom's connections, before going into the army.

My first film was *The Desert Rats*, Richard Burton's second film, in which I had one line, "Better 'ave a look at that hand" as an Australian medic. It was made at 20th Century Fox, followed by *Titanic* (the original with Barbara Stanwyck, Clifton Webb, Brain Forbes and the oh-so-young-Robert Wagner) in which I also had one line, "Sir the band is waiting on deck".

Interesting and weird, the difference in treatment of the "bit part" actor in those days and today. Now, a bit actor is largely ignored or in commercials, referred to as "the talent", cast from a tape made in the casting director's office.

In 1952, for *Desert Rats*, I was taken by the head of casting for all movies at 20th Century Fox, Owen Maclean, to meet the director, Robert Wise. Yes, a one line actor taken by the Head of Casting for Twentieth Century Fox, to meet the director! I was then transported to Desert Hot Springs for location shooting...in a Cadillac limousine! Just little ol' me in that cavernous car.

Standing at the bar that first night (and most nights thereafter) was the fine and most theatrical Brit actor, Robert Newton. His large, brown eyes had a mischievous twinkle, especially after several shots of good Scotch whiskey. I got to know him and a famous Aussie actor, Chips Rafferty. In those days Burton did not frequent the bar. Perhaps that came later with his wife (twice) and pal, Elizabeth Taylor.

My huge job was climbing aboard a burning tank with the wounded Richard Burton and stating, with great urgency, my "Better 'ave a look at that hand" line with an accompanying bogus Aussie accent).

Again, the next week, I was escorted by Owen and my agent, Glen Shaw, a kindly gentleman, (in those days one's agent also went to auditions with the actor) for *Titanic*. We were met by Brian Aherne, the tall, very handsome English actor who was to play the Captain, and the brilliant screenwriter, Charles Brackett. The film was to be directed by Jean Negulesco, one of the talented European directors who had escaped the Nazis.

We had a large cast on the set and a huge scale model of the Titanic, which they tilted on hydraulic jacks as the ship was sinking. Suddenly, one day, Negulesco, called a halt to the entire shooting and requested that the radio be turned on (a commercial radio, not the ship's) so that he could listen to a football game! Shooting was halted until the game ended.

This Romanian director was a sweet man who gently guided me through my one line as the ship was in its final stages of sinking. By now, the ship was at full list, probably some 30 degrees or so. I had to come to the Captain and say my one line, which was, as said, "Sir, the band is waiting on deck".

The best part of that job was, whilst sitting around the set waiting for my super important line delivery, I met and talked at length with the technical consultant on the film, an English Commodore who had actually been on the ship during that fateful journey! He was generous with his time and modest about his accomplishments. From what I'd heard from others, he had bravely saved many doomed souls that night.

When feeling wretched about being so old, I do often muse on the luck I've had in knowing such time-spanning people, looking into the still tortured eyes of a survivor of such a tragedy as the Titanic, one feels the shuddering cold, the screams, the gasps of human beings quickly succumbing to the freezing, dark waters. As an actor, yes, it did help me in the delivery of my one line, or so I thought. Perhaps the beginnings of my "method" acting? Possibly, but just as possibly, simply a real and vivid history lesson.

Ma had a pal, a producer, Bill O'Sullivan, at Republic, who got me into my first Western, as well as several other films at Republic.

The Eternal Sea was one with Sterling Hayden, a famous sailor like Errol Flynn as well as an actor. It was about the Navy in WW-2. A couple of lines.

The Sea of Lost Ships (about the U.S. Coast Guard). Again, a couple of lines, with John Derek. This was my first film with John.

Then came *The Outcast*. *The Outcast* was shot in Colorado using horses untrained for gunshots. Slim Pickins played one brother. Slim had been a rodeo clown. A magnificent rider. At one point, a "chuck wagon," an old Western version of a meals on wheels truck for cast and crew, was brought on set, being pulled by a team of four spirited horses. Suddenly gunshots were fired in a volley from behind them, spooking the lead horse, who reared wildly and then led the rest in a frantic attempt to escape the roar of the guns with which they were so unfamiliar. Racing away down the meadow with nobody in the driver's seat, they were headed for god knows where at breakneck speed.

Slim Pickens saw this mini-stampede unfolding, and quickly and instinctively jumped on a nearby horse and raced to the scene. Galloping alongside the lead horses of the chuck wagon, he vaulted from his saddle like the true rodeo cowboy he was and wedged himself between those lead horses, digging his spurs into the ground, banging the two horses' heads together and, in short order, stopping the runaway team! Much ado was made of this noble, now mythical feat. I sometimes wonder if anyone is still alive besides this geezer who was actually there to see that spectacular feat.

The night immediately before I started location shooting near Canyon City, Colorado, a Mexican actor named Nacho Galindo and I were drinking in a funky bar in Canyon City, then a small town in the foothills of the Rocky Mountains. I looked, in my youth, a bit like John Derek, the star of the movie. An hour or so after Nacho and I had arrived, some rednecks came in with their girlfriends, already half loaded. Upon seeing us at the bar, one of them started cat calling across the room, thinking that I was John Derek, "Hey, I hear the Hollywood pretty boy can't keep his hands off the local high school girls! Pervert!" That got my attention. "And who's that wetback you're drinkin' with? We don't want no spics in here!"

As he uttered this last, he came sauntering towards us, still calling Nacho and me names. Of course "queers" was one of them and so on. He then stuck his boozy face next to mine and invited me to go outside so, as he put it, "I can kick the shit of ya". I declined the invitation and suggested to Nacho that it was time to "exit these parts". We turned to leave, the redneck swung. I saw it coming and I came "up from the basement", as they say, with a swinging punch straight out of a John Wayne movie, lifting him off the floor with the force of it. He landed on a table top, spilling jugs of beer and prompting his girlfriend to start screaming. Amidst all the jumble and clatter, we were detained by the bouncer or somebody, arrested by the Sheriffs and sent to Canyon City jail.

My hand was starting to swell from what proved to be broken bones, it was two in the morning by the time we were booked, the call for the location shoot forty miles away was at 6 AM. A quandary.

The director, William Witney, had not taken to me from the beginning because I was cast in the picture by the producer, Bill O'Sullivan, my Ma's pal. I was, to Witney, a British RADA trained actor who had no business being in a film of his, playing the younger brother of Slim Pickens and Buzz Henry, both rodeo cowboys. He had evidently not been told of my days as a ranch hand on the Kentucky Ranch in Paso Robles.

So there I sat in the "hoosegow", as they used to call jail in the old west, with my broken hand sore now and swelling mightily. I thought my Hollywood career was over before it had really begun. I also knew that in the morning, now rising, I was to shoot a scene whilst riding a horse at full gallop and firing a Winchester '73. Fat chance of that with my hand, which now looked like a full-sized baked ham. Thankfully, a deputy came on duty who had, with a buddy, been drinking at that same bar and had witnessed the incident. Self-defense was my plea. I was released and sent by studio car to the distant location.

As the car pulled up in the dust, William Witney stood, looming like a huge, stopped locomotive in the distance. I got out, walked slowly to him, holding my ham-hand across my chest and waited for the sentence... "You're finished in movies, asshole!" As I was resigned and waiting for the ax to fall, he looked down at my hand and then into my eyes and quietly said, "Whaddaya say killer?" His admiration was more than evident. "Guess we're gonna have to change that shooting scene for ya."

I had just joined the club of Hollywood tough guys...The crew as a group, laughed and I was escorted to breakfast. I didn't do another Western until an episode of *Little House On The Prairie* in 1977. This was 1954. The smell of horse dung and tobacco spittin' gave way to the U.S. Army, the stage, the screen and soap operas...

CHAPTER 9

The Soldier

I am not afraid of death. I cannot remember the last time I was. I have used at least five or six of my nine lives. I'd be very pissed off if that final shot was used at this point, even this late point, because I don't think I have really finished what I was put here for. A conceit albeit, but treasured in my old age

Some of those nine lives almost lost:

At Frinton on the English coast, my mother, being always the gutsy "just do it" type, didn't just coax me into the waves; there was a push, or pushes. I was terrified. I never quite got over that fear of waves. Years later, when body surfing in very carefully chosen wave-sets at Zuma Beach, California, I was thrown upwards on a huge, unexpected one and then crashed down into the sand, head first, underwater. I felt something snap, lost consciousness and for some reason, ended up on the surface, sputtering and regained both consciousness and composure. I made it back to shore. Many years later, during a lung x-ray, the doctor, staring at a lump of something in the bones of my neck, asked if I had ever broken it. Remembering Zuma I said, "Maybe."

Decades after that, I began teaching disabled scuba divers. My first experience with a quadriplegic, was a young man who had broken his neck body surfing, coming off a big wave at... Zuma beach...not as lucky as I.

Another life used was in the U.S. army. No, not combat - I was a peacetime soldier-between Korea and Vietnam.

In advanced Infantry training at Fort Carson Colorado, We were on maneuvers up in the Rocky Mountains, an idyllic place for the otherwise dreary regimen of drills and learning weaponry and infantry platoon tactics. One day on the mortar range, we were loading and firing an 81-millimeter mortar. It's a sort of tube into which one drops a round with an explosive packet on the back side which then hits a pin at the bottom of the tube and the projectile comes blasting out and goes down-range for, in the case of some mortars, miles.

The ritual is to have the gunner lean over the sight on the barrel and the loader, hold the round until the weapon is aimed, then when sighted, back away from the weapon, call "clear". The loader then drops the round in, the explosion takes place at the bottom of the tube and the round (also with an explosive warhead) comes blasting out with great force.

I was the gunner. I did NOT raise my head off the sight and say, "Clear". The loader dropped the round in, the projectile came blasting out. As I raised my head from the sight, the round, on its furious journey, missed my forehead by less than an inch and in the process, took my helmet along with it, depositing it a hundred yards down range, a tangled mess of charred steel. The helmet was obviously not fastened to my chin. My most eloquent comment in my temporary shock, was not constructive: "You dumb fuck!", which was repeated several times in case repetition could be a learning experience I suppose.

I notice that now in the military, helmets are fastened to chins. I suppose the incidents of a mortar round accidentally taking them off compared to soldiers losing them while running are substantially less. All the World War Two movies show soldiers holding their helmets, unfastened to the chin when running. I was told that that was because in World War One, shells would explode next to a soldier and if he had his helmet fastened it would take his head off. The practice of unfastened helmets continued through my era and into the Vietnam War. Lucky me.

Another time in the army, an over enthusiastic young trainee, on maneuvers, jumped up and fired point blank at me, the "enemy", with a 30.06 caliber M-1 rifle. The round was a blank, but in that blank there was a wad of material. That wad hit my cheek and drew blood. Not a deep wound - it did not put out an eye. He was court martialed. One was not supposed to fire into someone's face at ten feet...on manoeuvres. He was a bit too enthusiastic about soldiering..They used to call it, 'Gung Ho!", an expression dating from our imperial past in China, I believe.

So much for the peacetime war stories.

I had set out at the beginning of my service to do a sort of tribute to my father, who had been a Royal Marine Officer in WW-2. I volunteered for induction in June of '55, not to be a hero, but just to get it over with, as I knew my number in the draft was coming up. As I entered the service, I called my Dad in London and asked him if he had any advice.

Ian Coster, the film critic, then with three children, had not been drafted into the British service. He volunteered as a Private, for the Royal Marines. I'm not sure my mother ever forgave him for feeling that necessity, when most guys 38 or so, minded their families and joined the Home Guard and watched for the "Jerry" bombers. But not Dad.

Years later, I thought about it as I volunteered for the draft. There were a lot of guys "eating it", in Korea, I couldn't just body surf in Malibu, remembering even the few from my high school who didn't come back...perhaps so it was with Dad; was it the fact that at twelve or so, during the Great War, he, as a little New Zealand boy, heard of so many of his brave fellow New Zealand men and boys being slaughtered?....He had to do his bit in this new war...He could not sit idly by. Likewise, I felt the same. Even though only eleven years old as WW-2 ended, I always somehow felt a tinge of guilt that I had not "been there" doing my bit....childish....nonsense...but it clung.

Upon completing Officers Training School, my dad volunteered for the newly formed Royal Marine Commandos. Led by Lord Mountbatten, a blood royal and with whom dad went on to serve in India and Burma. "Pay attention to the training. A lot of Americans got their heads blown off in the war, because they didn't," was his graphic reply to my request for advice. I, like so many other sons, did not write often enough. I have a few shoulda-woulda-couldas, but that is a painful one of them...Shoulda written dad.

On returning from basic training, to Ma's apartment, I was met at the door by my sister, Georgiana, then about to enter college. I was decked out in my "summer tans", as the street uniform of that day was called; tan cotton twill for enlisted men, with no jacket. I felt good, with my light blue "infantry" colors showing on my starched uniform, a pair of Corcoran Jump Boots that I had bought for myself (not organizational G.I., but allowed). They were Paratrooper, custom made, comfortable, absolutely super and were polished by me to perfection! I did look and feel proud.

In basic training I had been posted to "Sykes Regulars", a legendary regiment from days of old, now active as a training regimen. We were taught well. With my capped head held high, I climbed the stairs to my mother's door. My sister, standing there, hugged me a little awkwardly and then the reason for her being there became clear: "Did you hear?...Ian ...father...has died"

The words hung there in the confines of that staircase hallway "Oh, Jesus, when?"

"While you were in training, I'm sorry we couldn't contact you"

For a moment I felt her almost unexpressed pain. She having NOT gotten back to England would never see her father. She was three when we left.

The proud, starched young soldier stood there...just stood there. Shock. Gut tearing shock...and remorse. All of that. I didn't cry. The pre-storm, after-storm effect hung suspended on that dim lit staircase. He would not live to be proud of his soldier son. Nor would he have the opportunity to laugh at and be proud of his artist/actor son. None of it, after spending a very short 13 months with him, he was now gone. Writing of that moment

- when I so hoped my ears had deceived me - still strikes a forlorn chord sixty-four years later.

To paraphrase Tennyson, "Belated discovery of the love of a parent is so much better than never having had it." Ian's dear Kate and my half-brother, John, saw to his burial. His former boss for the entire war, Lord Mountbatten, read "the lesson" at his funeral.

***

My serious soldiering began in 1955 at the home of the 3d United States Infantry, "The Old Guard", the Honor Guard of the US Army.,

My duties there at Fort McNair in Washington DC ran from being a member of the world-famous Drill Team, the first to ever toss rifles with fixed bayonets over one another's heads...I never quite made that death defying position, limited to the best few on the team. The dreadful repetitiveness of the drill made my mind wander.

Eventually, I asked for a different duty. I was posted to Fort Meyer, Virginia, home of the Arlington National Cemetery. My duties included meeting dignitaries at the airport and train station, being in the personal escort for President Eisenhower on his last inaugural parade, and burying veterans at Arlington National Cemetery. There have been lots of movies featuring those burials - firing rifles into the air over the casket - something so primitive about that ritual. Strange how people need that. You could just as easily go down to a beach, get drunk, sing songs of "so long"...

Years later, my brother, brother-in-law and I did just that for the wake after the passing of ma. We roamed down the beach at San Diego at night, singing songs of lust and loss in her honor. We imagined in our at-least-a-case-of-beer state, that she would have loved it. It was so irreverent, as was she at her best.

But not at Arlington National Cemetery. We dressed in our finest and we were the finest. As we handed the carefully folded flags from the casket to the next of kin, the widows, sisters, and mothers were grateful and we felt their pain...as much as we could and as long as we could. Then at a given point we were allowed to request "off" that duty and go back to the line company. Walking guard duty was a relief from those ever-haunted faces.

Every Sunday there was a parade. We would wheel in our "Squads Right and Left" drill, another unique practice in the Old Guard. The only other unit in the army still to practice it are the Cadets at West Point. It's a beautiful maneuver like a formal, wheeling, gliding turn of cavalry horses instead of an angular change of direction. In my vivid imagination, I could almost hear the pounding of polo pony's hooves on the turf from the decades before we arrived at Arlington. I could see the great General Patton, the former cavalry officer, astride his magnificent horse there on that field before World War Two and his armored victories. Patrician elegance!

The greatest parade was in honor of the retirement of General McAuliffe, who had said "Nuts" to the Germans at Bastogne during the Battle of the Bulge. I glanced sideways down the line of blue-scarfed soldiers as they read the orders from across the field. From the speaker on the stand wafted the sounds in waves, cutting through the chilly atmosphere. The echoing words recounted his and the One Hundred and First Airborne's stunningly heroic stand against the German army with a handful of freezing soldiers. His reply to the German commander's demand to surrender, "NUTS", was heard around the Allied world.

I looked down the line at this mix of green young soldiers like myself and hardened veteran heroes of many wars who served as our officers and non-commissioned cadre. The tears of emotion were sliding silently down their cheeks and mine. Those sergeants and officers were picked, we thought, for the Honor Guard, because of the (deserved) medal-ribbons bedecking their chests...What a sight. All these heroes marching on parade in honor of another comrade.

Before that, in the summer of '55, I returned to training with renewed commitment. I did well in the Colorado Rockies. In the late summer and early fall of 1955 and was one of four soldiers in the division picked to go to the U.S. Army Honor Guard in Washington DC and Arlington Virginia.

While in Fort Carson, Colorado, in the pine woods and valleys of the lower Rocky Mountains, we even got to brush shoulders with the original Green Berets Special Forces, a tough, experienced group of veterans from WW-2 and Korea, with lean and lined faces and distant looks. As they passed by, little did they know how soon they would be in Southeast Asia, the first of our troops, as "advisors" sent there; a long time before the public knew about what was to become the Vietnam War.

I loved the foothills of the Rocky Mountains. I loved the smells, the challenges of the military as well as the sheer wonder of simple survival in the open country. My leadership skills were becoming evident, also my sense of excitement with infantry tactics. The rest of my regiment was sent to Korea, where the war had just finished. It had started and stopped several times...this time, though, they were convinced that it was really over. As of now, there is still no peace treaty.

But the three others and I went off to Washington D.C. with much eager anticipation to be in the "Old Guard"! I was determined, even as a "peacetime soldier", to be the best.

Eventually, in my final year at Fort Myer, Virginia, I achieved a certain notoriety having been awarded Battalion Soldier of The Month, then Regimental Soldier of the Month. I was also supposedly the first soldier to be awarded Colonel's Orderly...ten times in a row. Colonel's Orderly was awarded when one was considered by the Officer of the Day, to be the finest of the super spit and polish of all the guards posted that day.

Our duties included guarding the houses of the Chairman of the Joint Chiefs of Staff, Army Chief of Staff, and a host of other Generals and Admirals. They were magnificent houses, with two and three floors, multiple servants, and sweeping porticos and gabled roofs... all the grandeur of the 19th Century still intact.

When one was awarded Colonel's Orderly, one was relieved of having to walk guard on that round, and, instead, got to escort the Regimental Commander around for a day, and then receive a weekend pass. Good stuff. Our Regimental Commander was a war hero. He seemed to be amused at my continuing appearances as his orderly.

As a Private First Class, I entered the Non-commissioned Officers Academy at Fort Belvoir, Virginia. I managed to attain second in my class, losing first place by four points. The fellow who won went on to West Point, the premier army officers' school in the country. I was not a U.S. citizen and therefore could not be an officer; as an alien I was unable to gain a "classified" security clearance. Irony: I was in the President's official escort team with a rifle which could have been loaded, and a fixed bayonet, not one hundred feet away from President Eisenhower...without a security clearance! I did on one occasion, mention that security loophole to my Colonel. He, astonished, replied, "That stays in this office, right, Coster?"

I did, in my last year at the Third Infantry, achieve my final goal; to be posted as a Sentinel on what was then, The Tomb of the Unknown Soldier (now named Tomb of The Unknowns). I had earned a reputation from my Colonel's Orderly awards and had just completed the NCO Academy. Our Colonel said, "Coster, what can I do for you besides a three-day pass?" I said, "Put me on the Tomb, sir." He replied, "You're a little marginal on the height." A Sentinel was supposed to be 6'2" tall. I was barely 5'11" plus my shoes, which had huge heels and our Old Guard taps on the inside for clicking our heels....the only regiment in the US Army allowed to click heels! (generally, a no, no, because German soldiers used to click heels). But I was posted there on his command.

I went up to the tomb and reported to the officer in charge - then a 1st Lieutenant, now a Sergeant. Our Sergeant of the Guard was the second highest decorated enlisted man in WW-2. This fine soldier is now buried near the Tomb of The Unknowns. I reported for duty in that sacred barracks beneath the tomb. The training was all at night. I started to learn the steps, the pauses, and the rifle drill.

A day into that training, though, I got a call from my sister saying that Ma was quite ill and that she'd had to stop working and needed financial help. I made, at that point, $105 a month. One could not take a job while on The Tomb.

Through the graces of a lawyer buddy from Pomona College, Tom Slutes, who was finishing active duty, as a draftee, I got his part time job as a bartender at the Officers Club - a tale for another afternoon - and had to leave my beloved Tomb of The Unknown Soldier, the greatest disappointment of my life up until that point. But I actually WAS posted there! Apparently, most army records were lost in a fire during the early 60s, but thanks to mentions in the post newspaper kept by the Regimental Historian some of my exploits are still on record.

On a visit with my grandsons, who seemed mighty impressed when I took them backstage at the Tomb, I was made to feel welcome and the boys witnessed the sentinels preparing for the Changing of The Guard. It was there that the Sergeant of The Guard told me that all records prior to the 60s had been lost. Fortunately, to this day, I still have as one of my most treasured possessions, that medallion as a Sentinel on the Tomb which bears my name on it, given to me as an honor for simply having been posted there.

At the end of my active service I was eligible for American Citizenship.... I never considered I was not American, as my mother's family had come to America in 1681. But I was still British! The Colonel, when he found out my new status said, "If you stay in, I'll help you get a direct commission. We need young men like you, a lot of our young officers are leaving for private industry."

After assuring him that I was deeply complimented, I thanked him and said, 'If I don't get a job as an actor in three months, may I take you up on that offer?" He laughed, said "Of course," and then wished me well. I enjoyed serving under that magnificent officer.

Looking back, I cannot go on without mentioning a couple of others under whom I served.

When I arrived at Fort Meyer to report to The Old Guard, I reported to the "top kick", the lead Master Sergeant in the Company. He was a tough old bird who I was soon to find out was one of the few survivors of the infamous "Bataan Death March" in WW-2. I stood before him at attention and noticed him looking at me quizzically. I soon found out why. I had done a few movies before entering the army. The last one, *City of Shadows* with the famous Irish actor, Victor McLaglen, of John Ford movie fame, had just opened on the post.

The Master Sergeant without a trace of a smile said gruffly, "You were pretty good." I, surprised that my slight fame had escorted me to the grounds of Fort Myer, thanked him. Then he popped the question, "Tell me something Coster, are all them actors in Hollywood. tooty fruities?" My humor, almost ever present, got the best of me. My reply in a distinct lisp was, "Not me Sergeant! I just had an operation!"

He laughed an Irish laugh from his gut and from that moment on we were pals.

He seemed to appreciate my efforts to be a good infantryman. My cherished memories are of his recounting the days of The Bataan Death March - eating maggots for protein! He was not bitter...surprising considering the terrible cruelty with which the prisoners were treated. He explained, "The Japanese only expected about 25,000 American and Filipino soldiers to surrender. It turned out to be over 175,000. Yes they were cruel, but also afraid."

How charitable I thought. The atrocities from that march and other Japanese war crimes were only partially dealt with in subsequent international trials; the American government apparently feeling that the public had had enough with "war criminals" after the Nuremberg trials in Germany, decided our public didn't need recounting of the horrors perpetrated by our new allies whose country we were now helping to rebuild.

Young blood, young glands: In the gleaming white floored barracks of Fort Myer, the talk among horny young men often, inevitably drifted to women. There were a few of us at eighteen to twenty-two, not many, who had experience in the mysteries of the sexual female and the delight therefrom.

One of the exceptions was a guy we shall call Fred. He was a virgin, about to be married on his next furlough. When we wise old men of the world found out that state of innocence, we descended on Fred with our merciless humor. "Are you goin' down on her buddy? 'Cause if you don't, another guy will when you leave. Then she will throw rocks at you when you go home again."

He left to get married, returning sometime later to the interrogation of his teammates.

"Well, did you do the deed?" 'Yeah, actually I did, I went uh, down there and then..." "THEN!" - an echoing chorus of the same word, after which a pause and then without a trace of embarrassment, his almost whispered, simple, reverent explanation: "Well, I got a hair in my mouth and I sorta threw up." Speechless at this revelation, we hesitatingly, trying to stifle imminent guffaws, inquired as to how he coped with this extraordinary result of his adventurous love making. His answer: "Well, I actually got a towel, wiped her off and we started again...just kinda went back to it."

To a man, we were stunned. The whole cynical, fucked up bunch of us had to admit that his was a love, a devotion that would last forever. So much for making fun of a naive soldier from Iowa.

Don was also a virgin. We, the same tawdry group of "veterans", insisted that he should learn the ways of our limited world before subjecting his future wife to the possible brutality, certainly the insensitivity, of an inexperienced lover. He agreed in principle. We took my old Studebaker to a peninsula in Washington DC, on the banks of the Potomac, where there was a lovely park. The rest of us exited the car, affording Don a bit of privacy with a floozy we had picked up in a bar. She was loose, but lovely. A perfect first lay for the imaginative.

Not knowing how he would fare, we stood a not-too-voyeuristic distance away and awaited the outcome, so to speak. Suddenly from the Studebaker came absolute shrieks of delight. One "whoop" followed another, He then jumped out of the Studebaker and leapt and whooped a wobbling way to the end of the peninsula and back then dived back into the back seat with his much pleased and most surprised new amour. We tactfully waited until all the ardor possible from a country boy had run its course...Again, the cynical assholes of Company "B" had been hoisted on our own petards.

One hillbilly buddy of mine who could never remember my last name, Coster, always referred to me as Cosmo. "Cosmo", he said to me one day during a rare moment of reflection, "ah believe that when y'all die, they gonna cut yo head open in an autopsy and find inside nuthin' but hairy pussy!"

Not altogether true, but of course yet to be proven one way or the other.

One totally un-cynical experience was a brief liaison with an African American, Grace, a Corporal in the Women's Army Corps. We met on South Post; now primarily burial grounds as part of Arlington National Cemetery; then, among other things, the HQ of The Women's Army Corps. She was lovely to the point of my having to look away from her in order to not seem like some freak who had a vision problem. More than that unique beauty was to be discovered. A flavored social conscience, which when revealed in conversation, was enlightening to a white guy who's experience with African American culture was limited to my time at the Hightower School of Music. We started dating; more of her sensitivity became evident. A quiet but penetrating intelligence was also apparent and stimulating. Dark, mysterious, and hurt-holding eyes were seen there in the shadows of my car's interior, where most of our private, affectionate talks took place.

Yes, there was at that time in the mid-50s, something of the "forbidden fruit" aspect to the whole affair, but more than anything, I adored her with an increasing intensity. The whole brief, romantic interval between two soldiers ended when one night she said to me tearfully, "Nick, I can't go on with this...I can't take being stared at every time we go out as if I am some sort of street walker with a white man..." Washington D.C. in 1956 was still a Southern town. People did stare. With great regret, perhaps to this day, I acquiesced. We hugged a forlorn farewell and I never saw Grace again.

Another adventure while in the Honor Guard was my purchase of a beautiful blue uniform at a thrift shop, again on South Post Fort Myer.

In Company B, where I spent most of time after leaving the Drill Team at Fort McNair, we had the newly issued grey-green uniforms (the first issued to anyone in the U.S. Army,) but no blues. Those were reserved for Company A and the Tomb Guard. They were also organizational equipment, one could not wear the blue uniform off post.

I liked the look of that blue uniform. It was also a practical matter. With little money and a full social life in Washington, I could not afford even a blue suit for winter and only a seersucker blazer for summer. I went to the thrift shop and there beneath other trunks and boxes was a trunk which, when opened, still smelled of moth balls from long ago packing. It, this impeccable blue uniform I uncovered, was made of a superb woolen broadcloth, such as is unknown in officers' uniforms today. It had been an Artillery Officer's. I took it to our regimental tailor - yes, we actually had a tailor to ensure that we, with our trim waists, (mine was a svelte 28 inches!) were complimented by the uniform. He was amused that a draftee enlisted man should want such a glamorous uniform and proceeded to remove the artillery and officers striping and replace them with our Infantry yellow.

Outfitted in my lovely blues, I was able to attend all the Washington functions I had grown used to, and it served as an elegant substitute for the dinner jacket I could not possibly afford.

I dated, briefly, a young beautiful blonde from the State Department. I took her with the little funds I had, to the opening of the movie, *Oklahoma*. It was a glamorous affair, but my pride was somewhat damaged when afterwards on the street, arm in arm with my State Department sweetie, an old lady, adorned in pearls, came up to me and through her overpainted lips asked me, "Doorman, would you get me a taxi?" I got her a taxi. My gal was amused, but I think that the allure of a dashing Private E-2 was lost on her...or perhaps it was just one that got away...there were a few...actually, quite a few.

I recently told the star of that movie, Shirley Jones, that story. It brought a bright smile to the face of that still beautiful woman.

My dress blue uniform paid off another time.

I was at a very posh cocktail party on Dupont Circle for some high muckety muck and there was another blue uniform at the end of the room. I made my way over to salute and greet General Omar Bradley, the last of the Five Star Generals. Here was my hero. He was the guy who got the two prima donnas, General George Patton and Field Marshal Montgomery, the British hero, to work together. Largely unsung publicly, he was, nevertheless, one of the great generals in our history.

He looked down at my gold braided Honor Guard uniform and quizzically asked, "Son, what rank are you?" The 3d Infantry cocked hat on our epaulets looked, when buffed down, a bit like a Major's oak leaf. "I'm a Private E-2," I said. (That grade at that time had no stripe.) He chuckled and with that wry Midwestern smile said, "Well you coulda fooled me. You look like a Major!!" I, the 'Major', thanked him and turned smartly...the crowd around was amused...and so was I. Flattered and amused. Many times on the streets of Washington, we in our bespangled Honor Guard uniforms were saluted by other foreign soldiers and sailors. We were instructed to salute back, not break out laughing...we were ambassadors we were told.

A man in the wrong profession: We had as Company Commander, a First Lieutenant whose name escapes. He was the best field officer I ever served under. Our primary mission, as said, was the defense of Washington. To be prepared for that mission, we spent many hours on maneuvers in the woods of Virginia and in training for riot control on the streets. This man was a leader, a born and experienced leader who had been awarded a battlefield commission on the fields of Normandy. He had not risen rapidly in rank. His English grammar was not suitable to the halls of West Point or the Citadel. He was kind, but when called for, strict and demanding. Ultimately, he served as long as he could in grade without being "passed over", meaning without promotion he could no longer serve as an officer. He would have to retire or return to the ranks as an enlisted man, a Sergeant. He retired. It was a great loss to the army and to us...the young, the needful of his experiences shared.

His replacement? Captain Andre, a lean man in his thirties with sharp Anglo or Germanic features, a thin nose and pale blue secret-holding eyes. Probably a scholar. Not a born field officer. Our introduction came at an assembly in front of the barracks. The entire company stood at parade rest and was called to attention by this new commanding officer, who, we found out later, had come over from Intelligence. He had not seen Infantry duty in some years, but his branch was indeed Infantry.

In order to attain "field grade" (Major) he had to serve once again in command of an infantry detachment at his present rank of Captain. In front of the crack Honor Guard of the United States Army, Captain Andre called attention...We heard not the sharp, trumpet sound of an authoritative Infantry commander shouting, "ATTEN-SHUN!" but a crackling, weak, pathetic, almost squeaky boy's plea; "Atten–hut". The snickers, giggles, then outright laughs, started in the back of the ranks...it spread. Unfortunately, the eyes of the embarrassed Captain fell on me first. I will never forget that angry look and neither did he.

I was the leading soldier, not only in the Company, but the entire Regiment at the time. I was called in to be "interviewed" by the new commander. Looking down at a folder, obviously my record, without looking up, he said in a low voice, "This is all an act to you, isn't it Coster?" His intel-background showing in his "interviewing" technique. "It's all a show. Do you really believe in what you are doing here?"

Half innocently I said, "'Not quite sure what you mean sir...If you mean do I believe in the use of force as a national policy, no sir, I believe that the United Nations was formed eleven years ago in order to prevent that necessity. However, as we have seen in the recent Korean War alone, the prevention of war with adequate arms, with an adequate army, is still a necessity. I have tried, even in peacetime, to be prepared as well as I can be. My record before you proves that, does it not..." and then pointedly... "SIR?" Still without looking up, "Get out of my office," was all he said. It was sad.

His revenge took the form of assigning me to guard duty. As a non-commissioned officer (after my distinguished graduation from Non-Commissioned Officers School, I was given a raise in grade to Specialist Four, equivalent to Corporal), I was not supposed to walk guard, but, instead, be Sergeant of The Guard. When I enquired courteously whether that was allowed, He looked at me with those cold, blue eyes and said curtly, "There are no Privates available." "Sir!" says I smartly, obediently - not smart assed-ly. I had learned to beware of rule breaking with this guy.

Then came a mad scramble to prepare for the toughest inspection in the army. I had not walked guard for months. In my nine straight wins of Colonel's Orderly before that, I'd had time to prepare the endless spit shining of leather (unknown in today's army - the "leather" is all shiny vinyl), the peaks of our caps, the boots, the Sam Brown belts...In those bygone days we had not just one single belt, but a "Sam Brown", which consisted of a belt with bayonet scabbard and shoulder strap...all leather. Hours of using Kiwi or Esquire polish with an expert measurement of water and a touch of spit and or alcohol (each had his own secret formula) one made the application with soft cloth done in ring-like motions...endless, tiny, motions which resulted in the mirror like shine of which we were so proud and for some, like myself, resulted in awards.

The rifle was another painstaking chore. Naturally, we all kept our weapons clean. But an Honor Guard inspection of that rifle was an anal-like surgical room examination. The rifle was grabbed suddenly by the Officer of The Day, the inspecting officer. (A game each time to see when he would actually grab it...If one dropped it or flipped it to him too soon, the rifle clattered to the ground, to the sneering looks from the Officer of the Day, as well from one's fellow troopers observing the clumsy goof.)

The trick was to watch like a fencer (a lesson learned from my days at RADA) the officer's eyes. Then one flipped the rifle into his hands just as he snatched it. Once or twice when the Officer of the Day was not quite as quick as he thought, the rifle dropped as he tried to grab it. Once the officer's hand was in motion, we were allowed to flip it. It was indeed a game. An Infantry game.

Occasionally, the Officer of the Day was not Infantry. The terror in the confrontation was evident in his eyes. On one occasion, the officer dropped the weapon, and was supposed to, by custom, pick it up. This officer did not. He was red with anger and when I stood there waiting for him to pick it up, he looked at me and said, "Pick the damn thing up!" I said, "As you were, sir. It is customary in our regiment for the dropping person to retrieve the weapon." "Pick the fucking thing up, dammit! And don't ever say as you were' to an officer again! Ya got that!" "Yes sir," I said genuinely. Never saw him as O.D. again.

For this born rebel, these two officers were the only ones with whom the term "run in" became familiar. Captain Andre and I never greeted each other warmly. His last embarrassment was when I returned to barracks having been awarded the rank of Acting E-5, a feat unheard of by a draftee in the Military District of Washington in peacetime. I had indeed made Colonel's Orderly (under stress). I'd had no time to do my massive usual prep, so other buddies helped me...for beer, of course. Together, laughing, we cleaned and polished the brass and leather, surgically cleaned the rifle. I won Colonel's Orderly for the tenth straight time.

The Colonel upon my arrival, asked what the hell was I, a Non-Com, doing on guard mount. I said, "The Captain informed me there were no privates available." He, looking at my straight delivery of this comic line, said... "Hmmm, well let's make sure it doesn't happen again." He then promoted me to acting E-5; a full Sergeant at that time with three stripes and a rock underneath.

Captain Andre's strange misfortune in being assigned to the 3d Infantry Honor Guard, was not a source of enjoyment to me and I am sure not for him. I've often wondered if he made it to the rank of Major. My favorite, everybody's favorite Lieutenant, whom he replaced, was given a rousing send off.

I was the only qualified trooper who when separating from the army, was not called in to Captain Andre's office and formally asked if I would re-enlist.....pity.

Postscript: Actually, there was one other: I was the second-best rifle shot in the regiment. I scored regularly in the 237-240 area (out of 250- meaning center bulls eyes at up to 500 yards-open-peep-sights) of the very difficult M-1 range tests. He scored regularly at 247! He was wined and dined for months to stay in the army. Promises of Olympic glory and soft duty abounded. He led them on until the last day and then took off like a free-flying bird. Two years of army life was enough for him. Captain Andre, after this elaborate deception, did not ask him to re-enlist either.

Unfortunately: the only picture not lost of me in new (in 1955) grey-green uniform only issued to The Old Guard. 3d Infantry Regiment.

My medallion as Sentinel on The Tomb Of The Unknown Soldier at Arlington, 1957

As a new Honor Guard on the drill team, 3 Infantry,
"The Old Guard", Ft McNair, 1955

CHAPTER 10

Live Theater:
Starting with an Aside on Russia

John Steinbeck was, in my California youth, my favorite writer. There was something about the touching simplicity of his storytelling, with its quiet poetic allusions, which appealed to this kid who had so adopted the western ways, and experienced, however briefly, work as a ranch hand in Paso Robles California. Very close to Steinbeck country. .

He wrote a book in 1947, the first of its kind, describing his travels in post war Russia among the people, not the diplomats and mucky-mucks. His, *A Russian Journal*, is an honest reaction to what he saw in a country trying to rebuild itself from the worst devastation of any allied country in WW-2. His tales of young farm women dancing with each other with fervor after working in the fields for twelve hours...dancing with each other because there were no young men ...only a few boys and the very old who still survived. The book was written along with the renowned photographer, Robert Capa, who supplied loads of telling pictures of life in those difficult but productive times.

The book upon publication in the U.S. was considered by the rampant right wingers as Communist propaganda. Welcomed by free-thinkers, it remains a superb piece of objective journalism.

On a plane to Moscow for my second trip to Russia, I read that book.

Why Russia? Why at that time?

As a boy during the war, we'd all heard about the brave Russians defending Stalingrad and other parts of their homeland. Before the bitter, fearful years of the Cold War which were to follow, they were our beloved allies, struggling against the Hitler hordes. I, being an immigrant and not quite at home in America, found, at six years old, companions in other immigrants. It is where I found a kinship with all sorts of Americana, distinguishing neither race nor religion.

Our first California home was in Studio City where Ma had that Republic job. At the bottom of the hill from my grammar school, was a Jewish Deli. I would turn up there after school, push my coins up on the counter and order Matzo Ball soup and the end of a Kosher salami. Why? I have no idea why I found such inexpensive, exotic delicacies more palatable than a chocolate milkshake. After several visits, the owner peered over the counter at this slight boy and inquired not unkindly, "What's a nice goy like you eating this kind of food for?" "Because it's good," says I...The concise answer was good enough for him....the rest of my life I have loved Jewish food....having no idea until recently how much of the food and indeed much of the culture of the American Jew, was Russian based.

The Russians love drama, music, and romanticism. I, in my middle years, did a soap opera, *Santa Barbara*, which rapidly became the most watched television show - worldwide - in history. From France to Nepal, from Italy to Azerbaijan, but most of all in Russia. In Russia, on Facebook to be precise, I met my third and beloved current wife, Elena Borodulina, who had watched *Santa Barbara* as a child.

We met on Facebook. There was no picture on her entry. She wrote to me several weeks or months in a row. Finally, I answered. We discussed Russian composers; perhaps she was impressed with the fact that an American TV guy knew something of Gliere, Glasenov, Borudin? I finally asked her to send a picture. She did. Not the expected, "Babushka" of thickened midriff and bandana on head and missing or gold encrusted front teeth....oh, no; there in the photo was a lanky young woman, relaxedly lounging on a Black Sea beach Astonished at this revelation, I wrote. "I'm too old for you!" She fired back, "That's your problem!"...that was almost 9 years ago.

I shall return to my "Russian Journal" on another "afternoon".

Post RADA, my time in the army and my days at Bob's and the Poodle I headed to New York to embark on my fledgling acting career. I struggled there for some years trying to get any sort of job on Broadway or Off Broadway. Leaving the army in the summer of 1957, I was hired at The Barter Theatre of Virginia founded by Robert Porterfield, a Virginia gentleman in the best sense of the word, who'd had a brief career as an actor, working for the Belasco Theaters in New York. The depression came and with it he retired to his farm in Western Virginia and took along a handful of hungry New York Actors to start the Barter Theatre. Gregory Peck and Ernest Borgnine were among those who became famous.

Barter, ha! It was, in fact just that: Barter. Depression farmers had no money for tickets, but they had eggs, pork chops, cabbages and occasionally moonshine, the Southern homemade whiskey made famous in dozens and dozens of movies. So, they bartered their farm goods for tickets and the actors ate! To this day, on opening night, they accept a certain amount of barter as payment, and backstage, after the show, actors and staff sip a ritual nip of the bartered moonshine.

Upon arrival at this lovely place of of hard work (11 plays in 10 weeks), we were admonished by the correct but humorous Mr. Porterfield (nobody ever called him Bob, who said matter-of-factly, "Now you all…I know that in youth, certain urges flourish, I would request so's not to embarrass yourselves and the folks hereabouts, that if you are gonna 'do it', do it in the bushes, not out in the open." And with that admonition, he would smilingly retreat to his office.

That summer fresh out of the army was to prove an amazingly creative one. Fine actors like Jerry Hardin, Marcie Hubert, and Mitch Ryan started there. Years later while working closely with Gregory Peck, we swapped stories about The Barter. The summer was also filled with ripe young apprentices who more than once seemed to enjoy the discovery of "life-in-the-bushes".

The bushes were, over time, supplanted by the comfort of a room in what had been an old southern girl's school, which were now the dormitories for The Barter Theatre actors and staff.

At that dorm, as a permanent "guest", was Ann Armstrong, in her eighties, a very dear pal and initial editor of the writer Thomas Wolfe. She and I - in contrast to the young damsels in other rooms who were so delicious and with whom conversations gave way quickly to wildly athletic sex - would talk endlessly about 'Tom'.

It was obvious that she'd never gotten over him. It was my introduction to the great southern writers. Before that, in high school, I had struggled with Faulkner. Wolfe and, then later, Flannery O'Connor became two of my favorites. It was from these southern writers that I began to feel my southern-ness. My Grandmother who visited California – traveling by airplane well into her nineties, as said - was my chief source of southern lore as well as an inspiration to my acting fantasies.

From *The Barter* I went to New York and for a month or so looked for a play…or rather any play that would have me. No luck. I headed down the coast a bit and auditioned for the newly reopened Arena Stage Repertory Company in Washington DC, where I spent two very creative years. There were a variety of classic and new plays, including many Irish ones, as we had in residence, the great Irish actress, Pauline Flanagan O'Casey, a bunch of Shaw and others. Hard work and much fun was had. A bevy of very good actors got their starts there under the eyes of the Arena's founder, Zelda Fichandler.

The Arena Stage was just that; one of the first of its kind since ancient times, where we performed within inches sometimes of the first row of seats! There was an incredible sense of intimacy. On opening night, a friend, George Grizzard, by then a famous Broadway actor, and a founding member of Arena, sent me an opening night telegram warning me of the "arena" setting: "Keep turning, honey. They're all around you!"

One night while playing an intimate love scene very close to the front row in Turgenev's *A Month In The Country*, a woman, enthralled by the delicious romanticism in the play, sat with her legs completely spread apart unaware (one hopes) that she had forgotten to wear panties and that her entire array of female gifts were on display right in front of my face. The wonderful actress, Astrid Wilsrud, was facing the other way. I supposed I must have at least sputtered before regaining my lines and composure, because the ever-sensitive Astrid after the scene, asked me if my digestion had been in distress.

Towards the end of that first year there, I began to realize - playing with all these well-trained New York actors - that I lacked understanding of "The Method", Stanislavsky's teachings started at The Moscow Art Theatre and continued by The Group Theatre, The Actors Studio, and other fine teachers.

The necessity for that knowledge became obvious when the great director Alan Schneider came to direct the Australian play, *Summer Of The Seventeenth Doll*. In rehearsal he stopped me and said "Could you take a different adjustment?" I thought my fly was open! The cast laughed. an "adjustment" meant, I found out, taking a different emotional approach to a moment or scene. (Example: quietly intense instead of burning with open rage.)

One night early in that first year at Arena Stage, in the dim light of off-stage, I sensed, then saw, the dark but radiant eyes of Alicia Justin Hamilton. That pseudonym in this story will be her name .

Her almost night-raven hair fell to her delicately carved shoulders. Is love-at-first-sight possible? I'd never entertained the silly thought. When she emerged from the shadows, the bare-backstage light in no way diminished her astonishing beauty. I was to find out in the months that followed, her original and thirsty intelligence matched that beauty.

Thus, started the actor, 23, and the schoolgirl, 17, along a path of high romance, which lasted throughout the school year of 1957 into the late spring of 1958.

Alicia was an art history major, and being forbidden by the school to date during the week, we met at art galleries. The Phillip's was our favorite. It resembled someone's home. There was a small settee underneath Renoir's *Boating Party*. We sat many an afternoon, learning of each other's lives, which short even in aggregate as both of ours were, provided hours of murmured memories blended with growingly affectionate whispers of love professed...for indeed it seemed that this "at first sight" was not limited to me alone.

And so, the fall and winter went. She would come to the show on the weekends and we would meet surreptitiously during the afternoons when time permitted. I was doing one play while rehearsing for another the whole season. Time was precious.

Those ridiculously romantic times included sloshing home late on weekend nights in deep snow, slinging snowballs at one another while dressed in our finest; of me carrying and depositing Barbara soaking wet on the doorstep of the imposing Holton Arms School. With a lingering kiss, the shivering lass scampered into the protective halls of the Holton Arms.

By the beginning of spring, we knew that we could not bear to be apart and secretly agreed to marry upon her graduation.

And THAT was where the plot turned melodramatic:

Miss Brown, the stern principal at Holton Arms, had caught wind of our engagement, which became not-so-secret when the Washington Post published our plans in "The Bands", an old-fashioned column announcing marriage engagements. Miss Brown and others called me into the office one night after a performance. There, also, was the "General".

Alicia had lost her parents while a toddler in a tragic nightclub fire in Boston in 1941 and she was raised by her grandfather, the "General".

As I entered, with no courtesy at all, I, alone, without Alicia, was told matter-of-factly that I would agree to postpone the marriage. If I married her, the General told me and then without her being the General's dependent, Alicia would give up her U.S. Army provided medicine and all therapy and I, Nicolas would have to pay for private medical care! Alicia had had an operation for a thyroid issue which had left her in need of regular therapy for affected tissue in her neck and chest and left arm.

How much do you make?" asked the General.

"125 bucks a week."

"Well," said he, "her therapy alone would be all of that...per week"

Then Miss Brown chimed in, "AND, because of her time and thoughts spent with you, she is so marginal in her grades, we might have to hold back her graduation." Her face was chiseled in momentary conquest. She and the General waited for my reply.

"It would seem I have no choice"

"Correct!" retorted the General, Miss Brown nodding in satisfaction.

And that was it.

We were not even allowed a tearful departure.,

Later that spring after the allowed graduation, I scurried down to Virginia to meet Alicia, on a planned stop she'd made -to see a school chum while driving back to Texas. We met, unbeknownst to the General, and had a tearful and not very private farewell at the Barter Theatre, yes, The Barter, where her schoolmate was appearing and with whom I had worked the summer before. That was the last, the final heartbreaking romantic interlude in that extraordinary romance.

That fall, Alicia sent the ring back to me...the engagement ring. The General had won his last battle.

Heartbreak does not adequately describe my despondency...

I did find out years later from a U.S. Public Health doctor pal of mine, that I had been lied to regarding the post operation disability: The truth was that since the operation had gone wrong in an army hospital, they were fully responsible for her recovery!

The news came much too late.

After college, Alicia apparently got married to a guy who was not socially connected and had no riches, as had been hoped for by Miss Brown and others.

Years later, at that Barter Theatre chum's wedding at the Plaza Hotel in New York, I finally met Alicia again. I was married by then, had kids, she had kids; she was divorced, I think. I think....Ha! I was incapable of thinking. I was struck almost numb-dumb for I realized that after all those years, I was still in love with her.

She wanted to come to the show I was doing at the time, *Blood Knot,* my first real artistic success in New York. Backstage afterwards, once more in dim light, did we have a remembered connection? I really rather think so. We went back to our respective lives, she in Texas, I in New York, and it would be decades before I'd see her again.

Before playing *The Little Foxes* in New Orleans in 1982, I was about to marry dear Beth after several years of being together. But just as I was heading for New Orleans, I suddenly thought, 'I CAN'T marry again without seeing, talking to Alicia. I cannot marry Beth with that interlude lingering. I simply can't. Whatever the outcome.'

I got her number and called her.

Alicia, without prompting, replied, "Yes, I'll come to see you."

I told Elizabeth Taylor, my co-star at the time, the whole romantic Romeo and Juliet-esque story, replete with the suicidal ideations that ran through my mind all those years back while trudging along the Hudson River late at night, almost responding to the lure of the cold, deadly but inviting waters below

Elizabeth was fascinated by the tale and also intrigued at what might happen at this meeting to come.

Alicia came. We met at a Mississippi riverside cafe before the show at dusk. With her was her husband of not-too-long, Leonard. He quickly but unhurriedly suggested that Alicia and I stroll upon the river walk...alone for a bit. What extraordinary sensitivity thought I...and quiet confidence, I mused.

We strolled, and for the life of me I cannot even remember what we talked about.

They came to the show. All was pleasant...really pleasant. Elizabeth was astonished at Barbara's beauty and composure. "MY GOD! What a beauty..." said she. "Look who's talkin'," says I. She laughed her bawdy laugh, that full throated, full-living laugh of hers

The next night Eliabeth asked with glee in anticipation, "How'd it go? What the fuck happened?"

I said after a pause, "It went well. I know why I loved her all those years ago...but I didn't get that old, craaaazy feeling anymore"

Years later I saw Elizabeth on Broadway in *Private Lives* with her ex, Richard Burton and when I asked how it was with Richard this time around, she replied with a knowing glint in her lavender eyes, "But I don't get that old, craaazy feeling anymore."

***

The summer of '58 I scooted to the Neighborhood Place whose modern acting classes had been founded by Sanford Meisner, also of Group Theatre fame.

By this point of my "career" I had already developed a sense of character; a blend of oneself into the role they are being asked to play. In a concert style reading of Sean O'Casey's *Pictures In the Hallway*, I had to portray an old man. I was 23 and had seen many mediocre college actors play old men and knew that I had to find something organic - particularly since we were without makeup - to make his age believable. I discovered by accident upon injuring my thumb in a separate incident that the bone ached. I started rubbing the sore joint, and then began fooling around with it, slightly bending the thumb out of shape as though arthritic, and in the rubbing of that "aging" joint, being seemingly unaware I was rubbing while talking and listening, I became an old man. It was effective and I never forgot how simple and honest the discovery of character can be.

Following Arena came The Charles Playhouse in Boston in the fall of 1959. Once again, I had tried to get a New York gig in early fall, but no dice. The Charles, the first of several repertory companies of which I was a founding member, was a trip! We had to pee out on the fire escape as there wasn't an actors' bathroom backstage - at least at the outset - nor, for that matter, was there regular pay! The kindly, struggling producer, Frank Sugrue, always tried to make up for it in other ways. For example, he would scramble between matinee and evenings on Saturdays to bring us take-out Chinese food, which we wolfed down quickly, trying to avoid spilling lobster sauce on our velvet tunics.

We somehow got through that first season, and I received my first ever "brilliant" review from the then Boston Globe theater critic, Kevin Kelly, for the English play, *Epitaph for George Dillon*, in which I played an insecure, broke, upper class actor (type casting) who is sponging off a lower middle-class family and is eventually nailed by the bright, socialist daughter, played by the great Elizabeth Wilson. The play was directed with amazing dexterity by the young Artistic Director, Michael Murray.

At the Charles, I directed my first play, Sartre's *No Exit*. The play is about people in a simple square room slowly discovering that they're actually in hell. Marcie Hubert, the elegant actress who had been with me at the Barter Theatre, played the role of a lesbian. I didn't want a clichéd short stocky woman with a mannish tweed suit. Instead, I was looking for a slinky, tall attractive gal in what might be considered yachting clothes. Marcie fit the bill...except...she couldn't identify with her character killing her friend, her lover. She was so dedicated to the truth in her work, that she called me one night late and said she just couldn't get the emotional depth of the sadism involved in the killing. I thought for awhile... "Have you ever, in the middle of the night, awakened to the sound of an ambulance or fire engine's siren and wondered, in fact speculated on the intensity, the severity of the injuries or fire damage occurring? Even just a little perhaps?" A very long pause. Then, "Thank you." Somehow that image triggered a forgotten sin of thought. She was received, as was the play, with immensely satisfying reactions.

A moment of reflection: I caught the Asian flu during the run of Edwin Justus Mayer's *Children of Darkness*, about a young woman who is brought up in Newgate Jail, where her father is the jailer. She is torn between a nobleman who is rich and can get her the hell out of there and a young romantic who is a prisoner as well - played by none other than this guy at 25...fairly good looking (ha) and thin and muscular. But all those attributes did not save me from the flu and its almost disastrous consequences.

In the middle of some speech, I suddenly realized that the flu had reached the far reaches of my intestines and had to escape - and it did! - right into my velvet trousers. I could not turn my back to the complete audience, because the stage was a slight thrust. I could only back upstage so far. I sped through my lines hurriedly and raced offstage to find water and rag. LUCK! The breeches were not only velvet, they were black...I cleaned, I re-entered for my next scene with the huge water-spot barely showing... More than enough of that.

Along with *No Exit*, I directed on the same bill, Strindberg's, *The Stronger*, an open act play about two women confronting each other over one robbing the other of her husband's affections. The accused never talks. For the entirety of the performance. I had them rehearse as if the other DID talk, then shut her up for the final rehearsal and performances. Fun stuff. All her reactions therefore became as if she WERE about to speak, and then didn't rather than anticipating that she would never talk as indicated in the play.

The Charles Playhouse, was on Warrenton Street behind the Shubert Theatre. It was owned by the mob. There were three floors. The top floor was the theatre, below that was a floozie bar, beneath that, was a gay and lesbian bar (highly illegal in those days). Of course, the actors loved THAT bar. We did have fun being part of the basement–in-the--building world of the underworld.

Frank Sorvino was the supposed owner. A giant of man in all directions, he was curiously protective of his flock of thespians on the top floor. He and I hit it off. From my previous experience with gangsters at the Poodle Hut, I knew how to speak without fear or condescension.

As we started to rehearse, *Epitaph for George Dillon*, Frank asked what it was about. I told him of George's patronizing behavior to his hosts while sponging off them and then his eventual destruction. Frank pondered for a moment and said quietly, "I knew guys like him." The use of the past tense did not go unnoticed by me. He came to see me in the play, and said afterwards with a nod of approval, "Yeah." From Frank, that was an accolade to be cherished.

From the Charles Playhouse, followed summer stock tours all over the Eastern Coast and Maryland. Madcap races from one theatre to another, arriving just in time for a quick rehearsal before opening. One theatre had a corrugated iron roof...It started raining at the beginning of the show; a torrent of incredibly noisy rain drops which sounded like golf balls falling. The noise drowned out even the actors who bellowed their lines. One jaded old actor was heard calling as if to the Gods, "Jesus, it sounds like two skeletons fucking on a tin roof using a beer can for a condom!"

There were many more plays that summer and beyond, with many, many more rainstorms.

CHAPTER 11

My New York Trojan Horse

As said, I had a great deal of trouble being cast in a New York play, but finally my new agent, an aged gentleman (whose name eludes me in *my* aged-ness) who had seen me in a number of plays at Arena Stage, called and said they wanted me to take over quickly the male lead in a play by Maurice Valency, famous for translating *Giradeux and Anouilh*. It was not a strong play, but the lead male was a Greek hero and feeling heroic, I accepted. A well-known actress, Nancy Wickwire, was playing the female lead.

Nancy, like me, trained at the Neighborhood Playhouse utilizing Sanford Meisner's method acting (which concentrates on playing off and with the other actor), was a dream in terms of "relating to" in rehearsals. However, on opening night, which came much too quickly -one week of rehearsals for a difficult classical part - Nancy, the dream partner in rehearsals, completely ignored me on stage and faced the audience like a 1930s Theatre Guild actor, playing the prima donna. I was too young at the time to respond to this surprising alone-on-stage style.

Not too long after that, while working with Olivier, I did learn what to do when other actors don't or can't relate. Olivier simply took command. He would play to an imaginary character. He would even enhance the seemingly absent performer to the extent that the other person could have "phoned it in" because they became unnecessary! Only rarely has that tactic become urgent in my career. That as well as a skill at improvising, saved me a number of times.

So, Nancy not relating was just one unsettling experience that night. Upon my first entrance, which was as a hero returning from the wars, the tape that was supposed to emulate the crowd cheering broke, resulting in a sound resembling a repetitive frog "errp, errp reep, reep". The audience for whom all reality was instantly destroyed, roared with laughter. The play had devolved into an unintentional comedy. Then a short time later, the scenery chose to fall...on me. Yes, it actually came apart and pieces of it fell on the now ignominious Greek hero. The audience once again found it extremely amusing.

All these surprises affected this young actor...I'm not sure to what extent, but I kind of remember in a slight daze, struggling to "get through it" without pissing my pantaloons.

Walter Kerr, the leading American theatre critic at the time and after whom a Broadway theatre is now named, wrote, "Nicolas Coster played the second act as if he was half asleep," and indeed I was at least "half" asleep; dazed and hopeless.

He never mentioned me again until years later, in *Twigs*, where he actually selected me as one of the best performances of the season! It was at that time I played opposite the great Sada Thompson, who deservedly won the Tony and did relate wonderfully to me - on and off stage...for an entire year - at the end of which time she said affectionately, "Oh Nicky, it's just as fresh as it was when we started, all those months ago." And indeed, it was.

Years later, in Michael Sawyer's brilliant *Naomi Court* at the Manhattan Theatre Club, run by the adventurous Lynne Meadows, where I played opposite the late Brad Davis, an enormously gifted actor known best for the film *Midnight Express*, that same Walter Kerr wrote the most complimentary review I've ever received, including in that critique, even a mention of how much he had like me in *Twigs*.

CHAPTER 12

Olivier!

In the Fall of 1960, I read for yet another Broadway play, *Becket* by Jean Anouilh. Lawrence Olivier and Anthony Quinn were the stars. Quinn was leaving the show to do a movie and Olivier was switching parts from playing Becket to King Henry. Arthur Kennedy, the legendary actor, took over as Beckett.

A lot of the cast were also being changed.

A line of actors stood in the alley between two theaters and I was one of the last. When I finally walked out on stage and started to read the prepared scene, the casting director stopped me and said, "Oh could you skip to the next scene?" I miffed and not even hiding it, said, "Yes, if I can read this one as well, as it is the one I PREPARED as told!" "Of course," was the curt reply.

I read, finished and there was...silence. Nobody said a word. Not even the usually dismissive "Thank you" which signals they either hated you or were coldly indifferent. Then, finally, that same casting director wryly said, "Well, aren't you going to read the scene you PREPARED?" I, astonished, said, "Yes, of course..." and did so.

At the finish of what I knew was surely the end of my Broadway career (for being so cheeky in my insistence on reading the prepared scene), Michel Shurtleff, the brilliant casting director, whom I was in the years following to know and admire, said with a kind laugh, "You had the part after the first scene." "What part?" I asked. "How would you feel about being a standby for Sir Lawrence Olivier?"

I was twenty-six years old and amazed.

I knew that I would never open the show. If Sir Lawrence were ever ill or injured, they would postpone, but in the event of his falling ill during a performance, I could conceivably finish the show. What the hell...To standby for one of the greatest actors in English history? Absolutely!

Olivier was learning the role of King while he was still performing the part of Beckett. He was not the fastest or the most accurate line-learner. I had virtually nothing to do except rehearse with the understudies once or twice a week, but I was there every night watching my hero perform. I would literally stand in the darkened wings off stage like Anne Baxter in the movie, *All About Eve* (without the hat and raincoat she made famous).

The stage manager asked me if I would consider helping Olivier learn the lines of the King (I had learned them already...in those days being a "quick study"). I, of course, eagerly agreed. Thus, began a pleasant and increasingly close relationship with Sir Lawrence, the actor and a most admirable human being.

One night, as we line-learned between the matinee and evening performances, He, hearing my English accent in the part, asked if I had any relatives in England. "My father and a half-brother and step mum actually, but he, my dad, died about five years ago." Oliver suddenly looked sharply at me, and said, "Not IAN Coster, the newspaperman?" I said "Yes, indeed, that was my pa." He laughed and said, "Why the fuck didn't you tell me before?" I said, "Well, so many of the company here seem to have their noses half way up your bum, I thought I would be the exception."

Oliver laughed a mighty laugh and we were chums from then on.

Recently, my age-old pal, the great screenwriter Robert Towne called me raving about an article my dad had written about Olivier and Vivian Leigh back in 1939 or 40. Robert said, "Your dad was REALLY good!" I read it and agreed...I could see my dad's fondness for the two growing legends as well as good reporting.

I was honored to be asked to give the toast at Olivier's wedding reception to Joan Plowright on the stage of the Hudson Theatre. I lifted my glass, and, trying to quickly recall my knowledge of English heraldry, could not for the life of me remember whether Joan was to be called Lady Olivier or whether Vivien Leigh, from whom he was recently divorced, was still Her Ladyship.

The English crown does not, as the head of the Church of England, recognize divorce I thought....Hmm...and in that instant before the toast, I elected toward the positive. I said after a brief hesitation, "To Sir Lawrence and...LADY Olivier" I noticed a twinkle in Olivier's eye as he noticed my ever-so-brief pause. Afterwards he said to me, "Nicolas, you made the right choice. Joan is indeed now Lady Olivier and Vivian is now Vivian, Lady Olivier." Quaint, I thought, that Vivian loses a husband and retains her Christian name which now precedes her title...Shades of Henry the Eighth.

On stage, Olivier was a tiger. The stage was his territory, if you wanted a piece of it, come out and get it, he wasn't going to give it to you. If you were good, he would share the stage with you. If you were not, you may just as well have phoned in your performance; In that case, and I saw it happen with shitty or lazy actors, he would command the stage, own it.

One night he did in fact injure himself. On stage in the horse-riding scenes, Beckett and the King rode fabricated horses while walking under the horses' robes on stilts...tricky stuff for a young man. The still very athletic Olivier at fifty-four, was being 'creative' in making the horse seem to be independent of himself and In doing so, he twisted his knee badly and I, standing in the wings as usual, heard a muffled cry of agony. He came off stage hobbling and sweating. Ever the humorous soul, he looked at me as he passed and whispered, "Not tonight Nicolas," and continued into the darkness.

Somewhat later he said to me, "Nicolas the reason I said that in such a hateful way, was that the only time I ever missed a performance was in *Coriolanus*, and Albert Finney was my understudy. And we all know the rest of THAT fucking story!" He snorted and I felt complimented. Albert Finney had been greatly received in the part and went on to deserved fame.

I never did go on for Olivier.

I once asked him if all the stories about him were true or apocryphal, to which he replied, "If they were witty, they were true!" A lovely wit of his own.

Eventually, during the run, another player with a smallish part left the show suddenly and Jack Schlischel, General Manager for David Merrick the producer, in his infinitely wise financial and tactful way, said, "Nick, you don't do much except hang around here. You wanna take this part? "For how much extra?"I asked, the super savvy businessman. "Twenty-five bucks a week extra," he replied in an extravagant gesture. In 1961, when being paid 125 bucks a week total salary, 25 bucks was a nice piece of change. I, having just gotten married to a gal whom I met in Lee Strasberg's acting class, took the offer.

That gal, Candace Hilligoss from Huron, South Dakota, didn't look like a farmgirl but certainly retained elements of country humor as well as memories of her mother's telling of Great Depression experiences. These tales of woe and homeless wandering became, at my urging, the story, *Dakota Ashes*, I say, "at my urging", not to glorify my husbandly caring, but to illuminate certain facts left out of her book in which I appear as a fictional shit of monstrous proportions. It was unnecessary, I felt, and extremely hurtful.

When I went to NYU film school during the run of *SeeSaw* in 1974. I took a screenwriting course from the terrific teacher, Michelle Cousins. Eventually, when Candace noticed some of my script writing, I suggested she take that course independently of the whole certificate program. She was at a loss for subject matter, I suggested, "Tell those South Dakota stories which fascinate all who hear them."

She did enroll, stayed for years, and wrote *Dakota Ashes*. I cooked, shopped, and ran the kids to their lessons while working in the theatre and teaching scuba diving. I resented none of it. She was obviously happily consumed by her love of writing. When she finished *Dakota Ashes* and showed me a copy, I was genuinely complimentary, including the phrase, "I am so glad I was here to help you with this marvelous story!" Blankly, she looked at me and said, "How did you help?" Stunned and remembering the years of support in every way I had gladly given, something turned off in me. The help never was acknowledged. Her psychiatrist kept pleading with me to "Stay with your family"" and "She has no ego...too fragile." I remembered and coined the phrase, "Insecure people can be quite dangerous." By the fall of 1977, I could no longer go on with the charade. Her friends and mine were well aware of the difficulties.

I repeat here and elsewhere, I shoulda left in a more straightforward manner. Quite understandably she felt betrayed. Very soon after moving myself to California, I met Beth.

Returning to *Beckett*...I was to play a Baron who, when we all invaded France, had to come leaping up some church steps to Olivier as the King and say the memorable line, "My Lord, the Bishops are awaiting!"

Just before my entrance, an actor named Ferdi, who played yet another Baron, asked me in hushed tones whether I could make some noise on my entrance as he had been directed to turn on my entrance, but he was quite deaf and had trouble hearing the preceding actor's entrance. I, ever willing to please my fellow performers if possible, rationalized that because of my long ride and the attendant fatigue, I could easily stumble a bit in all that heavy armor and with shield and therefore make the necessary noise. Method acting training pays off sometimes.

I came on my opening night with tremendous gusto but weary from my imagined exhausting ride in a storm (ah, the boundless limits to a properly trained actor's imagination!) and stomped up the steps, clanging my sword and armor and breathlessly said my line. Olivier cocked his head and gave me a quizzical look not devoid of disdain, before saying his own line. After the scene, during intermission, he called me over and said, "Nicolas, what was that God awful fucking racket you made on your entrance?"

I, not wishing to rat on Ferdi and his deaf request, replied that as a method actor, I had summoned up a vast history of that terrible ride preceding my entrance to the steps of the church...I was exhausted and stumbled over my armor and shield. Olivier, never the fool, sensed something in my elaborate excuse. "Now Nicolas, what was the real reason?" I sheepishly admitted that Ferdi had requested that I make a racket on my entrance that he might hear it and so facilitate his turn.

Olivier with a snort, said, "Well, fuck Ferdi! The stage steps are painted wood, not stone! When you came stomping on those boards, the timbers betrayed our secret to the audience and thereby destroyed the illusion of the stone steps of the church and the reality of the scene."

He was right...of course. Another lesson learned.

In Detroit, while on tour with the same play, we played a giant cavern of a movie theatre, and Olivier sensed as he walked on stage that Detroit was not overwhelmed with his honoring them with an appearance. The audience was not as attentive as might be wished. The tiger in Olivier emerged; He changed timing, energy and even the movements (blocking) and in a few short minutes, excited the audience with his oh-so-special qualities and kept them riveted for the entire performance. Eyes on fire, voice trumpeting from wall to wall and his athletic body writhing in pain, or leaping in victory, he was indeed the improvising, inventive Olivier that is now his history. He taught a whole new audience what it was to spend a unique and exciting night in a live theatre.

A whole generation of us imitated him...the staccato delivery of blank verse, the silken, flirtatious use of his eyes...all of which he was aware. I remember watching him as he made up his eyes...very carefully as if for a film, accenting the corners of the upper lids with a dark liner which gave his already depthful brown eyes an even deeper intensity. For the King in *Becket* he actually changed his dark brown eyes to blue with contact lenses in order to look more like an English King!

His final, amusing (to me), makeup touch was gluing red crepe hair to his armpits so that that hair would match his auburn wig! Meticulous. Never saw him trying to peel that sticky shit off after a sweating performance...In fact perhaps that is why I sort of remember him doing away with that particular character dressing after a while.

CHAPTER 13

Antics of Live Daytime Television

During that run of *Beckett* on Broadway, I was asked to do my first Soap Opera.

Young Doctor Malone was one of several TV soaps that had come over from radio. There were still some old radio actors who delivered their lines in some cases with precision if not freshness.

Richard Chamberlain, whom I had known at Pomona College as one of the drama people or "DP's" as they were jokingly called (there were many Displaced Persons or DP's after WW-2, thousands of whom were within months, starving, disheveled and homeless....so the appellation applied to to the theatre students was not particularly complimentary) was a huge star on nighttime TV as Dr. Kildare. I suppose NBC wanted a sort of equivalent on Daytime....I was picked as that magical M.D.

Dr. Matt Steel was my name, and daytime lover and super understanding physician was my game. I found it challenging and money-making. The salary so exceeded my 125 bucks a week on Broadway that it was a joke. We were broadcast live, coast to coast and many a story has been told about the goofs on live TV. I was both responsible for and the butt of many of these jokes. I did learn how to handle those moments from a distinguished actor, Martin Blaine, one of many radio trained actors of his generation who graced our show.

There was a scene on *Young Dr. Malone* in which a gambling raid at a private mansion party takes place. The sheriff is supposed to break in the door, pull out his gun and say, "This is a raid!" The sheriff came in, tried to pull out his gun and it got stuck in the holster. In his distracted panic he forgot his one line, "This is a raid!". In some incomprehensible tongue known only to him (perhaps), he uttered a few sounds which we heard as, "Uhhhhh...This...ahh...This could...Youuhhhh".

Not relieving this poor man's agony with any haste of movement, but strolling over to him after leading the camera to "follow me" with a wink,

Martin Blaine with his thirty years of radio, slowly and comfortingly put his hand on the peace officer's shoulder, did a 180 degree 'Jack Benny take' to the audience (all of us) and said confidentially, "Is this a raid?" Guffaws were heard throughout the studio. The management was not pleased.

On the *United States Steel Hour*, one of the reigning primetime shows of its day, I was playing my first lead on evening television. Maurice Evans, the leading British-cum-American actor of his day, was playing a British officer taking apart a German mine on the coast of Britain. I, his son, also an officer, was taking apart another one just down the beach. If either were to make a wrong move, the other and the British army would know what not to do in the aftermath of the explosion.Tense stuff.

Evans, a master of technique on stage and screen, was mystified by the mechanical terms of the take-apart-process. During the trickiest part, he simply stopped, then after a pause during which the beloved director, Paul Bogart, said over the mike (which was plugged into our radio-telephones on stage), "Evans is up! Evans is up! Cut to Coster!" ("up" meaning forgot, forgetting). When they did indeed "Cut to Coster", I saw the red camera light go on while another part of my mind was witnessing the end of my fledgling career on national television. I heard myself inventing gibberish about grey spanners and four-inch screw drivers. I did hear from the control room snickers of wonder at my improvisation if not my acting. My debut on evening live television; Evans was most apologetic. I looked to the future.

On *The Secret Storm* years later, I was playing Dr. Paul Britton, an English professor who, having married his student, Amy, played by Jada Roland, an unforgettable, brilliant and sharing actress who at nineteen was a six year veteran of live television, was supposed to come home and announce that the family NEWSPAPER had been sold; tragic news. I came in the door, something distracted me, and I said "I have very sad news....the HOUSE has been sold!"

Dear, ever humorous Jada, began to laugh, but controlled herself professionally, and said with her eyes tearing up from repressed humor, "WHAT did you say?" I, ever quick on my feet, said. "What DID I say?" She replied, "YOU SAID the house has been sold." I then realized my goof and tried to cover it by saying, "Oh, I have been so upset, I meant to say....err mean to say..." Jada, now well into the torture, said with arched eyebrows twitching, "WHAT did you mean to say?" I blurted out, "The NEWSPAPER has been sold!" The volume of my delivery was enough to be heard in the rear of a Broadway theatre, for indeed, even the cameraman jumped. Until the day I left *Secret Storm*, my pals there, when they caught me doing something foolish, would call out, "The house has been sold!"

That same beloved Jada, and I started a forbidden TV romance; we were the first professor/student affair on television; subsequently investigated by the United States Senate for "immorality on television!" Yup, thems was the days....One could not use the word 'pregnant'...it had to be 'with child'. A husband and wife could not be pictured in the same bed...it had to be in twin beds. Oh, how far we have come! While world curing vaccines have been developed, Daytime Television allows sex in the bathroom, the kitchen and certainly from the "missionary position" to the implied if not explicit oral.

Once when making appropriately "polite love" (hugging) on a bearskin rug in front of a fire, Jada and I entwined were shocked to the point of being lifted off the floor. Still hugging and dropped again when a camera moving hit an open electrical circuit. ALL the lights in the studio went black. Jada and I started to laugh, the laugh of the ages. Minutes passed on the live but dead show. When circuits were fixed and the lights returned, we bit our lips and kissed the episode goodbye.

On one of my many daytime soaps (I hold the dubious distinction of having played more romantic parts on daytime than any actor alive or dead...thirteen, I believe, at last count, including my present fun-time on *The Bay*) *Another World In Somerset*, a spin-off of *Another World,* I had a confrontation with our Napoleonic producer after stopping him from bullying an extraordinary actress, Alice Hirson, my friend to this day. He was brutally abusing her verbally when I, in a rare (sure Nicolas!) show of physical might, told him to "lay the fuck off, or I'll put you through the wall!" Shortly thereafter, mysteriously, I went missing in the story line.

However, this Daytime Cat-with-12-Lives (*One Life To Live* was to be another soap in my long career). was picked up as the same character, Robert Delaney, on the show, *Another World*, by the producer, Paul Rauch, certainly the most wildly creative producer at that time. He seemed amused at hearing of my heroic defense of damsel Alice and put me to work opposite the delightful Susan Sullivan. At that time, *Another World* was the number one show in the country on Daytime. My "Robert" and Susan's "Lenore", went on to become daytime favorites. When asked once in an interview, why I thought our relationship was so popular, I replied, "Because we made making love, fun!"

I had many wonderful partners on Daytime: all but one with whom I got along. Students have asked me how it is that I managed to make believable, sometimes with actresses of lesser talent, a love-attraction. I tell them the task, sometimes easy, is to find one single quality in that person, then magnify it a thousand times and voila! believability! For, indeed, you are using the actual person not some remembered or imagined being.

John Considine, one of the great and enduring wits in my life, played contractor to my architect on *Another World*. John, who went on to write movies for Robert Altman, another brilliant wit, got a bit bored from time to time with the repetitive exposition-laden dialogue in Daytime. Because he and I were great pals, and he sort of knew I had enough concentration to cope with distraction, he developed a pattern of intentionally trying to distract me.

For instance, he would stand off-camera when I was in the midst of a love scene and make rude noises with his lips as if to imitate the most primitive coital sounds imaginable. I reached a point at which, effortless as my concentration was (WAS is the operative word), I'd finally had it. I came storming off-stage and with a fierce competitive glare in my eyes, said, "I'm going to get you motherfucker! I am going to do something so bad to you when YOU are on camera that will break you up!" ("break up" as in unintended laughing during a scene). Tall handsome John looked down at me and said in his most patronizing manner, "I cannot BE broken up! 'never happened, never will" The gauntlet was down.

Within a few days, I had a scene in which I, as an architect, had to present to the "Widow Alice" an elevation of her new cottage. My contractor, played by John, was to show her the portfolio. Instead of the expected elevations, I had inserted wildly pornographic photos from a then current sex magazine called "Screw". When John opened the portfolio to show the grieving Alice, there in front and center was a couple entwined like two boa constrictors, devouring each other. John looked up blankly at me with his large Greek eyes and then without a trace of breaking up, turned to the next page, expecting the relief of the actual drawings....but NO, the next page was an even more explicit oral act, actually with the hairy, not pretty body of the editor displaying his seemingly endless tongue and skills therefrom.

John broke. He was choking with laughter....the entire camera crew took pictures....the studio broke up. It was not long after that that I conveniently got a job again on Broadway. So much for naughty Nick on Daytime. Actually, no...there was one other incident:

The one leading lady with whom I did not eventually get along was an actress with a photographic memory. I was doing a Broadway show at night, traveling to Brooklyn to do the TV show at 7:30 AM. In the early morning rehearsal, I was acting, fully emotionally involved, as is my habit even in rehearsal, and this actress (who, in the interest of diplomacy or cowardice, shall remain without name) of course knew every line at that ghastly, early hour, including my own - she knew the entire script - but devoid of any emotion. When confronted with my inaccurate line readings, she, with a nasty edge, made a comment on that fact. In return, I said, "Well, dear lady, at 4:30 this afternoon when we actually have to DO this epic, I shall know them and indeed be there with fresh readings, whilst you, in your infinite exactitude, will be giving exactly the same, duplicated reading you are giving now."

This, as you can imagine, did not go down well. A little twerp of a kiss-ass-actor sitting nearby came up to me and said, "Oh, Nick, that was really out of line." I said, "Really? Well, then, just watch! You'll see that later she doesn't listen or even watch what her fellow actor is doing; her performance never changes. It's fixed from the moment of memorization of these unmemorable lines."

That afternoon with him on set with everybody else, I had a scene as her husband in which I slammed the bust of her father to the floor in a rage, left the room, went upstairs, changed into a suit and tie, and, with my briefcase in hand, came back downstairs to confront the angry wife again before leaving. As I re-entered, we played virtually minutes into the scene before she noticed that I had NO TROUSERS ON! Yup, that was it...the veins stood out on her neck in rage. The twerp on the sidelines was aghast. I turned to him and said, "I rest my case."

The studio was roaring with laughter. The producer was not joining in on the frivolity; he came storming out, seething, "The network is watching the dress rehearsal. How dare you engage in such antics?" Quite to my astonishment and relief, the whole focus was deflected from me when the women of the cast, unaware that "Network" (studio heads) was seeing them without full makeup and some still with hair curlers on, were furious! That female stir-up took the day.

A parade of soap operas started for me. As I have said, the money was good, I could do plays when I wished to. Yes, the 60s, 70s, and 80s were good to me. Here is a chronology of leading, always romantic roles on soap operas: (I'm sure a Guinness Book of Records record)

    1960-62 - Young Doctor Malone - Dr Matt Steele
    1963-65 - The Secret Storm - Dr Paul Britton
    1965 - Our Private World (nighttime)
    1965 - As The World Turns - John Eldridge
    1965-68 - The Secret Storm - Dr. Paul Britton (again)
    1971 - Another World in Somerset - Robert Delaney
    1972-76 - Another World in Bay City - Robert Delaney
    1983-84 - One Life to Live - Anthony Macana
    1984-87 - Santa Barbara - Lionel Lockridge
    1987-88 - All My Children - Steve / Dave Andrews*
    1987-93 - Santa Barbara - Lionel Lockridge (again)**
    1993-94 - As the World Turns - Edwardo Grimaldi

2012-Present - The Bay, the Series - Jack Madison***

* Afternoon TV Best Actor
**Soap Opera Digest Award; 3 Daytime Emmy Award Nominee
***Two Daytime Emmy Internet Awards

With the superb Sada Thompson in Twigs on Broadway, 1971

With Zelda Fitchandler, early Arena Stage Company, Washington DC, 1957

With the magnificent Louis Gossett Jr, Bloodknot, 1964

Brief movie-star career, Warner Brothers, 1964

With Eileen Fulton, As the World Turns, 1965

With Christina Crawford, Marla Adams, Lori March, Jada Rowlands and Keith Charles, The Secret Storm, 1964

Our Private World with Jada Rowlands, 1965

With Dick Cavett on Broadway, Otherwise Engaged, 1976

With Shelley Burch, One Life to Live 1983

Leading lady, the gorgeous, oh-so-nice, Dorian Lapinto,
One Live to Live 1983

*With Ellen Geer as Laertes to her Ophelia, opening of the
Tyrone Guthrie Theater, Minneapolis, 1963*

My first job on an American Stage, The Barrett's of Wimbledon Street, Stella Holt Theatre, LA, 1952

Western, The Outcast with Nacho Galindo, John Derek, Buzz Henry, me (dying), Frank Ferguson and an unidentified cowboy

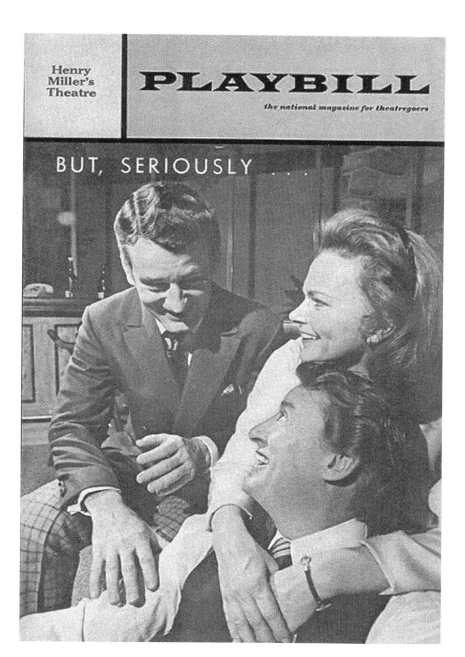

*With Bethel Leslie and Tom Poston on the cover of Playbill for the Broadway show,
But Seriously by Julius Epstein, writer of Casablanca, 1969*

Window shopping with my darling daughters,
Dinneen and Candace, during the Twigs Broadway run, 1971

CHAPTER 14

Beginnings of Boat Madness

B.O.A.T.: An acronym for 'Break Out Another Thousand'...so true..

After Pomona College and his Rhodes Scholarship at Oxford, my pal Edward Taylor, began teaching Advanced Studies at USC, overseeing a groundbreaking study on juvenile delinquency with Alexander McKeckron, and then started work with our mutual buddy, Robert Towne, on his various projects starting with the film *Chinatown*.

Edward turned up in New York to visit me.

In 1965, I had gone out to City Island, in the far end of the Bronx, to find a boat engine for a pal of mine who owned *Janet*, built in 1911 and sorely in need of propulsion. We found an old diesel. We also found an ancient hulk of a 1934, thirty-four-foot Marblehead cruiser sitting forlornly, rotting, waiting for some poor sucker to restore, to spend money, to have dreams of voyages to near and faraway places. The engine was the original Sterling Petrol with its individual cylinder heads of faded red jutting up from below decks. It was my first boat.

Her paint was peeling in great strips, the planks beneath were protesting their years of strain and then neglect by randomly protruding at intervals, begging for some young sucker to refasten, sand, then caulk, putty, sand some more, and paint. It was a first time for me, that kind of back straining labor, but was followed over the years by the saving of many wooden boats.

Joe Kolinsky the gruff, hardworking bear of a man who owned The Tri-Boro shipyard became the first sponsor of my boating madness. He helped, scolded, and coaxed me into some degree of knowledge of wooden boats...over many years and many boats. His hard-working Polish American background also provided me with that inevitable father figure of teaching, prodding and, in his case, insulting-with-good-intention, which pushed me from my ignorance of the sea and ships to unexpected pseudo--expertise.

Joe also was whimsically interested in my budding stage and TV career. It was curious to this fine common man that I, who worked so hard at wood restoration would rush to auditions and then the soap opera *Secret Storm*, followed in the summer of '65 by my first evening series, *Our Private World*...which was a flop. They had spun off an evening show from the hit daytime soap *As The World Turns* and I was the older of the two leading men. Eileen Fulton of great fame on Daytime was the leading lady (my wife). At the end of that summer of restoring my Marblehead cruiser in City Island and racing back and forth from the seashores to city chores, I had made a nice boat of the old hulk, and when *Our Private World* inevitably failed, I was asked back to Daytime - still as Eileen's husband, John Eldridge - to continue in that role.

The summer had provided funds for lots of things Candace and I had not had before. We had our apartment re-done, and Edward Taylor, The Rhodes Scholar from Pomona College, came to visit. No boating experiences I've have ever had could compare with the in-city-adventure of the summer of '65.

When Ed came, he immediately wanted to see "The Boat". By that time, she was afloat and had been motored down to a yard at the top end of Manhattan (the mad drive from City Island had been somewhat perilous to my career, missing or at least being late to a few appointments). The yard was in a curve of the Harlem River, just as it turns into the Hudson, near Columbia University's Baker Field. A highway and a railroad drawbridge separated the two rivers.

The journey began in the early evening with us loading a few bottles of Champagne, sautéed chicken, and other home-cooked goodies. With Candace, a willing boater and hostess for our guest, out we went into and across the mighty Hudson on a moonlit night. North of the George Washington Bridge, on the Western shore of the Hudson, lies the entrancing Palisades National Park, an expanse of green woods and rock abutments which grace the water's edge.

To these shores on a summer night steamed the Marblehead. I dropped the anchor; the near-shore waters were lapping gently at the wooden hull and we broke open the Champagne, set (replete with white linen tablecloth) the dinner table and discovered...NO CHICKEN! In my haste, I had left it on the table at our apartment on 110th St.

"My God!" says I, "I forgot the bloody chicken!" It was to be the highlight of the meal. Ma's cooking skills including a stint at the pre-war Cordon Bleu School in Paris, along with her naturally absorbed Southern style, had found its way into my cooking habits. I prided myself on chicken, fish, and grills. FUCK! I looked at Ed and apologized to him and Candace. Ed didn't give a shit. He was having a grand time with this mini-voyage unknown to most in New York City. In my compulsion to be a good host, and always the innovator, I said, "Let's go get it!"

"What?" says Candace. "How? It's so far back."

"Not if we take the boat back to the seawall this side of the Hudson at 125th Street. Eddie can take a taxi back, get the chicken and we'll meet him at 125th."

Both of them looked at this Captain-gone-mad and, I guess, because of their youth and similar madness, said, "OK." It was about two nautical miles back to the high stone banks at 125th St. The rusting, elevated subway arches formed a canopy over the cobblestone streets and the quaint abandoned remnants of bollards and 19th Century, merchant dockside life with tiny, steel doored shops and decades of abandoned car wrecks. which in the 60s, seemed to be everywhere. A dangerous place at night for some, with drug peddlers, their sometimes-desperate clients and the ladies of the night plying their last-chance trade there, where cops were few and various skills were abundant.

As we neared the seawall at 125th Street, we could see the residents of Harlem who had come to the shore to escape the awful summer heat of that August night. As we arrived, a murmur ran through the crowd: "He's in trouble!" "Somebody call on the phone box!" Concerned folk came to the edge of the bank and called out to us, "You OK? Need help?" A few beers can exaggerate the drama of the moment. There were stacks of coolers full and the now empty Rheingold cans scattered like cylindrical tinsel in all corners and gutters.

Calling back to the well-meaning folk, I said, "Nah, we're OK...Just comin' back for the chicken"

"He's comin' back for the chicken!" became the rippling call which echoed along the banks of the Hudson...a vocal beacon which that great river in all its history was surely unaccustomed to.

Eddie jumped off the boat with helping hands. The shouts of help had become a community laugh of enjoyment. "Go get the chicken!" became the battle cry as Eddie stepped into a taxi.

Soon after that, fire engines arrived. Some well-meaning soul had indeed thought there was an emergency. "No, not necessary," I called as I circled the boat just offshore...the sometimes-savage surges of the Hudson could destroy an old wooden boat tied even for a short time to the stone wall at its banks.

In an astonishingly short time, another taxi appeared. Out stepped Eddie emblematically holding aloft a great covered enameled pan of chicken.

"He got the chicken!" went the cry. Amidst the laughter which followed, were cries of delight, more than one jolly critique such as "They are mad mutherfuckers" and from the devout side of Harlem - caring moms, "Bless y'all! Gonna tell my grandchildren about this one!" Eddie stepped aboard to accompanying greetings and cheers and with the merry crowd wishing us good eating, we sailed once more to the quiet, pristine shores of the Everglades Park. Edward Milton Taylor was to experience over the years, many more boats of mine, but I never forgot "The Chicken" again.

Another nautical-night-lesson learned: NEVER hand the wheel to a guy who tells you he has been an experienced Naval hand with many years as a helmsman.

On this outing was a buddy, Louis (LOOEY!), a superintendent in an apartment building belonging to a rich man in the Bronx. From Puerto Rico, Louis was a good-natured, lean sinewed, strong but skinny young man in his early twenties. He had brought along, as his guest, the daughter of the apartment building owner who employed him. His work included maintenance, boiler cleaning and scrubbing many floors. The young woman was upper middle class Jewish and crazy about "Looey". Also aboard were an assortment of types from the shipyard and my apartment building on 110th St. ready for an evening cruise down the East River, from City Island, around Hell's bend and up the Harlem River.

Chicken was to be eaten (this time not forgotten!) and booze, somewhat cheaper than Champagne, was to be drunk. Most of the gang aboard were consuming vast quantities. Someone got sick aft of the bridge and an old U.S. Navy man offered to take the wheel as I went to tend to the "technicolor yawn", as my nephew Geoffrey used to call vomit..

An amazingly short time later, I heard a crunch. A sickening crunch and knew immediately that the hull of the 1928 34' Elco cruiser, which I had recently restored to near perfection, was injured. I seem to be - throughout my whole life - better in emergencies than regular, daily life. That night called upon those talents.

I raced below decks to survey the damage. A column of water was flooding in from the forepeak hold. Just in front of that column, was "Looie" and his employer's daughter, standing up, naked, hastily pulling their undies up above their knees as they were being drenched in what Louis called afterwards, "the biggest douche in the world." Pushing them aside I saw the great hole in the hull. Impossible to stop, was my opinion.

I tore back up topside and with the re-clothed Louis by my side, got everyone into lifejackets, called the Police and Coast Guard and then tried to figure out how to save the night.

We had hit a sunken object towards the side of the channel. Our noble naval coxswain had not been looking at the charts which clearly pointed out various barges both floating and not. He missed the floating and struck the "not".

Hastily, Louis and I looked into the darkness (we had one flashlight). By now the water had flooded the below decks compartments. "Titanic" was imminent. The dark waters of the fast-current running East River at night are not a treat to be savored.

In one's youth, one is capable of extraordinary physical feats. Louis and I were young. We each took one life jacket, then the long length of anchor line, unfastened the chain at one end and took the remaining nylon, tied it to another life jacket and decided to swim to a nearby darkened barge. It seemed to be floating. At least in the darkness, we could make out the superstructure above water which was good enough for us. With instructions to wait for us or the police – who were on their way, (but not for some time) - Louis and I leapt into the water from what was left of the bow. We swam furiously against the current. The longer we swam, the longer the anchor line became and it was heavy, the life jacket tied to the end barely kept it afloat. Exhausted even in youth, we just made it to the barge. We hoisted our adrenaline filled selves up the side of the rusty barge and tied the line to the bollard, We called into the night, "Make sure your life jackets are secure. We're coming back for you!"

We swam back holding onto the supporting line. A great and loyal neighbor, Larry Schneider, a tough product of the Lower East Side, was there and enormously helpful getting those in near panic over the side into the water and strung out along the line as we started edging our way to the safety of the great black barge.

Cops in a boat eventually arrived at the barge. *The Elco* had lasted afloat for 19 minutes...warm blankets, coffee revived us. I heard afterwards that poor Louis was fired by his furious boss, either for fucking his precious heiress daughter or for risking her life? Perhaps both. I never found out his ultimate fate.

A postscript tribute to my brave comrade:

When I asked Louis why on earth he had chosen to engage in the sexual act with that pulchritudinous young gal, standing up in the forward most part of the boat instead of the newly made-up bunk in the cabin just aft, he replied with his natural, easy-going manner, "Aw, man, I had just come from cleaning the boiler and didn't want to dirty the sheets." At my look of astonishment, the very bright and perceptive "LOOEY" said hastily and with great sincerity, "I did wash my dick, man." And so, he had by the tap first and then by the frothing, sea-fountain-douche surging through the ruptured planks on a sinking boat during his passionate if hasty lovemaking.

The next afternoon as I lay my bruised and exhausted body in well-deserved rest, my agent called and said in mock anger, "YOU MADE ME FALL IN A SEWER!" I dazedly, "What the fuck are you talking about?" He continued, "Yeah, I just bought a paper at 57th and 7th. I was stepping off the curb and I see in the headline of The Daily News 'TV STAR CRUISER SINKS, 8 SAFE'. I figured it was Desi Arnaz or somebody and it was fucking YOU, you asshole! What the fuck. You scared the shit out of me!"

That was the one and only accident or near accident in my succeeding 50 years of boating. There were however, some other rough times in the open sea, to be told....perhaps yes, again, on another afternoon.

CHAPTER 15

Laertes' Moment

Hard work, fun, wild creativity, the best of theatre was at the 1963 opening season of the Tyrone Guthrie Theatre in Minneapolis, Minnesota.

Minneapolis had not had a professional theatre company since pre-WW-2. For reasons unknown to me then and now - stupid me never thought to inquire - in 1963 they asked the foremost British stage director at the time, Sir Tyrone Guthrie, to come over and start up a theatre which they named in his honor.

Guthrie was a smidgen over 6 feet tall, with a nose quite close in shape to a California condor and a wingspan to match. He was a man who shunned formal wear, but when obliged to wear a dinner jacket, wore, in protest I assume, "plimsolls", the oldy-Brit word for tennis shoes; white canvas tennis shoes.

I had filled in a gap in employment by reading for and then losing a part in a Broadway show to an unknown but obviously handsome and charming actor named George Segal, who went on to a fine degree of fame. However, the wonderful Charles Blackwell, Production Stage Manager, offered me the job of understudy for George and, interestingly, the job of Assistant Stage Manager. I accepted and learned much from the kind and skillful Charles. He went on to become a Broadway legend for those mentioned qualities. He also happened to be Broadway's first black Production Stage Manager.

Out of town on tryout with leading lady, Tammy Grimes, then married to Christopher Plummer (and because this is not, or tries not to be a gossip column, I shall not relate her raucous stories of THAT marriage!). Edward Woodward was the Leading man, *Rattle For A Simple Man* was the play. In Baltimore, most of the company went to a restaurant to have lunch. THEY, the restaurant, REFUSED TO SERVE Charles Blackwell! This is 1963! As a company, we stood up noisily, protesting and left.

Actors had been in the vanguard of unions for Civil Rights, when in 1954, they refused as a union (Actors Equity) to appear on the stage of Washington DC's then segregated National Theatre! Indeed, in 1954!...90 Years after the end of slavery.

"Separate but equal", a copout term and practice adopted by the Supreme Court in the late 19th Century to appease the South and yet pretend to appeal to the victors of the Civil War, was to create a poison of inequity in all areas of life in these not-so-United-States. Does it still infect?...one only has to observe and listen.

At the Guthrie, there was an attempt at integration. Two African American actors were among those of us "youngish" New York actors chosen to appear in the Minnesota theatre company; they were, Graham Brown and Janet MacLachlan. Leading, famous actors like Jessica Tandy and her husband, Broadway co-star, Hume Cronyn, were invited.

Some of my most memorable moments at the Guthrie - and there were many - included playing Hap in *Death of A Salesman* with Hume Cronyn as Willy and Jessica Tandy as Linda. Jessica's Linda was the most touching I had ever seen. Hume's Willy, was a masterpiece and utterly original. Arthur Miller the playwright attended and admitted he had actually written it with a little guy in mind for the part. A 'bantam cock", as he described the part.

By the by, a young graduate student from the University of Minnesota, Al Rossi, who played Howard in that *Death of a Salesman*, recently organized a Guthrie Theatre Alum party, to which came Joan Van Ark, Charles Cioffi, and others. Al, then a PHD candidate, went on to chair the drama department at Los Angeles City College. We're still great pals.

Of all the productions, for me at least, *Hamlet*, was the most memorable.

A reigning Broadway star, George Grizzard was asked to play the Danish prince, and I was asked to play, among other parts, Laertes. George, already a friend, was a superb actor of great stagecraft who fully understood Hamlet. By that I mean, his was in terrible conflict as *Hamlet* must be, but it was not lost in either the music of the text, nor buried so far beneath the surface as to be more mysterious than revealing. The best compliment I can remember of that *Hamlet* was from a local gasoline station owner whom we invited to see the play because he seemed interested in the new-found cultural addition to the Minneapolis scene. He said the next day, "Well, I didn't understand every word but I sure as heck understood what was goin' on!"

My well learned fencing at RADA came in handy as Laertes. George's fencing, in what became one of the most superlative sword-fighting scenes ever, took months of preparation. As in everything George did, he was exacting of himself. On top of this, George and I practiced the entire sword and dagger fight scene before EVERY PERFORMANCE...for six months! It was dangerous and unpredictable. Douglas Campbell, the fine actor and very good fencer, choreographed it.

Guthrie waited until almost the end of a rehearsal to add his final touch, which produced, in every performance, an incredible, audible collective gasp from the audience. Instead of Hamlet probing Laertes' guts with the final stab, Guthrie had Hamlet wound Laertes on the run. As Laertes mortally wounds Hamlet, Laertes, unaware he has been hit badly, turns, spinning at the completion of a cut to Hamlet and then suddenly pauses, then falls...STRAIGHT OUT AND DOWN INTO THE AUDIENCE! (The theatre was designed as a thrust stage, jutting out several rows from the proscenium.)

Always the showman, Guthrie had in fact planted four Minnesota football players in seats as audience members who stood up quickly and caught (thank God) my flying Laertes!

Another Guthrie touch...The night before the opening - to be the largest, most publicized in American history, when 140 critics from the Western world would be attending - Tyrone Guthrie stopped the dress rehearsal in the middle of the "player scene" in which Hamlet had urged the players (performers in the play within the play) to ridicule Hamlet's evil stepfather, Claudius. Sir Tyrone, leaping all gangly six- and one-half feet of him, replete with white plimsolls, called out, "I'm frightfully sorry ladies and gentlemen, I've fucked this thing up a bit!" With astonished looks from the cast, he then, breaking all convention, changed it.

The scene had, as played, been a little predictable. Guthrie had gotten an idea when during the scene in rehearsal the King, Claudius, had stood up and cried, "Give me some light!" Lee Richardson, the terrific actor playing Claudius, had accidentally bumped into an on-stage spotlight illuminating the players and THAT'S what Guthrie used, He said to Lee, "swing your arm wildly in frustration and anger when you leap up!" Lee did, and Guthrie had instructed an extra to spin the light as though hit, and as it spins, looking like a police car light, Lee cried, "Give me some light!" with added fury and the whole damn scene lit up...so to speak.

A most alarming time during the early stages of the *Hamlet* run was enduring a motorcycle crash after reading and seeing myself pictured with Ellen Geer, the brilliant Ophelia in the production. That moment when I realized (in character) she was nuts was captured and printed out as a FULL PAGE in Life Magazine...at the time the leading magazine in the world. With only little tiny TV sets on the market, and not so many of them, we had magazines...and everybody read them.

I was racing back to our lodgings to show my wife Candace the picture, clutching the Life magazine to my breast as I turned into the last curve on my beautiful black BMW motorcycle. As the whispering, silent, strong engine led me, I had no premonition as to what was coming; I had, in my haste to get home with the glorious news, left the kick stand down! In those days, there was not an automatic spring on the stand, so, upon reaching the last curve before our hotel, and leaning the bike over to accommodate the turn, the kickstand dug into the asphalt and my lovely bike spun out! Yeah, spinning on the ground as it headed toward its resting place... the curb. That cement curb stopped the missile.

Without a moment's hesitation, I, still clutching the Life magazine, picked up the accommodating, barely dented motorcycle and raced home.

For those mildly interested in the reasons for all that glee:

I didn't mention that Rita Gam and I were the only Lee Strasberg Actors Studio types in the Guthrie cast. Most were products of Carnegie Mellon, other rep companies and various universities. I mention this because that Method training came to the fore when I asked to talk for a moment with Dr. Guthrie.

"Yes, dear boy," says he. I said, "Well sir I have always seen Laertes played as a complete fool, a boob if you will and I feel his attraction for Hamlet is not that he's stupid, but rather, that he's impulsive...sort of gets thing done and with dash, and that's what appeals to Hamlet and makes them buddies...otherwise I see no reason Hamlet would bother with him!" Guthrie pondered that Strasberg-ian theatrical logic for a very brief moment, and then said, "Well, dear boy, Shakespeare rather shat on Laertes didn't he?" "But I can't play that," says I..."Do your best," says he....And that was that! Ha.TRUE story! But it spurred me on.

When we got to the scene where Laertes has committed treason, banging his way into the castle, being disarmed by Claudius, and then being confronted by Ophelia entering in her madness, dressed in weeds and so on ... "Helluva scene."

Dr. Guthrie said to me just before, "Now Nicolas, come bashing in like Errol Flynn in the movies! Don't be shy."...and with a twinkle, " I'm sure you can do THAT!"

And I did...slashing and bashing in I came. The King disarmed me. Then upstage came Ophelia, my sister, in her bizarre rags and weeds, which usually was quickly followed by Laertes' speech in horror at her plight. My immediate response as Laertes, not knowing she is now insane, was to break up in laughter! Which I DID! My Method madness then led me slowly upstage still not realizing my sister's plight, but as I got to her, suddenly seeing in her eyes, the sad remains of that wit and intellect and beauty now despoiled, then and only then, in a shocked and deeply moved delivery, I began my speech, "Oh, heat dry up my brains...."

THAT MOMENT made that full page in Life Magazine....

Guthrie, not one to dwell on emotions nor compliments, said quietly but earnestly, "Very good, dear boy."

My mother, in California, seeing the magazine but never having seen me on a professional stage, was very moved. This was the woman who had sacrificed all to feed, house and support her children's endeavors. I am most thankful that she did learn of her actor son doing something "first rate" as she used to say. I certainly felt and thrived on that constant support.

A memory...We lived in a small rebuilt (by her, we boys and a wonderful Mexican stone mason) stone and wooden bungalow in the country west end of Los Angeles...It was a four-mile trek home from high school and with no bus ride after practice for track or cross country, one did have to walk home. When it rained in the fall and darkness came early, I had to walk-wet so to speak...and at times cold and miserably.

It was just such an eve when I arrived home in the darkness, soaked through and shivering, and made the most of my misery as I entered the door. Ma was sitting reading (much of her more than 40-hour weeks were spent reading the works she had to synopsize), but even after work, she could always be found reading something.

So, there she sat by lamplight in an easy chair as I entered...grandly, like something out of *Way Down East*, she said later. Over her glasses, she peered at this refuge from a melodrama, playing my misery for all it was worth, and she said, "Get paid for it boy!" I was so fucking furious at her. I said sharply, "Damn right, I will!"...I'm sure that was in fact a wee bit of a motivator.

Her death was not sudden, she had rheumatic fever when young and yet accomplished herculean feats of strength physically and emotionally most of her waking life. Any issues of "cutting the cord" from this strong woman had, I thought, been resolved during the time I spent away at RADA and then the army days so long ago.

Obviously, I loved her deeply and forgave those fits of frustration when raising two obstreperous boys got the best of her, occasionally resulting in violence.

When at 14, I grabbed her wrists during one of these physical "releases" and said, "No more hitting!", she, massively frustrated, started throwing things - when the pot boiled so to speak. Frying pans and even electric irons (cold, thank God) and other missiles never hit their mark. She was, luckily, a lousy shot.

By the time I returned from RADA, the rage had ceased, never to appear again. A lack of provocation may have had a bit to do with the succeeding years of tranquil. civilized behavior between us. She adored Nancy Irvin, my second Pomona College amour. It was not only Nancy's brilliance, but also her modest manner and depthful beauty which attracted ma. She was almost as heartbroken as I when Nancy left me. She always wanted the best for me.

Some of my Freudian feelings were explored in later years of therapy. First with an unconventional psychiatrist, Dr. Pepi Miller, a former student of Jung, who told me, "Nick, don't confuse normal with average. You might be normal, but NEVER average." My second exposure to the science of mind, was when my wife had shall we say in the interest of tact a need for therapy, I asked her psychiatrist, Dr Jean Munzer (a pioneer in group analysis) whether I might need therapy. She asked why I thought that and I replied, "Because I didn't see this coming." "Good reason," she said. I spent quite some time in that groundbreaking group

Are all those conflicting feelings about Ma resolved? I rather think so. Her greatest problem, as I now see it, was being thrust into the role of dual-parenting, My dear, generous sister and her equally generous husband took care of Ma for years and years. My brother Ian and his wife Pat did also, before that. I was in New York for all those years and helped as I could.

A young, independent guy with THAT strong a mother, had to rebel, or so I thought. One muses now on two leaders who, (whatever one thinks of them politically) coming from single mothers, led the country through turbulent times: Bill Clinton and Barack Obama. Hmm, did they rebel at some point? Each got through law school successfully.

Which brings me to the subject of ADD, Attention Deficit Disorder: Odd turn in the path? Possibly not. Were these two strong leaders afflicted by this condition, or the other - the lack of having a father in attendance?

In early grammar school, I was thought bright, but lazy. In middle years, I was skipped past the 6th grade because of excellence in school. That skip however, proved fatal to my succeeding academic ambitions. I never caught up in math; all else could be quickly studied. With ADD you have intense but short-lived periods of concentration, and then, poof! What is happening outside the school window becomes more fascinating for lengthy periods.

Years later, when studying for my scuba instructors license, I had to learn algebra to discuss the Ideal Gas Laws and so on (Physics). Then when working to pass my Boat Captain's tests, I had to learn trig or whatever it was to calculate distance, set and drift (the effect of currents on course desired).

None of these symptoms were explored on a grade school level in the 1940s. "Lazy bum" was the appellation most often applied. Of course, as in Highgate when I first heard my parents' remark ("not good character"), I succumbed, at least partially, to that pronounced fate. Not in music, not in track and cross country...and as told, not in a well-executed life of planned juvenile crime. I, like many others afflicted with ADD, did get on. The army produced a disciplined environment in which to function well. Likewise, in the theatre. I thrived.

Many years passed then, with the help of the marvelous psychologist, Dr Stephen Johnson and his Men's Center group of eloquent and most giving, sharing guys, I actually read and talked about people who had achieved something in life despite their seeming disability. I bring this up because this ADD might have had an immense influence on the relationship between Ma and myself. One sharp person trying to communicate with another, when the other has a concentration problem she knows nought of? Yeah, that could warp a clear sense of understanding...'nuff said.

I loved dear Ma with such depth of feeling that even now it is difficult. The unstated affection, the understated credit for all that help. My glorious sister, Georgee is the living memory of all that was good in ma. I call Georgee, "The goodest person I know".

So then, at the Guthrie, I was so pleased that this woman, not long before her death, got an opportunity to see, in Life Magazine of all places, the fruits of my labor and of her love and unwavering support. My becoming recognized as an artist was indeed more important to her than all the bright lights anywhere.

CHAPTER 16

Life in The Theatre, Broadway, On & Off

It was 13 years after my Guthrie stint that I began working on one of my most beloved roles on the New York stage in the terrific production of *Benito Cerino* by the great poet, Robert Lowell, in cahoots with the unforgettable African American actor, Roscoe Lee Browne.

I say African American actor, not to distinguish by color, but to point to his distinction as a history changing African American and as an actor.

Roscoe Lee was to become best known for his role on *The Cosby Show*, but in the New York and Los Angeles theatre worlds, his performances were legendary. In *Benito Cereno*, Roscoe Lee created the role in 1964. I was overjoyed to play opposite him as the Captain in the revival in 1976.

The play was based on a true journal of Captain Amasa Delano, a young sealing ship Captain of the early 19th Century whose vessel comes across a derelict slave ship taken over by the slaves who have been attempting to return to Africa. They've murdered the Spanish crew, save for the Captain, Benito Cereno, who has been driven crazy. They are starving and are led by an educated slave, Babu, played by Roscoe Lee. I played the Captain, Amaso Delano.

His performance was a wonder. His wit, intelligence and intense purpose were there in every moment of every performance. Speaking of wit, one of the great stories about Roscoe Lee was about his encounter with a super liberal, super rich Eastside lady at a fashionable cocktail party. Roscoe, who came from an army officer father's (one of the first black officers) background, did not sound like a kid from the "hood". He could do such dialects and did, including a mock Caribbean which I especially adored, but his normal speech was that of an educated New Yorker. When an Eastside grand dame asked him how he happened to have such perfect speech (unaware of the patronization evident in her question), he replied, "Madam, we had a white maid."

Another time, when I asked him what he did with his demons (projecting of course, that I was cursed with a few), he replied in that delightfully pseudo-Caribbe dialect, "Well mon, I go to de window, I opens it, and says, Come iiiiiin!" This self-mockery, but with a real touch of pathos, led to us both into breaking out into laughter of a grand sort. We shared a dressing room and shared our many stories. And WHAT stories!

Roscoe had been the fastest half-mile track star in the world in the early 50s. He, in his celebrity capacity, got to know a young Congressman, John F. Kennedy. I, years later, got to know the Kennedy family when I taught John Jr. to scuba dive. His mother and then Caroline came to see my plays in New York for some time after that.

One of the stories I told Roscoe was of my seeing the young Alvin Ailey in Los Angeles at the Lester Horton Studio in the early 50s with a magical goddess of dance, Carmen De Lavallade, as his partner (together they subsequently formed the Harlem Dance Theatre, now Alvin Ailey Dance Company). She then married the great dancer, choreographer, Geofrey Holder. I've always adored dance. Carmen created some of the finest modern dances in history. She was recently awarded the highest American civilian award for art, The Kennedy Center Award.

One afternoon, Roscoe with a twinkle in his eye, said, as he was making up for the matinee, "Nicolas, I have a treat for you this afternoon; someone you mentioned you lust for is coming." He would not tell me who. Mischief was not an unknown quality for Roscoe. I said to him, "Interesting, for I too have a surprise visitor for you this afternoon." I, of course, did not tell him who.

Backstage at the American Place Theatre, into our tiny dressing room after the matinee, stepped two of the most beautiful and interesting women in America: Carmen de Lavallade and Jacqueline Onassis. Carmen and I are still very close friends to the time of this writing.

The last time I saw a Kennedy was at Lincoln Center not long before John's death. I heard a voice call across the lobby, "Mr Coster!" I turned and saw John, Jr. "It's been a while since you were my student," I laughed, "You don't really have to call me Mr. Coster anymore." He laughed. That charming, intelligent young man was a joy.

Off Broadway I was a part of the renaissance of black theatre in the United States. I had done the play *Blood Knot* by the great South African playwright, Athol Fugard. The wonderful J. D. Cannon, who opened in the part of the white brother, Morris, had left the play not long after. and I took it on for the majority of the remaining run, replaced when I went to be a Hollywood star (hardy, har, har), by the talented Alan Miller. I reclaimed the role in Los Angeles the next year after my short-lived time as a movie star ended with, *My Blood Runs Cold* at Warner Brothers, a film which killed the career of Troy Donahue and almost killed mine.

In *Blood Knot*, James Earl Jones opened in the part of the other brother with Yaphet Koto replacing him and then, eventually, Louis Gossett Jr. Yaphet was brilliantly intense...I cannot remember why he left, but Louis Gossett, a very young actor at the time, was marvelous. He and I spent nine months, 8 times a week, two on Saturday, back-to-back with a half hour break, two on Sunday, in this two-character, two hour play.

At times with all our fondness and mutual admiration, we would look at each other before the last exhausting show on Sunday and just say, "fuck you!" And then go onstage and do that wonderful, revealing play. I say revealing because it did just that. It was not about race, but about brotherhood rediscovered. It was the first integrated play ever done in South Africa. The loveliest compliment I've ever received as an actor came in that summer of 1964 from Dr. Martin Luther King's lawyer, Clarence Williams, who said in the soft light of backstage, "You understand, don't you."

After *My Blood Runs Cold* in late 1964, I was finished with movies for a while but got wind of *Bloodknot* being produced in Los Angeles by the actor Frank Silvera, half Hungarian Jew, half black, who started what became the first truly integrated theatre I'd ever been a part of.

Frank "passed for white" in the movies and on stage for most of his career, but in middle age, had found his blackness. He shared without guilt, his past, and his hoped-for future. *Blood Knot* took place in the shabby, spoiled, corrugated tin section of Port Elizabeth South Africa. In New York, that is what you saw on stage when entering the theatre. Tin roofs and the bleak one room of Zach the black brother. For Frank's LA production, a young black man low on funds and experience, but eager to be in theatre wandered in from the streets and, after a bit of quick training on the fly, was encouraged by Frank to "Create Africa in the lobby!" He did. He climbed the palm trees outside the theatre and took the fronds, some four to six feet in length, and cut and painted African masks from them.

These imaginative creations welcomed one into the patio and foyer of the theatre...wild, free Africa as you walked in with colonial, corrugated, tin ruins of shacks as you saw the stage. Quite the dramatic introduction to what was for me the finest theatrical experience of my life. From that experience of watching these modern, great actors and becoming a part of this "Theatre of Being", I coined the phrase "Good acting is selective schizophrenia!"

The Guthrie Theatre in Minneapolis had the requisite one black woman, one black man. Frank's theatre was truly integrated. Bea Richards, the great actress, was playing in James Baldwin's *Amen Corner* when I arrived. I saw it....many times and marveled at what was truly "being" on stage..

I was fortunate to share the stage with the magnificent Rupert Crosse, known briefly before his early death for his one movie, an Academy Award nomination in *The Reivers*. He was a tall, slender man who had known segregation as a very young soldier in the army. He understood, as well as any American can, the plight of South African blacks.

I was not simply hired because of my New York success in the role. Frank asked me if I would go over a bit of the play with Rupert onstage. I did. I quickly realized that I was on stage with one of the finest actors of our time.

One evening, in the middle of an extremely emotional scene with Rupert (Zach), a man in the audience, in the second or third row, started to heave with emotion. His chest rose and sank in despair. His eyes teared and he uttered sounds - unrealized by himself - that were revealing primitive torment. Rupert, facing him from down-center-stage, lifted his long, beautiful hand and with slender fingers facing me, like a gentle conductor softening the cellos, motioned for us to stop. He then raised both arms, the entire expanse being over six feet, and faced the man. When finally the man realized he was being beckoned, he looked back at Rupert. Rupert then with those endlessly welcoming arms, gestured as if to bring that soul to Rupert's chest; an embrace. A brotherly embrace of understanding across the space of darkened theatre. The man's breathing slowed, his tears dried, his whole being calmed. Rupert then turned back to me and I knew we were to continue. He knew. The entire audience knew.

I tell that story often to my students at the University of Georgia, where I have been most welcomed as a Visiting Lecturer for 14 years. It was the finest example of being on stage, never breaking character, taking a potentially disastrous distraction into a revelatory moment, one that none of us involved in will ever forget. Writing about that time, I still feel the surge of emotion over forty years later.

Thanks to *Blood Knot*, I was a proud part of a major turning point in American theatre, when actors of color were increasingly recognized for talent and not denied access because of the shade of their skin.

The summer of 1964, in a different town, late at night after the same play...As said, Louis Gossett Jr and I played most of the run in New York. He was intensely magnificent with the same penetrating concentration and theatrical freedom which subsequently won him an Oscar in the film *An Officer And A Gentleman*. We performed at a little theatre on 2nd Ave. The great actress Cicely Tyson was in a play upstairs at another little theatre. Down the street was *In Black America*. All over town a renaissance of African American theatre was blooming and it was wonderful to be part of it. Charles McCrae, who went on to found The Negro Ensemble Theatre, was our stage Manager on *Blood Knot*. I was pleased to be asked by James Earl Jones, who had become my friend, to do a reading of a new play...at the moment it's title will have to stay in my mind's attic with the countless other plays I did with The New Dramatists, The Women's Theatre and so on. Joseph Papp, whom I had met when he was a stage manager at CBS, then started The New York Shakespeare Festival whereafter, an explosion of finally realized talent came from Asian, Hispanic, and Black actors.

CHAPTER 17

Street Scene

One night, during the run of *Blood Knot* Off-Broadway, in the summer of 1964, I climbed into my sometimes-trusty 1954 Buick convertible, which, with tattered top down, had taken us to Gilgo Beach off the South Coast of Long Island many a summer's day. Powder blue with the signs of New York winter salt and rust-wear evident on all panels, I made my way toward the Upper Westside, heading for my apartment at 110th and Broadway. Up and off 2nd Avenue I went, through the gaudy night neon of 14th St. and its many tawdry shops lighting the way.

I can't remember quite when, but another car started following me along the way. Off 14th, as I was going across to the West Side Highway, the other car, an undistinguished American car of not-too-distant age, slammed into my back bumper at a stop light. I did not get out. My old car had sustained many a bump, mostly when I was parked.

I thought...a miscalculation by a tipsy driver? Forget it.

At the next light, the same thing. This time with more force. I looked in the rear-view mirror and could barely make out the faces of two young men. I could also see my face which just a few nights before had felt the force of a fist, when in an accidental mis-calculation, a stage fight had turned to injury. My eye was a mess. I looked not unlike De Niro in *Raging Bull*. My hair was long and I sported a beard, which was perfect for the role of Morris in *Blood Knot*, but also resembled a hippie after a bad night on drugs and a fall into some gutter.

I sped up. In those days and perhaps now, best to avoid confrontations with aggressive sorts on late night streets.

At a light on West 22nd, I was subject to the final slam. A teeth jarring slam on my back bumper. I could feel the entire bumper give way. The streets were by now deserted. I yelled through the open windows (my first mistake), "What the fuck!"

Within seconds the two in the other car leapt out and quickly approached my car. Not wishing to get pounded in the car - no time to raise the windows - I slipped out of the driver's side and into the middle of the empty, barely lit street. The two guys approached and in their steady, purposeful gait I could see their intentions were more than conversational. I reached for my wallet hoping that what remained of the Off-Broadway salary in my pocket would suffice the demands of the impending robbery.

"We don't want your money," says one, his intense blue eyes penetrating the darkness.

In my ever-present humorous state (notice how some idiots like me pick just the wrong time to make jokes), I said with the still lingering South African accent from the play, "Two of you, one of me...Not very sporting." Yup, I actually, when facing the imminent prospect of having the shit beaten out of me, came up with that ridiculous line. The jovial delivery did not succeed in halting the advance.

"We don't want your money, wise ass, we're just gonna kill you."

Stunned finally into an adrenaline filled silence, I turned slightly to present a smaller target as they got closer. Their eyes and attitudes vividly showed the effects of a newly prevalent drug, PCP, which even in my then racing thoughts of survival, I remembered produced in some, almost superhuman strength.

From out of the buried memories of army training came the slight martial arts moves I had never thought would come to use. As the first guy swung, a mighty swing at my already damaged face. I remember him being quite tall, his arm full and the swing coming with some velocity. I ducked and came up under his swing and for some reason unknown to me to this day, I aimed my hand with fingers extended toward his throat. His voice box was vulnerable; it received the full force of my blow. The fingers found their way straight into his throat and he fell gasping. As he fell, his head hit the curb and I heard the crunch of bone on cement. Blood gushed. I turned to confront the other guy.

He was charging back to his car. Before I could get to him, he was reaching inside the glove compartment for something....

I thought, "Whoops, he's reaching for a knife or something..." 2nd rule in the army (the 1st being: never volunteer for anything): If he's armed and you're not, get the fuck outta there.

I raced to my car. The engine was still running with windows down and I jammed it in gear. As I did so, I heard a "click" in the night. Again, back in the army, I had been an expert with a 45-automatic pistol. The "click" that summer night was the safety on a 45 being released. I glanced over my left shoulder and there was the remaining madman with his 45. I ducked, he fired. In that order fortunately. Hair was blown off the back of my head.

The round went through the windshield, splattering glass over the hood and dashboard. I stomped down on the gas pedal and sped, wildly zig-zagging, down the street as he repeatedly fired away. I turned on 9th Avenue. raced up the wrong way on a one-way street, trying, for once, to attract attention from the police...any police.

Some twenty blocks later, I caught the eye and siren wail of a waiting cop. He approached my car, saw the bullet holes, and ordered me out. Hands on the hood, I was searched and inspected. He saw my beard, and swollen eye and immediately assumed that I was some kind of hippie ne'er-do-well and started to cuff me. I told him rapidly of my recent adventures downtown, but he did not believe the tale.

I suddenly found myself again the actor in a jam, speaking in an imperious tone almost - a "My good man" sort of thing - explaining just who I was and just what had happened...a man possibly dying on the street back there...and finally the masterstroke, "If you don't believe me, call the Manhattan Squad and ask them who I am." This gave him pause. Thank God that in my drinking hours, one of my spots was The Triple Inn at 54th and 8th. Therein, along with Philly, the other partners, and William Marchand the writer, many actors, and students from the American Academy of Dramatic Arts, were the guys off-duty from the Manhattan Squad.

We partied together and they seemed amused by my theatre and TV stories, at that time filled with *Secret Storm* gossip. My character of Paul Britton, who was shtupping his student, Amy, was of particular interest. Most of their wives watched watched soaps while possibly ironing in their undies - an intimate, unique experience known only to the Daytime watching wife. Did these manly-men wonder what their wives fantasy lives included? I have had more than one strange, suspicious look from such a husband. But not from these guys.

They treated me like one of their own. They appreciated that I was an ex-soldier in this time of anti-war sentiment. I suppose they never thought about the fact that I was "in between the wars" and therefore had never been in combat. With these mysterious cops, nobody really knew what they did, only that they were tough guys and elite. When this camaraderie was mentioned to the suspicious old cop on 9th Avenue late that night, he responded.

Later as the forensics expert gazed at the giant pool of blood on the ground sans a body from which the blood sprang, he said quietly, "Not really likely that this guy is alive." They, including some buddies from the Manhattan Squad, concluded that his partner, the other guy, the gunman, had dragged his pal to the river and dumped him.

A five State alert gathered no further clues. No one with that sort of injury had been admitted. The press found out. The police in their investigation did not reveal the possible fatality to the newspapers. The next day I was once again mentioned in The Daily News, an article whimsically headlined: 'Actor Plays Street Scene' (an allusion to the play by Elmer Rice). Pictures of my bullet ridden old Buick were there for all to see.

In the weeks following the incident, I thought a lot about the bare and lingering feelings: the during and the after. I had to admit to myself, the innermost horrific thought: a feeling of exaltation seeing another man fall by my hand.

That, as I said, was the summer of '64...the summer of Selma, of Dr Martin Luther King. I had seen that history unfolding, and as I said, had met Clarence Williams, King's lawyer and confidant.

A primitive male feeling of triumph was tinged with this awful gut feeling of, well not exactly regret, for I felt totally justified (one justifies to save sanity), but a lingering feeling of I could've disarmed without overwhelming. I thought of Dr. King and his preaching of non-violence...What if I had just kept driving? What if?...another shoulda-woulda-coulda. I wondered that if it were to happen again, if I were ever confronted with a choice to join violence or avoid it, would I, like Dr. King and his brothers and sisters in peace, have their strength?

On a sultry evening some years later, in Natchez, Mississippi, an angry redneck waved a loaded 44 Magnum in my face. It was not a civil rights action on my part. Quite ignoble in fact.

I was a guest star in a TV series filming down there, and while drinking with a fellow actor, who went on to become quite famous and who shall remain nameless (the necessity for which one will see in the forthcoming saga), we were driving in my cheap rented Plymouth Valiant with a couple of bimbos we had met in a nearby bar, heading promisingly back to their trailer park to party.

Upon turning the last bend in the piney woods to the trailer park, there, in front of the gal's trailer in the cold light of an overhanging bulb strung bleakly across the driveway, was a sleek, brightly red, and striped painted Firebird with its engine already running.

"Oh, my GAWD," says the girl next to me. "That's mah boyfriend! We gotta get outta here!"

"Get outta here?" I exclaimed in disbelief, noticing that the boyfriend had already seen us and was fired up and screeching tires toward us, "He's got a Firebird with a monster engine and we've got a Plymouth fucking Valiant!"

At that point he had drawn up and turned, slamming on his brakes as he cut off our exit. "You got mah women in yo car," he says. From the closeness of our two rolled down windows, I could see the glint of a very large pistol...what looked like a long-barreled Magnum.

Summoning up my best Southern accent I said, "Ah have nevah intentionally had another man's woman in mah car! Hold your fire." With that absurd excuse, meant to be conciliatory in the best traditions of survival by Southern gentlemanly behavior, I said, "Ah am getting out of mah car and comin' to talk to y'all."

I slowly got out of the Valiant, with my buddy in the back seat, speechless, He being a Yankee had no idea what I was going to do. I hissed at him as I was leaving, possibly to face my death, "Stay put, asshole, and shut the fuck up, all of you."

With hands in the air, I then carefully approached the Firebird. In that moment of staring down at the barrel of yes, a Magnum pistol, I thought – like a slow-mo dream - of Dr. King. No kidding. As I got to the window, the irate redneck was obviously drunk and ranting away about his slut girlfriend and "I'm finally going to kill all y'all sons of bitches!" While ranting, he carelessly waved the pistol within striking range. The night on West 22nd St. came roaring back into consciousness. Whether I actually and methodically remembered the oath I'd made to "disarm, not overwhelm" I don't know, but I did refrain from striking when the moment came.

After quiet and gentle apologies were made for the mistake, I called to the girls and requested they join the Firebird king and suggested I might buy them all a drink as a peace offering. He accepted. In my rearview mirror I could see him ordering the girls into the trailer and then followed me to a bar downtown. We spent the evening drinking and telling stories of chicks, army life and other macho tales. I left him, head drooping onto the bar as I slipped away into the night.

I had already dropped off my sweaty, exhausted actor pal. He did not join us, as he had in the heat of the moment and fear of outcome...soiled his linens.

I am proud of that minor non-fatal victory. Not of my tacky reasons for being there - brains in the dick moment - but of a slightly irreverent, but active remembrance of the magnificent Martin Luther King.

CHAPTER 18

More Broadway Tales

Other New York theatre shows followed, including one by Kurt Vonnegut, *Happy Birthday, Wanda June*. Starting Off-Broadway at what was the Theatre De Lys, now the Lucille Lortel (a wonderful theatre loving woman who was a producer of *Blood Knot*), we moved to Broadway (very prophetically, if not logically) when there was an Off-Broadway strike. The play became a hit again. Kurt had never written a play before. I've never seen a playwright trust his actors more than he....If a scene did not quite work, being too literary or something, he would bound down from the balcony and talk, then bound back to the balcony and fix it...sometimes in as little as forty-five minutes! His photographer, who was documenting his foray into the world of legitimate theatre, was a beautiful young woman named Jill Krementz....I believe they stayed married till the day he left us.

He and I were close. He seemed to realize I got his sense of whimsy. I played the schmuck vacuum cleaner salesman who, when he sees the Ernest Hemingway-like character opening the door to him, feints dead away! Yes, I fell straight forward into the room and seemingly flat on my face. How? I was very strong and athletic in those days (1970) and bore the shock of the fall on my flat hands as if I were doing a push up... with my nose coming perilously close to the floor...about 3 inches.

All but one night that is.

That night I have no idea how I miscalculated the move, but I slammed down onto my nose and forehead and knocked myself out!

I was lying cold on the stage and William Hickey, that simply marvelous actor and teacher, who in the play played the deranged pilot who had dropped the bomb on Nagasaki, knelt and I awoke to his not too pleasant breath but oh so comforting manner..."Are you OK?" he rasped in that unique outboard-motor voice of his. When assured I was OK we got up and continued the play. I have no idea how. Kevin McCarthy was the

Hemingway character, a lovely gent whom I knew into his nineties. Keith Charles, a buddy from the soaps, played the other young male lead.

One night, a guy had an apparent heart attack in the audience. Keith and I were on stage together. I could sort of tell by the sounds and then looking down into the audience...(by that time, we had moved to Broadway - It was a much larger theatre)...I stopped, realized what was happening and called for the house lights as well as for a doctor. Yes the phrase, "Is there a doctor in the house?" Thankfully there was. He attended. They carried the guy out into the lobby and I turned to Keith and, in character, said, "Where were we?" With one of Keith's adorable twisted smiles, he continued. We continued.

Offstage shortly after, he asked me, "How the fuck did you do that, just deal with all that and then without breaking character, just turn to me and go on with it?" I told him of the experience with Rupert Cross in *Blood Knot;*. Ah, live theatre.

Great stage musical performers occasionally "stop the show", meaning they're so outstanding that the audience's wild applause literally stops the show. I had a few good laughs as in *Twigs* when I got locked behind the fridge, but I can't remember actually stopping the show...except for the experiences mentioned where I, not the audience, stopped the show.

There actually was one other time...

London, 1982, *The Little Foxes* with Elizabeth Taylor. The IRA militant arm was dangerous at the time. We had many blood Royals and high-ranking government and military figures in attendance. I was alone on stage with Elizabeth and I noticed that some guys with hats and raincoats were sliding silently down the aisles. As they reached the stage, I stopped Elizabeth with a gesture and said something really brilliant like, "Honey, we have to stop," (still in character as Oscar, with my southern accent) and asked the lead MI5 whether he would like us to clear the stage. He said, "We have to clear the house" I turned to the audience, ever ready to improvise and said, "Ladies and Gentlemen, could we all clear the theatre and adjourn to the pub next door?" They did, in a good British, orderly way, coming back later to continue.

Naughty Nick did not pull pranks on stage as did a lot of fine British actors, including Olivier. Once in *Beckett,* when he was still playing Thomas Beckett, (which bored him...in my opinion) he got a bit naughty. He, Olivier, liked physical parts. The King, whom he later played with super physical gusto, was far more appealing. During one performance, he went upstage to fill his water flagon at a fountain, and facing completely upstage so as the audience couldn't see (but in full view of the onstage actors and those watching from the wings), he faked pissing into the flagon and then turned to the audience and drank heartily! All backstage and some on, broke up.

John Mills, the fine English actor who came to Broadway to play Laurence of Arabia also could get mischievous on stage...making quietly provocative asides to cast members in non-critical moments. John was wonderful as T.E Lawrence. The play was called *Ross* and was indeed a fine play, written by Terence Rattigan, who attended rehearsals with great enthusiasm. The mix of famous British actors and Americans seemed to go well. I was asked eventually to play the part of a jaunty aviator in the *Royal Flying Corps*, replacing Jimmy Valentine who had done so well...It was almost a year and a fine experience. Prior to that, though, I was a standby, something I had promised myself never to do again. But, okay, I was offered a chunk of money...I had just gotten married and rather liked paying the rent. Perhaps a tad more importantly, I loved the play,

So, once again I was standing in the wings, the ever dutiful standby, but this time I was in costume as Ross/Lawrence. John Mills had been ice skating with one of his famous daughters (Haley and Juliet) and had had his hand skated over when he fell on the ice that previous afternoon. Apparently hurting terribly, he almost didn't make it on stage. As I stood in the wings waiting to go on, he came up to me and said breathlessly, "Nicolas, I'm going on." He did. He was splendid. The injured hand certainly ramped up the rape scene (the Turkish soldiers in WW-1 raped Lawrence) after which he was very much, yes, hurting.

Was I disappointed? Sure. But I also admired the British guts he displayed not only on screen in countless heroic wartime roles, but here on the Broadway stage before my eyes. Bless his soul, it was admirable. When the show closed, he gave a lovely cocktail party on the Queen Mary, just before one of her last voyages across the Atlantic...Yes, I actually saw the stewards serving the first class in those beachwood salons and staterooms which are visited regularly today as a tourist attraction in Long Beach, California.

My standby days behind me, I started working like a madman, never missing a performance until *Blood Knot* when a terrible back injury sent me crawling to a hospital. I did, years later, in 1982 (*Little Foxes*) have to leave a show to have an angioplasty. The great British cardiologist, Dr. John Coltheart, told me "You must have a bypass." I said, always the smartass, "Don't you have Roto-Rooter over here?" He laughed and said, "Matter of fact, I've just come back from Emory University in the U.S. and we've developed something called angioplasty." I asked pragmatically how long I would be out of for a bypass versus for an angio-whatever. "Possibly a week or so for angioplasty and months for a by-pass. "A not at all difficult decision. "Roto Rooter it is!" says I, and we did.

I might add that the ever-generous Elizabeth Taylor paid me my salary for that week I was out. My very caring then wife, Beth, joined me and we went to Cornwall where I recovered. We even ate at the Inn at Mouse Hole in Lands End, where Dylan Thomas (another of my favorites) spent his honeymoon.

CHAPTER 19

$\mathcal{T}$wigs

Back in 1971, during the summer of that year, I tried to get a reading for a play by George Firth, *Twigs*. George was already famous for *Company*, as was its director Michael Bennett, renowned as a director/choreographer for the musicals *Follies, Promises, Promises* and others. I could not get a reading. To this day, casting directors have their favorites. I was not then the favorite of that casting director. Giving her/him undeserved credit, perhaps I was "not right" for the part...a favorite euphemism for being an unfavorite. "No fucking imagination!" is the way I put it.

On this occasion, I got a hold of the play from a friend and knew I had to get a crack at it. George Furth, among others, including Marilyn Monroe, Brooke Hayward, Henry Jaglom, and Dennis Hopper, were all in Lee Strasberg's class in the early 60s. I remember the delicious wit of George Furth and our times together over the years at Joe Allen's, the theatrical haunt on 46th Street, where to this day, the famous and the not famous are made to feel equally welcome. Joe is rightfully proud of his many actor, director, dancer, writer customers who 'made it'. Some started as waiters at Joe Allen's...He made a point of hiring actors. A kind soul.

I called George and said, "Can't get a reading for your play. Could you...?" He did. I went to the Plymouth Theatre and read for the part of FrankI had played a lot of highly theatrical, energetic parts, but Frank was not that. He was kind, quiet and patient with the leading woman played by the magnificent Sada Thompson. She played two sisters respectively and finally their mother in three succeeding acts. Frank, who owns a moving company, is her leading man in the first act. Her character is newly without husband and in a near panic coping with moving into a new place. Frank takes the time to help her. I had envisioned Gene Hackman, to whom I had lost the part in *Any Wednesday* some years before, as perfect for the part. I think in the reading I sneakily paid tribute to him by doing a bit of "channeling".

At the end of the reading, Michael Bennet, already then a legend, directing his first "straight" play (as opposed to a musical), came down to the proscenium and said softly, "If you're not too expensive, you've got it." I said something really quick and bright like, "Nnnnnn no, I'm not uhhh…" and then he said, "In deference to Sada Thompson, would you come back and read with her?"

I did and the result led to a year of the finest, most rewarding long run in my theatrical life.

A truly grand lady of the theatre, Sada was the consummate professional. In my attempt to be a good father to my two girls, then 8 and 7, I tried, despite a ridiculously busy schedule, to be a good father. "Good father" did not mean to me "quality time" only, which was (and is!) a useful phrase for parents too busy with their own lives. "Time" just time, anytime and anywhere, was what I believed in. Having missed so sorely my father's time when I was young, I tried not to repeat that and many other mistakes of parenthood.

By then separated, I had my kids visit on weekends and any other times possible. To her great credit, Candace, their mother, never deprived me of visits at any and all times possible.

As a result, up 45th Street, to the theatre marched daddy and Candace Jr. and Dinneen. We would stop before the matinee and get an "extravagant" lunch at the cheap deli on the corner of 8th Avenue, and then, while I was making up in my dressing room, my girls would visit others backstage. BoBo Lewis, Sada's understudy, a wildly intelligent gal of indeterminate age and flaming, utterly mad red hair, had a lifetime of fun experiences to share. Sharply witty, pulling no punches, she made a point of remarking on my girlfriend, a flight attendant, Dee Dee Devine (actual name) who looked a lot like Barbie Benton, the matchless Playmate. Dee Dee and I had met on a plane. Her cat-like, inviting eyes had intrigued. We lasted a year. She wore, among other snappy outfits, a purple jumpsuit, not quite the couture of my ex-wife, Candace, who loved Oscar De La Renta and the like. All in the company found Dee Dee intriguing. Especially witty BoBo. "A purple jumpsuit? For you, Nicolas? Oh, come now!"

The company all liked my kids, especially Sada, who became great pals with my youngest, Dinneen. Dinneen was a wistful, graceful child who had blond hair like her sister and mother, a petite figure which later blossomed into an athletic body of almost perfect proportions. At the time she suffered from an accident which had damaged her hand and wore huge glasses to correct an eye issue. Above all else, she had a charm and quietly radiant personality. Not being as immediately glamorous as her older sister who became a Ford model at 14, she lingered sometimes in the background. She was, however, direct, probing, completely fascinated with life, music and people...especially Sada Thompson, with whom she would visit backstage before the curtain.

Sada, of the curious nature, would welcome this little creature. So as not to ever play favorites, I made time with each child. With Dinneen, we sat Tatami in a Japanese restaurant. I remarked at one point, observing her utter comfortability in that lotus-like position, "Honey, I believe in another life you were a Japanese princess!" "No, a Japanese cat," was her instant but relaxed and positive reply.

Dinneen, after being treated for long term orthopedic issues, has become a fine fashion photographer, just getting started when COVID-19 hit the world.

One day Dinneen brought Sada a present; a most personal and prized possession...her hairbrush...strands of childish blonde hair still clung to it. The value and innocent well-meaning of this gift was not lost on Sada. To the last time I ever saw that miraculous woman, she smiled in fond remembrance of the "hairbrush" gift.

My older daughter, Candace, is a woman of extraordinary energy, multiple talents including cooking and baking, the latter of which started on a Barbie Stove, no longer sold due to a few houses being leveled by fire from overcooked mini-biscuits, the work of 8-year-old fledgling bakers. She has multiple talents, was in the math club at the primo New York girls school Spence, and as mentioned, was a Ford model at 14. She saw to her own college education and more than anything has created a magnificent home on the shores of Connecticut for her swell husband, Andrew Smoller and her two sons, Nicolas and Christopher, my witty, handsome devils who are incredibly kind and patient with their "Popi". Beautiful and with a character to match, she runs that superbly re-created house with a gift for cooking and interior design, equaled by her blending of rich and not-so-rich guests, all made to feel wonderfully welcome.

One of her super rich friends remarked in admiration when seeing the tastefully and imaginatively done house, "Oh, Candace, what understated opulence."

Returning to *Twigs*, Sada was trained at what was then Carnegie Tech, now Carnegie Mellon. Her approach, like most great actors of her time, was largely instinctive and technically flawless. I, on the other hand, was trained first at RADA then at the Neighborhood Playhouse (with Sandford Meisner protégés, David Pressman and Charles Conrad, later briefly with Sandy himself), then Lee Strasberg, and even later with Frank Silvera and Milton Katselas. And of course, I've worked continually at The Actors

Studio in New York and still here in Los Angeles. I am steeped in if not obsessed with the "Method".

An illustrative moment of that method stuff came in rehearsal for *Twigs*: My character, Frank, was helping Sada's, this lonely but determined woman, move into her new apartment.

In the play and on the newly constructed set on which we were in our final rehearsals up in the Bronx, there was a scene In which, while attempting to help me move the fridge, she pushes the damn thing on a cart which then slides, carrying me all the way across and off right stage. As written, a grand comedy moment. As practiced repeatedly that day....It didn't work.

The cart worked but made so much noise on the newly constructed track that to me at least, the reality was destroyed....harking back to my advice from Olivier all those years before. I finally said, "This is bullshit. The track and all this technical stuff is destroying the illusion. It's like a slicky-Broadway comedy!" A pause...and then from the back of the scene shop rang acidly, the voice of the ever humorous and often caustic George Furth. "What's the matter with a slicky-Broadway comedy?" I said, "This play is much more than that...there must be some way of doing this moment which ain't phony!"

My blurt out stunned the assemblage. After another pause came not the anticipated "You're fired" but rather a sharp, not unkind retort, "Suggestion?" I thought and then said, "I don't know...it has something to do with the play itself...this well-meaning woman screws up the moment and is embarrassed....I don't know how..... it has something to do with this fridge and the clumsy handling of it."

I was standing, holding onto the fridge in my frustration, pushing it...Suddenly Bob Avian, then Michael Bennett's assistant, later a very famous choreographer, jumped up and said, "Sada, get in front of the fridge, Nick, get in back of it, Sada push it and Nick, you get trapped in back." We did just that. Organically. "Method" at its best; the moment with this little, formerly helpless woman, now eagerly, energetically pushing the fridge, trapping me between it and the wall without knowing it, and then calling to me, not knowing where I was, became one of the biggest and most genuine laughs in the show.

Sada of the sparkling, ever mischievous eyes, was a treat on stage. Despite her miraculously accurate technique, she would and did notice the slightest variation in my performance. A pause slightly different by me – in character - would stimulate a change of reaction in her...quicksilver changes within the form which each night gave a newness to a familiar set of motions.

A simple tale of mutual need and loneliness, *Twigs* became a revelation of great depth. It was my first leading role on the New York stage as a "nice" guy. I truly loved Sada Thompson.

Michael, nervous in directing his first non-musical, was nevertheless at the top of his form. He was acutely observant and had an uncanny ability to immediately spot solutions. For example, he looked at me in the very beginning of rehearsals and said, "You move like a dancer, a guy who's a moving man does not. Go get some heavier shoes!" I got it....them. I went to Macy's that day and got a pair of wingtips, thick soled, heavy brown leather shoes, which I wore in every rehearsal and performance to the end of the run.

I hate seeing on stage the bottom side of shoes with brand new soles and heels...obviously never worn outside the carpets of the theatre. It breaks the illusion. Mine looked as if l walked all over Manhattan in them. Method. Michael Bennett's natural Method.

Another Michael Bennett gift: *Twigs* needed some incidental music. George Firth and Michael enlisted none other than Steven Sondheim to create the now unforgettable score. Opening night, in my first major part on Broadway, I sat in a hotel room with Steven Sondheim waiting for the New York Times review. In those days, opening night parties were usually held at Sardis on 44th Street, smack in the middle of the theatre district. Moss Hart's brother still drank at the bar, Hirshfield's legendary caricatures of famous Broadway types adorned the walls, Vincent Sardi, son of the original owner, still attended like the head of a two star Michelin....It was quietly grand,

The front circle of tables was always reserved for and nearly always filled by the Broadway greats. On the opening night of *Twigs* the great musical names were there in deference to Michael and Steven and George; distinguished legitimate theatre folk, some who had been skeptical about this up-start musical director genius being able to pull off a "legitimate" play. In those days there was a definite perceived difference between the legitimate and musical theatre, now erased by the economic juggernaut of the modern musical's dollar power. What a night. With all the very often glorious opening nights since, nothing has quite equaled that one.

By the time I walked into the doors of Sardis that night, I had been an actor trying to be good and trying to make a living for 20 years. My first job at RADA in the summer of 1951, when I was 17, was in a BBC special about Queen Elizabeth 1 with Moira Lister. So, at Sardi's, though still just 38, I had no idea what to expect as I entered looking around for others from the company in the foyer. I turned, entered the main dining room...as I did so "the circle" stood up, legendary greats, Carol Channing, Julie Stein, other composers, stars, directors, clouded my vision; they were all standing, applauding.

The sounds have faded, the memories have not.

At the end of the run, almost a year later after she had deservedly won the Tony, Sada and I looked at each other with appreciative tears in our eyes and agreed that it was - that last performance - as fresh as it had been all those many months ago.

***

My next project with Michael Bennett was the musical *Seesaw*. I got an out of the blue call from him one day in 1974 asking, "'Wanna do a musical?" "How do you know I can sing?" I answered. "I used to hear you warming up your chords in the dressing room during Twigs." "Ah! But how do you know I can dance?" "I don't. Come down to the Uris Theatre (now the Gershwin) and dance with me."

I did so - literally! I got up on stage and did a polka and a waltz with the great Michael Bennett! Baayork Lee, who was the "swing girl" (a kind of chief of the chorus as I remember) then took me under her able wing. Baayork went on to fame as the director of many revivals of *A Chorus Line*. Tommy Tune, the legendary dancer, director who was making his Broadway debut was also most kind to this actor-would-be musical performer.

I was replacing Ken Howard. He had left suddenly for a TV series, *The White Shadow*, which made him nationally known. He graciously left me a full bar in the dressing room for entertaining guests, a great old-fashioned tradition, especially in the British theatre.

Candace, my wife at the time, an ex-Copacabana (night club into the 60's) girl who taught me in the basement of our apartment on 110th St. and Broadway to dance a waltz clog. Why? Upon seeing the show AFTER being hired, I was shocked to see the second act begin with a SOFT SHOE SOLO by my soon-to-be character! I learned with good teaching from Candace and much patience from Ms. Baayork Lee.

Opening night for me, I whispered to the wonderful Michelle Lee, "I can't promise you a singer or a dancer, but I CAN promise you a Nebraska lawyer! I kept my promise I did my acting job. The dancing? Ah, well....The soft shoe at the beginning of the second act went splendidly...for me. However, Michelle, who was used to Ken Howard's silken if not expert soft shoe, actually broke up laughing in her on-stage hospital bed! When we both left the stage, she apologized. I said, "No, No,! That was the whole purpose of the scene! I'm supposed to come to the hospital to CHEER YOU UP!" She thought, laughed again, and said, "Oh my God, of course!"

We got along beautifully. She was simply, bloody marvelous in the part. Unfortunately, vocal issues made her leave the show, but she went on to become a huge TV Nighttime star. Recently, I had dinner with Michelle after 44 years!...still the same fun and genuine soul!

Patti Karr took over. Patti was delicious, an expert dancer and a good singer. A consummate professional and most patient with me. One night, again, during the solo dance, I forgot where I was...musically. (I did not learn the dances by numbers as most dancers do, I learned them by the music.) That night, I don't know what happened, but in the middle of the dance, I got distracted and "went up" (forgot)...I looked to "the pit" wherein stood the great Broadway conductor, Don Pippin and as I improvised a number of racy turns and pirouettes, I looked at Don for guidance? He smiled at me and just shrugged his shoulders while never missing a beat of conducting. We all laughed about it later. He, in wonderment at my silly improvising at the time. Asked how I did it. I told him that I used to play a trombone!

Alas, I was told some weeks later that they were preparing the then movie star (*Thoroughly Modern Milly*) John Gavin for the role. "Need a star" was their reason. A Broadway musical with a fading box office needed a pump up. Despite lovely music by Cy Coleman and Ken and Michelle, it had not been a consistent sell out even before my arrival, so in the minds of Joel Kipness and other producers, John Gavin was the answer.

Also nagging Joe was the fact that Ken was 6 foot 5 inches tall, I a little over 5 '10. Joel said to me after my very good opening, which most admired, "Can you be taller? I said, "Mt Sinai (hospital) might be able to stretch me"....There was no sense of humor in this short, serious, restaurateur turned producer. So, while John rehearsed, I played. Then Michael asked me to stay on as "standby" for John. I told him they already had an understudy, why me as well? He said they really wanted me to stay, that they really loved what I had done with the role, and as John was also President of The Screen Actors Guild, he would likely be gone a lot.

Hmm....quandary. Settled quickly for lots of money and the proviso that I didn't have to BE there. Just call in at half hour and see if John was there. Wow! Good deal. It proved to be tricky...I enrolled in NYU film school, downtown and called in at half hour. More than a few times, John got stuck somewhere between cities and I rushed from Greenwich Village to the theatre! Breathless I would bound on stage...Ah me, ah, musicals. John never did another Broadway play. He went on - under Reagan - to be Ambassador to Mexico. A charming, generous guy who was very good in the role. Not just sayin. He really was!

I loved doing a Broadway musical. I had done one other New York theatre musical *Oh Say Can You See*, Off-Broadway in 1963. It was a satirical look at the Hollywood Canteen which entertained soldiers during WW-2. I played Bing Crosby, the most famous singer in the world at the time. Yup, I got the part because I had for some time - in fun - imitated that baritone, mellow sound of his. The reviews were fantastic. We were ALL good! I was thrilled. The critics did notice the startling similarity to "Ol' Bingo". I managed to not do an imitation, but an impression, made my own in music and in dialogue. And then the ax hit.

October 16, 1963: The Russians sent missiles to Cuba; patriotism was suddenly not something to be made fun of...certainly not in a theatre production where one paid money to be amused. Our production died within two weeks, but not before - on the basis of those fantastically good reviews - CBS Music bought the rights and we did a very good LP recording of the show.

Somewhere between boats and garages lies a copy of *Oh, Say Can You See* gathering dust. Sometimes when people find out I actually played the role in *See Saw* over 40 times, I can see their not-so-hidden astonishment. I don't sing at clubs, rarely in the bathtub and so very few remember my musical abilities - singing in choirs and playing the trombone in the canyons of Chatsworth.

So now, when questioned wondrously how I did musicals, I say, "All the tomatoes missed!"

Whilst making money in *Seesaw*, I studied Film Production at NYU. I was much older than the rest of our little team (the class was divided into squads who would work together making short films). As my final project, I made a commercial about *Seesaw*. It was shot in Riverside park and started on close up - just the faces - of a foreign woman getting into a taxi and asking to be taken to "Seesaw". The New York taxi driver corrects her pronunciation of "Seesaw", saying, "No lady, its Seeee Sowah," He with his New York accent. She, with several tries, eventually gets it. As this is happening, we pull back and reveal that the beautiful woman and the amusing, grizzled taxi driver are riding up and down on a seesaw in the park!

I got us an "A" in the course, but my ad was never used. *Seesaw* closed during my time at NYU. I finished there after these many fun, stimulating experiences and never directed another film...'till a soon- to-be of my own creation? Stay tuned...

CHAPTER 20

Scuba, Underneath the Sea, the Mysteries, the Other Life

In 1973, I had finished the long and satisfying run of *Twigs* and was thriving with the success of the soap opera *Another World*. All was good. I had returned at the request of her psychiatrist, to my wife, Candace.

In those heady years of Broadway, Off-Broadway and soap opera money, there were summers at the Cambridge Beaches in Bermuda and winters in the Virgin Islands with our two beautiful daughters.

On the American Virgin Island of St. Thomas, in the winter of 1972-73, I was just 39 and having fun on the beach near the newly constructed Frenchman's Reef when I noticed scuba divers exiting the water. I went to the instructor, Joe Vogel, a former Underwater Demolition Team diver (the forerunners of the Navy SEAL super warriors). He was massive and told me of their swimming for 5 miles in open cold waters and missions in Korea. I was there in the tropical calm of the Virgin Islands and never dreamed of the adventures to come from that casual inquiry on the coast of St. Thomas.

In those days' instructors were allowed to test your reactions under stress, a leftover from the Navy, a rigorous weed-out theory of elimination...a Darwinian approach to scuba diving. In the pool, he shut off my air without telling me...I breathed until my regulator ran dry, looked at him through my mask. Expressionless, he just waited with his hands clasped at the bottom of the pool. I came to the surface slowly, switched to my snorkel which afforded fresh air and breathed normally again. His only comment on joining me, was, "Yeah, you react okay under stress." Some, but not too many, stressful times were to come in the following 40 odd years.

From there came the enchantment of reef diving, the fantastic array of marine life unavailable in aquariums at the dentist's office. My first week of scuba diving ended with a night dive. Suddenly the colors brightened, the reds became startling under incandescent light. In daylight, as one descends everything gradually loses color. The reds turn brown, the greens and almost everything turns blue, and bluer.

I went back to New York entranced with this new multidimensional world and worked quickly and very hard to get my almost 40 year old body in shape to become an instructor. My buddy from jury duty, Gary Collins, with whom I got certified for scuba in New York City, became, eventually, my partner in founding Pan Aqua Divers, which is still there. Gary has since retired.

Gary took me to a fancy country club on Long Island and worked my butt off with a stopwatch and some loud urging and much more cursing to make the minimum times for the upcoming instructor pool tests for the National Association of Underwater Instructors. Panting, red faced, aching with fatigue, I tolerated Gary's well-meant scolding. Because of my limited availability, I was the first to endure and pass a most difficult NAUI Instructor course. I first had to build up some serious time at considerable depth. My diving after Joe Vogel, had been mostly tropical, relaxed tropical reef diving from 30 to 60 feet in depth.

Our other partner was Don Osias, a brilliant plasma physicist at Columbia University. Don went on to brainy work and scuba teaching in Oakland. I scrounged everywhere to find all the equipment for the courses we created...Great help was given me by the owner of the dive shop in the Bronx. Our new assistant was a PHD Marine bio candidate, again from Columbia University. Handsome, smart as hell, Jim Peterson went on to become the leading partner in Pan Aqua divers...still is, as well as owning The Dive Bar and another wine and tasty restaurant, Buceo 95, on the Upper Westside of Manhattan.

Then began a series of sometimes scary dives in over a hundred feet on a WW-1 wreck off Fire Island, NY, and then WW-2 wrecks off New Jersey. Those were most challenging at times...the wave height was often so steep that in order to get back on the dive boat, one had to wait near the stern, watch the boat rise-all 50 tons of it and then, as the stern splashed mightily back down into the sea, one quickly grabbed the stern platform and lifted tanks, weights, wet-suit, and fins, some 60 pounds of crap with all one's strength, up, up onto the dive platform. Huffing, puffing, I then lay there gasping for moments before climbing into the boat. One's brain was filled with recent memories of the depths: WW-2 tanks, jeeps, guns, lobsters as big as your arm scampering along among the machines of soldiers and sailors and marines who didn't make it past the waiting German U Boats lurking just off shore. Was it all worth it? Oh, yeah.

Voila! I began teaching and loved it all.

CHAPTER 21

John Kennedy, Jr: Scuba Student

As a scuba student John Kennedy, Jr was challenging. His mother had called the Westside YMCA in New York City where I was the Chief Scuba Instructor. The life-guard came breathlessly to me to announce her call. It was 1974. I was teaching a class in the pool and thought one of my pals was pulling my leg. "Yeah sure, Jacqueline Onassis is calling...get the fuck outta here!" "No Nick, I'm not kidding. It really sounds like her..." "Go on, quit this shit. I get the joke. Tell Gary or whoever put you up to this, It ain't funny. I'm busy!" "REALLY Nick! Go. Answer the phone..." I went. I answered. The voice on the other end was either she or a perfect imitation; that breathy, almost whispered timbre.

When John Kennedy Jr, age 14, came to the pool with two Secret Service Agents guarding him, it was the beginning of an adventure. The Secret Service agents stood at the side of the pool, as I instructed young John. At that time, I was the only instructor in New York to use the new Buoyancy Compensating Device, an inflatable vest with pressure relief valves for governing one's buoyancy underwater and on the surface. It had been used in Europe for some time, but that and a submersible pressure gauge for measuring the amount of air one had in the tank, were new to America. We had a pull rod on the side of the tank which, when we ran out of air, would give us an additional few pounds to enable a return to the surface....supposedly.

The failing of that device lay in the fact that when diving on wrecks and brushing against objects, the pull rod could be "pulled" prematurely. Then when needed, the air was already used. It happened to me at night in 60 feet of dank, cold water off City Island. The pull rod was down, I was out of air and in the dark could not tell which way was up. I, remembering some advice from my instructor, the magnificent Phillip Quarles, breathed out a few bubbles, watched - by diving light - the direction they travelled and followed, breathing out slowly in order not to burst my lungs on the way up as the air inside them expanded with my ascent.

I barely broke the surface, gasping for air and then breathed into my new Buoyancy Compensating Device in order to stay afloat. I thought about both pieces of equipment and swore that when I became an instructor, I would ensure my students were trained on and used that safety equipment. The other leading instructor at the time in New York, said "You're ruining it for the rest of us economically. It's too expensive." To which I replied, "That's kind of like telling a guy traveling across a lower California desert in a jeep, 'Oh, don't bother having a gas gauge...just remember - under stress - how much gasoline you have.'"

John Kennedy Jr. stood in the pool and said quietly, "I actually know how to dive, Mr. Coster, and I never use all this stuff, but I am going on a National Geographic dive with Al Giddings (a world-famous underwater cinematographer) and he insists I get an American certification." To which I replied, "And where did you learn to dive, John?" "With a Greek naval Captain off the Christina" (The Christina was Aristotle Onassis' massive yacht.)

"Well, here at the YMCA, we use the BCD and the submersible pressure gauge and an extra regulator...in case your partner's fails, you can feed him or her without removing your own regulator at depth-risking, never having it returned, and someone, or perhaps both of you, drowning...It has happened."

"I don't need it." came the defiant response. I paused. To this day, I have no idea what happened exactly, but I heard this voice coming from within which sounded like his father....weird, replete with New England accent saying sharply, firmly, but without large volume, but enough to alert the Secret Service men in attendance, "Let me put it this way, John; Put on that equipment or get the hell out of my pool!" The Secret Service guys looked a bit shocked, but stood fast. John quietly put on the equipment.

He learned well and quickly. We went on a training dive off the point in Brooklyn on a fellow instructor's boat, who, when seeing John and the Secret Service escort, stood practically at attention as we boarded. He was a retired Marine and was impressed.

John was a natural athlete and did well. He was also raised well and respected all levels of society. This working-class Brooklyn environment seemed to fascinate him; a far cry from the mahogany and polished brass and crystal of the Christina and the islands of Greece.

I always told my students, "If you forget the tables and you will (the tables being a card calculator from which one could determine how long and how deep one could be at depth in the water without contracting the dreaded, "bends" - decompression sickness from nitrogen retention), then call me, come by and I'll review them with you.

A couple of years after teaching John, I was doing a Broadway play, *Otherwise Engaged*. The doorman called over the loudspeaker, just before one matinee, and said, "Mr. Coster, John Kennedy Jr is here and wants to talk to you. About a SCUBA LESSON!" I could hear the cast and crew laugh. I came down and John said he was going on yet another expedition and had indeed forgotten how to use the 'tables'. I said, "Sure, I'm offstage for about 45 minutes during the show and we can review them then." He stayed and we reviewed. During this very pleasant reunion, He relayed a story to me:

"You know that equipment you made me wear and then gave me to use?" (His mother had been so generous to me when I finished instructing John, I had insisted on his taking the BCD, double regulator, and pressure gauge with him afterwards.)

"So, I was diving with that Greek Captain in 180 feet of water (a very great depth on scuba) and HE RAN OUT OF AIR!" "My God!" says I, "What did you do?" "I actually fed him off the spare regulator you gave me, partially inflated the BCD and we got to the surface...just barely before I ran out of air".

I looked at him and understood that would have been a double fatality.

I cannot describe how sad I felt when hearing about the loss of his life in an air crash. This magnificent young man...dead in a flying machine.

During his training I would go to the Onassis apartment on 5th Avenue to do theory work. His mother, sister and I got to be friendly. I went for supper, they came to my shows, I took Jacqueline to Joe Allen's and one day, she had me join her for tea. At that tea was a close friend of hers. I walked into the drawing room and there sitting elegantly but without affectation, was the greatest British ballerina of all time, Dame Margot Fonteyn. She, upon extending her hand in greeting, said, "Oh, I'm a great fan of yours!" I, staggered that she'd recognized me, said incredulously, "You're a fan of mine?" She said, "Oh, yes, I have watched you for years."

The last time I saw Caroline was when I was doing *Otherwise Engaged*, directed by Harold Pinter, and starring Tom Courtenay on Broadway. She came the night that all the lights in New York went off. A gigantic power failure. We finished the performance by candle and flashlights. The audience cheered wildly.

On darkened Broadway there was not a taxi to be had. Dark streets and near panic in the crowds prompted me to walk Caroline home...from 45th and Broadway to 82nd and Fifth Avenue, a considerable walk. A lovely walk. I have not seen her since.

Since teaching John Jr, scuba has become an astonishingly huge part of my life, extending to the teaching, and transporting of disabled persons to scuba dive. Another afternoon...

CHAPTER 22

Pinter, Gray, Courtenay and Cavett

In the summer of 1976, I returned to read for a Broadway play, *Otherwise Engaged* by the fine writer, Simon Gray. Tom Courtenay was to play the part originally created on the London stage by Alan Bates, a classmate of his at RADA. In the same class, some years after my attendance there were Tom Courtenay, Alan Bates, Albert Finney, and Peter O'Toole. All of them had graced the halls of Gower Street. I was to read the part of the brother.

I read for a role in the play and once again at a Broadway reading got cheeky. I walked out on stage and to the astonishment of the casting director, said, "Do you mind if I read for the part of the critic instead of the brother?" Silence was deafening. Harold Pinter, the director, finally said, "By all means."

I read. The role was an acerbic, nasty bright, bastard who, in 19 minutes of non-stop, virtuosic diatribe, becomes shit-faced-drunk, but wittily so and insulting. Typecasting. I got the part.

Rehearsals were a hoot. Lunches across the street were civilized and fun at the Theatre Bar and other haunts of Broadway. At one such lunch, joined by Harold, his fine writer wife Lady Antonia Fraser, Simon Gray, Tom Courtenay and our young assistant stage manager, I led off the discussion on a very high literary level popping the question as to whether the calling of a guy by the name "wanker" would be understood by most on this side of the pond. It was generally agreed that it would not, thereby robbing the moment and the aftermath of understanding, ergo, humor.

This was in the winter of 1975-76, and at that time, without all the now familiar across-the-Atlantic slang from Monty Python and countless other Brit films, most across the pond slang was relatively unknown. We needed a "wanker" replacement. Not necessarily British, but something that at least sounded British. Clearly not 'jerk-off', the graphic American down-to-crotch name for it.

Furrowed brows on the talented foreheads of Lady Antonia, Pinter and Gray followed. The puzzle was met by the feline, ever present humor of the brilliant Tom Courtenay, who suggested, deadpan, "What about pull your pudding?" Chuckles, but hardly a glance of appreciation to that contribution. After a number of lame other attempts, from out of the corner came the unobtrusive voice of our youthful American assistant stage manager, "How 'bout whack-off?'"

To a person, the assemblage turned and applauded. Ah, the wonders of new-English! For it is not indeed an American expression, nor British, but it SOUNDS British and was readily understood by all....including the audience.

Harold Pinter was a gentleman and a joy to work with. It was Harold's first experience with a mostly North American cast. The fine Canadian actor John Horton, the Swedish-cum-American Carolyn Lagerfeld, my scene partner, the glamorous Bostonian Lynn Milgrim, and the remarkable John Christopher Jones, a patrician New Englander, as the working-class lout. My character's 19-minute virtuosic turn getting progressively drunk until at last, he throws his drink into his girlfriend's face and dress, after which she peels off her wet blouse, exposing a lovely pair of breasts to all present. Again, not done too often on stage in that day...save for the exceptional *Hair*, which, of course, had exposed far more a few years earlier. The play was very well received. Jackie Onassis came to see it...the last time she was to attend a play of mine.

Tom Courtenay got terribly, clinically homesick during the middle of the run. He was sociable with those he liked. We became fast chums. I finally advised him, watching his ever-decreasing energy even on stage, to "Go home, Tom." He was miserable. He finally did return to England. The much-admired talk show host, Dick Cavett replaced him...or tried to. One thing a good actor does not do, despite having a necessary healthy ego, is to let that ego or let 'performance gratification need' get in the way of creating character. One should remain valid, honest, and true to the playwright's intention of character.

The essence of the character, as written by Simon Gray and impeccably performed by Courtenay, was his complete inability to express pent up emotion, (a perfect example of that repression can be found in the German film *The Lives of Others* as played magnificently by Ulrich Muhe). Opening night, after patient direction by Harold Pinter, Cavett came on and at the end wept textbook 101 tears and thought, proudly, he had conquered yet another field of play...Nope. at the curtain, there were even some hisses. Not the accolades he'd expected.

Always conscious of the audience, he stopped the curtain call and proceeded to give what he must of thought was a humble in-person connection to his fans, which was a mini talk show-monologue. Embarrassment not hidden was evident on the faces of the rest of the professional theatre actors standing with egg-on-faces alongside him...un-referred to by him. Always reverent, I finally said loudly, "In the immortal words of Abe Burrows, we have just missed the 11:10 to Westchester," and left the stage.

Furious, I confronted Dick offstage and said, "Are you an actor or fucking Buddy Hackett!" Ever the quickest with a retort, he replied with his finger pressed to his nose to produce a nasal-gravel like sound, "Is that a criticism?" I laughed...

In his book later, he accused me of wanting to play the leading part. I did not. Mine was flamboyant, revelatory, and very satisfying. There are some parts which I have never felt I could play as well as the actor playing them. This one by Tom Courtenay was chief among them...ah, and of course Paul Scofield's Lear.

Broadway, Off-Broadway. Repertory companies, summer stock tours, many years, eight performance weeks from 1957 through 1977; tiring, often frustrating attempts to get work. I had appeared in many New York theatre plays and musicals, ending with Simon Grey's *Otherwise Engaged*. Being fed up with Dick Cavett, and admittedly disappointed in not getting a somewhat expected Tony Award nod, I departed for a fresh look at the heretofore elusive Hollywood career.

So, in late 1977, I left my beloved New York for a number of reasons, not the least of which was those many years of working every day but Monday. The memory of rejections fade at least until the next time one comes calling. Then the opened scar tissue stings once again. But since then, and now especially, one dwells on the creativity experienced, the camaraderie and the fun...God, the fun.

CHAPTER 23

Elizabeth not Lizzie

Roscoe Lee Browne once said to me, "Nicolas, you don't drop names, you BOMB them!"

Well therefore, here comes the air-raid about my pal, Elizabeth Taylor.

As said, we went to Byron House primary school in London before WW-2. I don't remember that young girl as she was two years older than me. In 1982, she was playing the lead, Regina, in *The Little Foxes* on Broadway. The show was about to go on tour to New Orleans, Los Angeles, and London. Many of the cast were changed for one reason or another. I was offered the part of Oscar the ne'er-do-well brother of Regina.

I went to see the play. It was superbly directed by Austin Pendleton who, some years before, had directed *Benito Cerino*, the show which starred Roscoe Lee Browne and myself. Backstage I asked the doorman to announce my wish to meet the legendary Elizabeth Taylor (not yet then, "Dame"). I said," Would you tell Ms. Taylor that probably the ONLY actor who ever went to Byron House School with her awaits her attendance?"

He did so. From down the hall came the shriek of delight! Thus, began a remarkable friendship.

On stage, the consummate professional who, when one of her three leading men missed or fluffed a line, would jump in silkenly and save our ass. Between Horace, played so well by J,D. Cannon, Robert Lansing as Ben the oldest brother, and me as Oscar, we had about a hundred and fifty years in the theatre! Well, La Dame Taylor was as crisp, focused and commanding as if she'd been there (on stage) all her life!

Backstage, off-stage, we hit it off together. Never an affair (for those who might wonder), but super close and with whom wit abounded, the closeness and respect was exemplified the night after Beth and I got married, Elizabeth cooked us a wedding dinner and then washed the dishes herself! I noticed that she was wearing the fabulous diamond ring Burton had given her while scrubbing the cutlery! It had a chip in it.

I said, "Jesus, Elizabeth, how much does that chip knock off the price of the ring?" She with a sly smile said, "Oh, about a hundred thousand." That was January of 1982. Imagine what that chip alone would be worth today!

We dined together in New Orleans, London, and L.A. In London I took her to Joe Allen, then newly opened. Elizabeth came with Muhammad Ali, who had been to the show that evening. My character, Oscar was a fearful bigot. At dinner, I asked Muhammad (who sat in the first row where I from the stage could see the massive fists resting inactively on the arms of his seat). I asked him what his reaction was to me saying all those awful things. He said, "I turned to the guy next to me and asked, 'did he say, BIGGAH?'" I silently imagined being flattened by just one of those enormous, lethal looking fists.

I paid the bill!! Yup. When asked why, I replied, "Royalty does not carry money." It was a pleasure.

Maureen Stapleton who played Birdie until we went to London, (she wouldn't fly and my beloved Sada Thompson replaced her) was a robust, wildly entertaining guest of mine at dinner in New Orleans. What a great and endearing actress. We talked of Marlon Brando, her buddy, and other things from the past and our hopes for the future. I remember eating alligator for the first time. Like veal but lighter. "Rather like rattlesnake," I said deadpan.

In L.A. I got a private glimpse of Elizabeth's enormous shoe and clothing collection! Ah, the memories contained in those massive storage closets.

I last saw that wonderful woman at her birthday party given for a few hundred of her closest friends, as the saying goes, at where else but Disneyland. I miss very much her mischievous intelligence and ever-present sensuality.

CHAPTER 24

The Great Gregory Peck

In the past chapters, I have twirled off memories of staunch heroes who are at least legends in my own mind, who have influenced my visions or delusions as to 'what is a man'. A near perfect man to me was Gregory Peck. People used to ask me what he was like, I replied, "He is everything you hoped he would be"

And he certainly was that to me.

At the close of *Benito Cereno* with Roscoe Lee Browne, and after a fabulous tour of Europe representing the United States in our Bicentennial celebration, I winged to Hollywood for a brief looksie before returning to start rehearsals for *Otherwise Engaged* in the Fall.

I used to ship my motorcycle by air freight after emptying the gas tank. No longer possible after 9/11, now it has to be empty of ALL liquid and crated in a box. Back then they put it on a pallet and along with a small empty can, would fly it to Los Angeles or return it to New York. I would then walk a short distance to a gas station, fill the jug, put it into the waiting bike at air freight, go back to the gas station, fill the tank, and speed off to the coast of my youth.

All that effort - tedious (even as I read in re-telling), was worth it for indeed I did not have to rent a car. It made my many trips to Hollywood to seek work and visit family infinitely cheaper.

My agent called and said that I should meet Darryl Zanuck Jr, the producer of the film, *MacArthur!* starring Mr. Peck. I went. Zanuck had seen me on Broadway, and with that I got the part of Colonel Sid Luff, aide to the General.

I loved every minute of it!

I was even able to use my seafaring knowledge in one scene where MacArthur pulls off the, "I Will Return!" promise made when he escapes just in front of the Japanese invasion of Corregidor.

On his "I have Returned" moment, as we descended down the ramp of the landing craft, the boat operator had mistakenly taken a sandbar - in over 6 feet of water - for the beach! I knew it. I have the actual picture taken of that moment when, just after Greg hit the water he started to sink, I yelled to the actual Marine standing by him, "Marine! Grab Mr. Peck!" he did. I meanwhile snatched one of the former Presidents of the Philippines, who was aged and about to fall head first into the water! Greg, always the wit, said, "I always thought MacArthur could walk on water."

We got to be close, Gregory and I. He had started his career during the depression in the same theatre in Virginia, the Barter Theatre. Good talk followed. After the film finished, he invited my then wife Candace and me to dinner with his friend, Garson Kanin, the famous playwright, and director. at a very fancy New York restaurant. He did not see the play *Otherwise Engaged* in which much is made of a suicide. Apparently, Greg had lost his own son not long before...Kanin told me of this sadness in a moment alone.

My best and most savored story about Greg is this: President Truman fires MacArthur and in the film it is I who have to tell him. His biggest emotional moment in the film. But after the rehearsal, he turned to the director, dear Joseph Sargent and said, "I want Nick to have a big closeup here...What he's doing is very important." I have never gotten over the astonishment I felt at that act of artistic generosity!

It did, as well, afford that fine actor a moment to anticipate, by the look on my face, the ax that was about to finish the lengthy career of this genius soldier.

Another moment: I was on set about to do the finishing closeup in a scene with Gregory. The assistant director came to me saying, "Greg has been dismissed for the day, I'll read his lines off-camera." A practice not unknown to this day. Greg heard this news just as he was leaving. He said, "Wait a minute, I'm coming back." He did. He went quickly to his dressing room, changed into his entire uniform again and returned to the set so that I would have GENERAL MACARTHUR TO WHOM I COULD RELATE! He had no on-camera lines, but he stood there for me. Now THAT was a professional. a caring professional.

A quick tip of the plumed hat to Marge Dussay, God rest her sweet soul: From *Facts of Life*, through *Santa Barbara* and especially in *Macarthur!* where she played the General's wife, I had the mysteriously enjoyable pleasure of working with dear Marge. An elegant, kind, and beautiful woman. I say "mysterious" because it is a mystery to me as to why we did not over those years become closer friends. Perhaps because I never had an onscreen, big time romance with her? Or was it because luckily and occasionally in a man's life, there are woman friends who, though immensely attractive, are never the object of desire or the follow through of such an impulse. She did not flirt, nor did I, but we both paid compliments politely masked as with the tilt of an 18th Century fan silently signaling a discreet welcome. and enjoyed the reciprocity. We discussed highly personal issues which shall forever be confidences, and today I still remember her bright eyes and sweet smile.

While we're at it, another fine professional gesture: Robert Redford in *All The President's Men.* I played the fancy lawyer who denies representing the Cuban bandits who broke into the Watergate. At the rehearsal as is customary, I turned and faced the "star" as he came up from behind me in the courtroom. He whispered, "You don't have to look at me." "Thanks," I said and proceeded to treat him like an annoying mosquito over my shoulder. That gesture helped me mold a character.

When asked how it was working in *All The President's Men*, I say, "Like working with a triumvirate of non-egos! Alan Pakula the director, Gordon Willis the Cinematographer and Robert Redford were just that. I have never worked in a better creative atmosphere.

CHAPTER 25

Back to California, Hollywood Hopes

I arrived and once again found refreshing the rides up the Pacific coast on my motorcycle as I had done so many times since my adventurous youth. In my mind at least, I was looking for a more satisfying relationship than the oft separated one with Candace. No excuses...a more honest separation from Candace would have been more ethical. But after numerous messy separations the result was, I was not brave, just exhausted.

Joe Allen's restaurant, our favorite haunt in New York City, had a newly opened branch in LA. I entered the charming lightly classy restaurant on West 3rd Street. A weekend night, the bar adjoining the sit down area was full, and the charming patio replete with leafy trees, mostly young people, showbiz hopefuls, showbiz "have arrived" and those perennial "civilians" who perhaps hope that through osmosis some of the glamor will rub off.

Aside from those subject to that cynical appraisal were the just plain curious, out for a good time...no scanning the place with desiring eyes, no self-consciousness preceding the silently sought-after meeting with guys...or gals. Just folks with jobs who find it mildly exhilarating rubbing shoulders with those in show biz.

The eyes were almond curved, the skin was a light bronze, the hair long and full, streaked with blond but revealing the core Latina brown base. Tall and full figured, there stood Susan. Beside her was a much shorter, but at first and brief glance a very pretty girl, Beth...the name I was to find out later. Both of them looked to be in their twenties. Early twenties. I sauntered (is there any better verb for a male pretending to be confident approaching two beautiful women?) over and tried to strike up a conversation with tall Susan. With her advantage of height, she could scan the room for more worthy escorts. Her lovely eyes never came to rest on me for more than a quick perusal. After a slightly awkward pause, I realized that for Susan the potential rewards of the night lay not with me but elsewhere.

In the pause, I looked down at the gal beside her. She was a real beauty! My god, how could I (in my elevated search) not have noticed her first? She, being fully aware of the whole ridiculous scene and my unskillful compromise evident in my NOW noticing her, said, "Don't do me any favors!" The first salvo in what proved to be many, honest and often humorous observations of my inadequacies over the years.

"Busted huh?" I said in reference to my quick change of focus from one girl to the other. "Yup" was the concise answer. It could have ended there, but it didn't. "Well, since I've been caught in tactlessness, would you at least let me buy you a drink?" "Why not?" We drank and talked, and talked of many things...we were rarely apart from that night onward.

We married, she saw me through mishaps and successes, helped me with my kids who came to live with us for years. I could go on. After 35 years of ups and a few downs, we grew apart. People ask me what the hell happened. At a loss, I try to describe it like a navigational course gone wrong: If you are 1 degree off at the beginning, later, you are 60 miles off. You have to course correct. We didn't.

Did we both take each other for granted? Probably. I committed, eventually, errors and infidelities for which I shall be forever remorseful. Some are obvious in this memoir. I try to make 'amends'...I've taken a number of friends to AA. Sometimes I stayed and listened. Years ago, I did attend Overeaters Anonymous. The same good book is used. I lost almost 30 pounds until a sort of facist like sponsor, bored the hell out of me with his relentless bullying. However, 'making amends" is still my favorite of the 12 Steps.

In deference to Beth with whom I am still close, especially after the death of our son, I shall tell no more tales. Wit, ah, the wit, intelligence, and natural beauty...that's Beth.

My house with Beth and my kids was on Gardner Street, west of Hollywood, Not West Hollywood, per se, still LA City. When I built the enormous pool in that house, I was teaching scuba diving to the famous and up and coming in Hollywood as well as our disabled divers with whom I started in 1982.

We had several of my friends come and stay in the guest house... sometimes for months, one for over a year. They all had one thing in common, their relationships with wives or girlfriends had just finished. "The Guest House Gang", they came to be known. One was dear John Considine, who like the others had a lovely wit.

As he was moving in, I rushed from the pool (which occupied most of the back yard) into the den, which had an old glass sliding glass...the door was not tempered glass. The darkness inside the house concealed the fact that somebody had closed it and I went through it, the glass shattering into large pieces. One such piece, like a guillotine dropping, silently sliced through almost my entire lower left arm.

I, the old scuba instructor knowing first aid, clamped my hand on the spurting wound and called to John and Beth who were preparing the guest house. They came over and immediately freaked out. I calmly asked them to get the car as I would need rapid emergency aid at a hospital.

We went to Cedars Sinai where we met a Nurse Ratched from *One Flew Over The Cuckoo's Nest*. Seeing me holding my thumb to the wound as we entered the treatment room, she commanded me to let go. I said meekly, "I'm a scuba instructor and I think I should not release my pressure until we have a hemostat or tourniquet." She, responding with increasing agitation at anyone not obeying her instantly, said, "Remove your hand!" I hesitated for a moment and then released the arm from pressure on the artery.

Blood spurted mercilessly from the gaping wound all over Nurse Ratched's pristine uniform. It was in the height of the AIDS epidemic, so all attending were horrified at the spewing of raw blood. Especially Ratched, whose face contorted with rage while rushing from the room.

A fine hand surgeon at Cedars sewed up my arm, and then after surgery, when asked how long my arm might be paralyzed, he said, "Well, at your vintage, I'm not sure if you'll ever regain usage of that hand."

I got back home and decided on my plan of attack. Lots of Vitamin B-1, a nerve food (five tablets a day!) and then I think I invented water aerobics. I got in the shallow end of the pool with my cast on, wrapped in saran wrap, and started waving my arm back and forth in the pool while doing jumping exercises. I actually melted the plaster on the cast which understandably pissed off the hand surgeon. But my hand and arm remained useless, hanging like a pathetic almost lifeless part of a gangling vine.

Stubborn Nicky kept it up. Finally, after a few months of this, with my arm still hanging by my side, I said to Beth, "Maybe I should try to get a job on Daytime again. Perhaps I could stick the useless hand in my pocket and I could be one of those actors who just gestures with one hand whilst leaving the other in the pocket (doing God knows what)...hmm, jaunty!

I got an offer from *One Life To Live* with a marvelous cast and a classy producer, Jean Arley. I was to be Anthony Makana, gangster, café owner, in love with Delilah, a dark haired endlessly long-legged beauty played wonderfully by Shelley Burch, who was in "9" on Broadway at the time. The tasteful Jean, our producer, allowed me to create a sad but clever and charming gangster a bit of a distance from the cliché. He was educated at an Ivy League college and had the trappings of a gentleman. Gatsby-esque? Perhaps a touch.

As to Delilah, I remember, (in character of course) being rejected constantly by her and so turned to the very light blonde gal, Samantha, with a smile like a forties movie star. irresistible red lips offset by magical blue eyes and that lighter than light blond flowing hair, Samantha, played by the intelligent and adorable Dorian LaPinto, was most desirable. That fun role lasted a year. My dressing room mate was Bob Woods, again a terrific wit. We talked of army days...he had been on heavy duty in Vietnam as a Green Beret. To the day I left I laughed as he recalled ol' Nick moving into ABC Studios on West 67th St. New York City with a giant propeller I had been sent for an old PT boat look alike as well as the huge bronze propeller was an AR-15 rifle given to me by a friend whose wife demanded he get rid of it....or something.

So there was Bob, who taught me to field strip (take apart and clean) the AR-15 army rifle. Mine had been a Garand M-1 as well as a Springfield 1903, (a lighter rifle) on the Drill Team in the Honor Guard. When I left *One Life to Live*, Bob gave me his Special Forces Medallion as a keepsake...I was very touched. Today it rests with my medallion as a Sentinel on the Tomb Of the Unknown Soldier.

Wonderful times, lovely actors, probably the best all-around cast of all the soaps.

And then came the call...

CHAPTER 26

Santa Barbara

In LA, I'd had lots of employment in plays, movies and TV; big, Oscar nominated, star-studded movies like *All The President's Men*, *Stir Crazy*, *Electric Horseman*, *Reds*, *Betsy's Wedding* and others...but then one day a life changer.

Bridget Dobson and her super husband, Jerry, had created a new series for NBC daytime, called *Santa Barbara*. They talked, I listened and I liked what I heard.

I was in New York at the time, working on *One Life to Live*. My eldest daughter, Candace, was also in New York, living in an apartment with a bunch of young gals her age (eighteen). She went on to college there, secured a good job, got married and still lives in the area. A shining, optimistic gal.

Dinneen, her younger sister, by then flowering into a beauty with her own style and temperament, stayed with her mother in Beverly Hills while I was in New York. Usually, I took both girls everywhere I went, but this time, she liked the school and it would have been unsettling for her to join us for so long.

Ah, *Santa Barbara*...When I came aboard to play Lionel the profligate son of, OMG, Dame Judith Anderson! Yeah, the grand Dame herself. She had played, a bit before my time, the title role in *Hamlet* on Broadway! Her Medea was a legend. She sat regally and accepted my bow upon introduction. We did for the most part have a grand time. Of course, at the outset, though, we had to establish some territorial prerogatives.

Most of the cast had not done a whole lot other than some television. She started in with me in a most patronizing manner, assuming, I'm sure, that I was just another aging still sort of pretty face from Daytime TV. I quietly changed the subject and slipped into a few anecdotes about my New York stage career with yes, Olivier, and she quickly understood things before I had finished elucidating on all nine (at that time) Broadway shows.

She was most impressed with my having been a founding member of the Tyrone Guthrie Theatre in Minneapolis.

When she retired from the show, she was replaced by Janis Paige, the famous musical theatre star (*Pajama Game* on Broadway among others) and films and her own TV series. Her legs, which were entwined under a table were still noticeably shapely. She was much too alluring to be my mother for God's sake...she was only 11 years older than I...Days with Janis were a joy from start to finish.

One cannot omit mention of Louise Sorel as Augusta. I can remember forever, the jewel-like brown eyes - inquiring, constantly inquiring eyes - the smoothly shapely body with curves in all the intended places. We were, I like to flatter myself with the phrase, the 'William Powell and Myrna Loy of Daytime TV'; witty, unpredictable, adventurous, sometimes damaging, but ever humorous. We "danced" together effortlessly, as the saying goes. In the story we were both more than a bit risqué. I perhaps more than she when it came to dallying with the opposite sex.

My mother, then played by Dame Judith, finally denounced my profligate ways, and threatened to disinherit me if I did not get a job. So, I did. I became the host of a local TV show in Santa Barbara and could show movies, chat, whatever I wanted.

Then the Dobson's came up with a wild story conceit: I, riddled with guilt at being indiscreet in an affair, became impotent and was to tell my TV audience of my plight, begging for cures. Hmm, yeah it was groundbreaking alright...also possibly career breaking. Fuck! The "Lion" Lionel, couldn't get it up? What would that do to one's romantic image on the small screen? The subject of impotency had not been dealt with openly on Daytime TV (or pretty much any TV) before.

I said, "Ok, I'll do it as long I can on the TV show, within the show, say to the audience, "I'm going to reveal something that has troubled me, but I must say that this condition, impotency, affects hundreds of thousands of men in this country alone. In most cases it is treatable, So If you are afflicted with this, or a loved one is, find a physician, or therapist and see to it....while I joke, remember something can usually be done."

Well the Dobson's, in their infinite wisdom, allowed me to do it....I received piles of very positive mail.

So, on the show within, I drank monkey gland potions, spiraled in ritual dances dressed in weird headdresses and so on...fun stuff. My television wife forgave, I regained...em, sexual clarity...and the show went on.

At the end of that siege just described, I was to give an on-air apology to Augusta, at the end of which was a quote from a poet, whose name escapes me; I thought it not quite apt and called the fine writer, Frank Salisbury, and said, "It seems a bit acerbic...." He asked what I might think of as a substitute. I said, "Maybe one of the romantics or even one of the First World War guys" "Who, Owen?" "Nope, was thinking Rupert Brooke..." He thought and then said 'Send it to me." I did, he said okay and I did it. Now, how many soaps have writers who discuss such poets as Elliot, Cummings and Brooke...One wonders.

Before those episodes, Louise as Augusta, for reasons I can't remember, went suddenly blind. She was already not talking to me because of one of my escapades. I, thwarted in my attempts to visit her, decided to be sneaky and gain entrance. At the time, the movie *Terms Of Endearment* was popular with Jack Nicholson as the retired astronaut and Shirley MacLaine as the female lead. I, as Lionel, decide to gain entrance to my blind wife's house pretending to be an ex-astronaut....the twist, more than suggested by Cyrano De Bergerac, was that I get the milkman, played hysterically by Ronnie Schell, to pretend he's the Astronaut while I, hiding somewhere in the room, am feeding him the lines to say.

All worked fantastically. However, Louise actually being able to actually see, could never get through a rehearsal without breaking out in gales of laughter at Ronnie's antics....He, in character, completely messing up my instructions, stumbling over the most simple poetry I was feeding him...It was glorious comedy.

Louise had, shall we say, a "misunderstanding" with the Dobson's at a given point, and left the show. Pity for all. (In the interests of tact, no more about that. I'm sure Louise will deal with that in her auto-bio!).

My next leading lady was the entrancing Lenore Kasdorf. She was petite with gorgeous, sensual eyes and...was it auburn hair? What is happening to this old guy's memory? Doesn't matter, the "mattering"' thing is she was not only attractive, but also possessed a gorgeous husky voice, reminding one of Jean Arthur, the 30s movie star. She didn't play sexy, she just was...she exuded it.

Unfortunately, the powers that were, did not feel (ironically) that there was a great deal of appeal from that match...chemistry, or the lack of it. "Balderdash!" as British characters used to say! I knew better. By that I don't mean to imply anything other than the chemistry on screen. Actually, in all those years on *Santa Barbara*, with the host of lovelies I had occasion to know, I never did have anything romantic to do with them off-stage (just to clarify for those most inquisitive).

In Lenore's case it wouldn't have happened because she was wonderfully proper and also a friend of Beth's – my real-life wife. However, I thought, though, quite a different relationship from that with Louise, that it was most romantic and to her everlasting tribute, she was extremely generous on screen. In explanation of that last kudo:

I got in a terrible car accident. I was in a coma, hanging out the driver side door of my VW Scirocco, over the Hollywood freeway! Yup, truth! I had made a left turn onto a bridge going over that freeway and a guy going 90 miles an hour or something came over the top of the hill in the opposite lane and smacked my car into and through the railing on the bridge. A friend of mine who ran a towing service at the bottom of that hill had seen the wreck just after it happened and told me weeks later when he asked what ever happened to the VW, I told him of the accident and he aghast said, "I passed by that wreck. I thought the guy was dead!" Nope...another one of my nine lives. I returned to *Santa Barbara* in about a week, but my memory had been severely affected.

On screen, I had a number of scenes with Lenore. I covertly explained that I was rough on the lines and would she mind if I looked at the Teleprompter when my red light went out. (The camera had a red light, signaling that indeed, your camera was on.) She assured, "Nicky, anything you need, of course." So, I looked...However, after a certain amount of times when the control room caught me glancing at the prompter despite what I thought was my speedy, sneaky, technique, Bridget Dobson called me to the office and asked if perhaps I'd been partying too much...I said, "Maybe...sorry."

I studied twice or three times as long from then on. Nobody else knew of my horrible limitation. My memory did improve in the weeks following, but to this day, I have not had what was before, a very quick ability to learn lines...well, most of them anyway.

Even Harold Pinter, as we were about to open *Otherwise Engaged* in Boston pre-Broadway, said, "You are going to learn THESE lines are you not?" I did. For indeed, one of the bad habits one used to get from learning so many lines on short notice, was if one had that devious talent to paraphrase. Even Olivier did it. I saw him elegantly paraphrase Jean Anouilh. I understood he could even paraphrase Shakespeare!

My next and final leading lady on *Santa Barbara* was Robin Mattson. Robin was and still is a delightful woman whose wit and intelligence shines through. I'm not sure she took too kindly to having this older guy picked as her next leading man, but she surely never showed it. Robin and I had fun plots and did well, Alas, by that time, though, we had gone through several writers and producers and had to suffer through crappy story lines, with many of them going on way too long, leading inevitably to falling ratings.

Still there was, in this period, a chance to play with fun plotting. One episode had Robin and me (in character) running from the police, and ending up hiding in a traveling Shakespearian troupe's costumes. When the police followed us in, we got on stage as Romeo and Juliet and had the Friar marry us! For the vows, I delivered, at my suggestion, an entire sonnet. The first time, repeated later by others, for the delivery of an entire Shakespearean sonnet on a daytime soap. Later, when her character was pregnant, we were scrambling to get somewhere and ended up in a veterinarian's treatment room, where she had the baby on the vet's examining table.

So much for serious soap opera...But that was the point in *Santa Barbara*. We mixed, at its best, serious, and timely topics with some of us providing the comic relief.

Eventually we got a new producer, one who'd been very successful on another show for years, and who chose to bring a kind of overly fantastic quality to the show. By that I mean he had obviously studied the show and knew it had a kind of quirky quality, but he possessed no real sense of humor and brought an artificial element into the writing and producing. Phony might be a more accurate word.

The Dobson's were long gone, Mary-Ellis Bunim, a tough but fair woman had done well, but left to spearhead the reality show genre. So here we had this affected but formerly successful producer and his magic wand which was to transform the show into ...something.

He presented a storyline to me which had me falsely killing myself for insurance money, and then (here is the disgusting, uncharacteristic part) I was to attend my own funeral in disguise and laugh. As a character, I got away with a lot of mischief primarily because I obviously loved my children. The spectra of my laughing as my children grieved at my funeral was grotesque.

I told the producer that it was awful. He disagreed. I said, 'Then, I'm outta here!"

"What do you mean? You can't just quit!" he threatened. I reminded him that it was I who wrote the contract in which it clearly stated I could leave if dissatisfied with content.

I left without much further fuss..

All My Children beckoned, I spent a delightful year there. My deal included first class tickets to and from New York in order that I might commute almost once a week to see my family. I was playing Steven Andrews, super sophisticated international assassin. Susan Lucci, the already legendary Erica on *AMC* was being deceived (as Erica) by her husband who concocted a plot pretending to be killed by my character in order to cash in on a huge insurance policy.

The plot went awry for reasons I cannot recall, Travis, the husband played wonderfully by the dashing Larkin Mallloy, betrayed me, the hired assassin, and I beat him up on a penthouse rooftop. Erica left him and escaped to a little town out in the countryside. I followed her, checked into the same rooming house under the assumed identity of Dave Gillis, a mechanic.

A big switch and challenging character change for me to play. I was there to track her down and kill her to show her husband the price of betraying the fierce and revengeful super killer, Steven Andrews.

Simple? Straightforward? Of course.

The hitch in the predictable, written by the legendary head writer, Agnes Nixon, who had also created *Another World,* was that I, now as the mechanic Dave, asked Erica, now hiding as an anonymous waitress at a local coffee shop, out for a date. We went out in my van and ended up out by a lake. In the country-clear night we gazed at the stars. Much to her amazement, Dave points out constellations. The wonder is evident, as well as their being taken with each other.

Susan and I rehearsed briefly as was the way in live-on-tape shows, and then we went to do the air show.

I, in the meanwhile, went off to do a little homework. I called the husband of Jada Rowlands, a friend who had played my great love Amy on *The Secret Storm* all those years before. He was an astronomer at Columbia University. I asked him about the constellations listed in the script; "daystars", as he called them, were not visible at night. "Ah," says I, "can you give me ones which would be visible at night?" He did. I went back to the show and only on air did I romantically describe a host of constellations!

Bless Susan, she listened, registered surprise (which she truly was) and then we proceeded to fall in love (on air). She adjusted beautifully to the changes and complimented me afterwards on my surprise stimulus.

Eventually of course, Dave had to be caught. I was killed in a kitchen!

As a fond goodbye treat, Susan had a surprise for me. A five-thousand-dollar farewell dinner! I did not find out that figure from Susan. I, lacking her class (ha ha!), found out that sum from a whispering waiter. They served Dom Perignon as table wine. Did I cry? Of course.

As it was, after a year, I really wanted to spend more time in L.A with Beth and my son, Ian, as well as my daughter, Dinneen. I had been commuting almost every weekend in snow storms and other hazards. Growing fatigue was also an element.

So, I reached out to the re-instated Santa Barbara producers. The producer of my parting had departed and all seemed hopeful. I had good story lines with Robin Mattson ...but the show was already flagging.

Lane Davies escaped to do what turned out to be a short-lived comedy playing an airline pilot. Our young Olivier. He was tall like Colin Firth and as mysterious as Heathcliff. He was and still is a hugely popular figure in Eastern Europe and elsewhere. I say, "still is", because he does films in

Kazakhstan, Azerbaijan and recently performed the lead in the big musical *Man of La Mancha* in Prague. Above all, in my opinion, he is the consummate gentleman.

On the occasion, years earlier, of the Dobson's being locked out of NBC because of their feud with that network and we were shooting the show on stage at the time they arrived at the gate. Word quickly got to the set of their peculiar plight. Some, I suppose, fearing network reprisal, stayed on stage, ignoring the situation. Lane Davies, and I, being reared as Southern gentlemen, along with that beloved Yankee gentlewoman, Judith McConnell, strode from the stage to the gate where we waited for the adventurous rebel couple. We greeted them, assured them of our support, which was never needed...ha...a glorious empty gesture.

One muses upon just how many soap actors would have become so much more with a good break on film or Broadway. Tommy Lee Jones, Meg Ryan, Ray Liotta and even Leonardo DiCaprio, who played briefly on *Santa Barbara* during my absence, all began their careers on Daytime. Robin Wright, was an ingénue on *Santa Barbara* for a few years until leaving for a film career, bearing children and then an even better career! Robin, my dearest pal on Santa Barbara and beyond, did tell me years later that I'd probably stayed on the show too long. I did one major film, *Betsy's Wedding* during that time...was offered others, but could not accept them because of contract obligations.

On one occasion, when Mary-Ellis Bunim was producing, I had an offer for a very nice feature film, but when she told me I was written in very heavily for months, I said ok. She, surprised, said, "But we can't keep you from doing it...by contract." I said my contract had always been a handshake, adding, "That still stands." She registered some degree of surprise on her usually cryptic face...We got along...tough as she was, I have a feeling she never forgot that moment. She died early. Certainly, one of the most able producers I ever worked with on Daytime.

Have I painted myself as morally irreproachable? Sorry, don't be fooled. I have only mentioned those times in which I stood up to the challenge....It's much more fun writing stuff that, though true, is totally specific and flattering, ignoring the horrendous failures and slips on the ice of moral challenge which did occur...this is not a Russian novel, it is a flavored memoir.

A couple of other much needed mentions from the *Santa Barbara* days:

One of the most terrific romantic actresses I've ever known was the hugely popular, Judith McConnell. She started her out as a beauty queen from, I believe, Pennsylvania. Playing Sophia, she was my big secret affair on SB. During our tryst, we were stuck in a gigunda earthquake. Much hugging, more fearful tears were in evidence. It really was like a 20s movie with Mary Pickford...except as remembered, Mary Pickford did not have amours with married men...on or off screen.

Harley Kozak, ah, Harley. Mary on the show; tall, fair, and infinitely bright in mind on and offscreen, she did indeed, "light it up". I adore Harley. We actually had dinner together long after the show went off the air. She had, by then, become a very good writer. I'm kinda sorry our lives took us on different paths to the exclusion of dinners, talks and idea swapping. UNTIL! A recent celebrity cruise with Santa Barbara fans and several cast members...what a grand time!

She and Lane Davies were the biggies in the early years. They had a magic, almost palpable chemistry. Harley's character, for reasons known only to the producers and writers, was killed off, dying in Lane/Mason's arms from a huge falling metal letter "C" from the Capwell sign atop the hotel owned by Lane/Mason's father, C.C. Capwell, played most dashingly by (finally) Jed Allen. By "finally" I mean there had been three C.C.'s before Jed. Peter Mark Richmond, a fine actor whom I still see often as a fellow member of the Academy of Motion Picture Arts and Sciences Foreign Language (now called "International Film") Committee. We see and judge many foreign films eligible for the Oscars every year and also enjoy the receptions and dinners which sometimes accompany the season's displays.

I shall digress...I honestly feel that our Committee is one of the very few uncorrupted groups in Hollywood. A pompous, perhaps fatuous remark? To some perhaps, but I bloody well believe it and could probably prove it if pushed. I know of no one whose vote is influenced in any way. The post-screening receptions are simply a nice way to know the actors, writers, directors and sometimes composers who appear on behalf of their films. The Committee does admittedly include a disproportionate number of men and women over fifty, err, over sixty...And why not! All whom I know are still sharp and have distinguished careers and therefore knowledge of film. Also, an unavoidable fact is that so many younger members are out working! Yeah, 7:30 PM in Beverly Hills is not a great time for ambitious, working filmmakers to say "Stop shooting, I have to go judge a film".

Charles Bateman was the third C.C. A handsome and very dear man...a gentleman. I'm guessing the producers maybe wanted a guy with more of an edge...and in stepped Jed Allen. Jed was terrific. He looked very handsome in a tuxedo, or in anything really, and was a powerful, energetic force on screen. The rivalry between his C.C. and my Lionel was hearty and most times a lot of fun.

A. Martinez as Cruz came a bit into the run. I don't know whether Brian Frons, the then head of Daytime on NBC, would admit it or not, but we did in fact have a conversation in his office a couple of days after I arrived about story where I floated the idea of incorporating a Latin Lover character into the SB mix. He jumped at the idea. And so, it went.

Martinez became one of the all time great Daytime lovers (and fine actors) in TV history. An incredibly admirable man and eloquent political activist as well, he and I are pals to this day. Recently, I went to see him playing on stage in the part that had kick started my New York career as Morris in Athol Fugard's *Blood Knot.* Louis Gossett Jr, with whom I had played all those years before, directed and A. Martinez was simply marvelous in "my" role. In his typically generous manner, he presented me to the audience on stage after the performance. What a guy! What an actor! On social media, his contributions to the world of political discourse are most often profound

Another little contribution for which I might take a bit of credit, was getting us included in the Battle of the Daytime Stars. It involved performers from all soap programming, on all channels, and so of course it had loads of gorgeous guys and gals competing in scanty, sweaty clothes for track, field and water sports. I decided to relinquish my role as an athlete and instead chose John Allen Nelson, who played my son on the show and with youth on his side, to fill in for me. I then took on the job of coaching track and field. The magnificent Joseph Bottoms competed in and coached the water sports. Sneaky Nicky called in a favor from a gal pal of mine, Cary Gossweiller Payton, who was on the ill-fated Olympic team in 1980 (they were held out by President Carter from attending the games in Moscow due to Russia's invasion of Afghanistan). Cary is a wildly talented athlete as well as, it turned out, a super coach, so between all of us we went in with high hopes.

The result was we finished in a respectable 2nd place. A special tip of the hat to Robin Wright who gave her all. In her final sprint she pulled a hamstring but finished. I carried her off the field...my first and last time I ever carried her off or on anywhere! Todd McKee and Julie Ronnie should also be mentioned. Both contributed greatly to that event and indeed the entire show

I have no evidence for this excessive claim, but Santa Barbara's fortunes took a dramatic upturn after that. It put our show on the map and introduced our stars to a worldwide audience. It also cemented the bond of brothers and sisters in the cast. I had a lovely house at the time with a large pool and we had many a good wholesome party there after that; some parties not so wholesome but enjoyable ...for most. The rest is confidential.

If I have not said much of Marcy Walker as Eden, there are reasons...I never wanted to write a bitch book about personalities. It might be noticed that I have mentioned negatively thus far only one actress in all my years in soaps.

I'm not sure what it was that made our relationship sour. I had met Marcy years earlier when she was really young. She came to my house on Gardner Street to rent it with her boyfriend at the time. I was going somewhere, perhaps to England to do *The Little Foxes* and needed to rent the house for a few months. Marcy came with a couple of friends and looked. She was pert, cute as hell with a short, curly hair style and very bubbly personality as I remember.

The Dobsons early on created an affair between Marcy/Eden and me which was short-lived. Marcy apparently hated the idea of her Eden having an affair with an older man. I suppose she had never seen the films of Luis Buñuel...Ha!

I, ever the professional plunged in, so to speak, unaware of her displeasure. I did realize that she was cold and indifferent (why do those two always go together?). Shortly thereafter, I heard from other sources of her feelings on the subject. After that show, she did other soaps, never achieving her fabulous success on *Santa Barbara*. I believe she lives a quiet, religious life elsewhere in the country. Practically all other cast members of *Santa Barbara* have attended various reunions...not she. To her artistic credit, she was indeed fabulous as Eden; strength when needed, glowing, sensitive, beautiful always.

Richard Eden, our Brick Wallace, must be mentioned. A muscular and handsome man, Richard was a rock on SB, consistently good and an absolute pleasure to work with. He went on to do wonderful work on the *RoboCop* television series. We are still very much in touch.

I cannot talk about the fine people on *Santa Barbara* without touching on the contribution of associate producer Mary Dobson, daughter of Bridget and Jerry. Mary was one of the smartest, kindest people I've ever worked with. It was she who put together my "reels" for Emmy consideration. I managed to get three nominations while on that show. Two as lead actor and one as supporting. I have no idea why I was suddenly relegated to "supporting" but that was after Mary was gone.

A proper mention for my well-loved TV son, Warren, played initially by John Allen Nelson. He looked like me. To his credit, he had few of my faults and more charm. He had a healthy handsomeness and never any apparent vanity. We are, to this day, good friends. The greatest compliment he paid me was inviting me, a licensed minister, to officiate at his wedding in a glorious, huge, and ancient castle in France.

Nancy Grahn played Julia on the show. She was and is a sleek, sharp brunette with a flashing wit whom they paired with Lane Davies for a while. She has made millions on Daytime, and is still appearing as a leading actress. I often wondered whether she, with any luck, could have left *Santa Barbara* or the soap that followed and become a movie star and or, a huge

Nighttime star. She has it all; looks, intelligence, charm As far as I know, she has worked constantly for over 35 years.

We, myself along with some of the alums from *Santa Barbara*, are, at this writing, working on an Internet series, *The Bay*. Involved are Lane Davies, A. Martinez, Judith McConnell, and a handful of stars of other soaps.

We tried. Our names got the show off the ground. The Executive Producer/Creator, Gregory L. Martin, and his partner Kristos Andrews (also the young leading man), have tried valiantly to make it a success, winning multiple Daytime Alternative Programming Emmys along the way.

It's been a difficult nine years. We've been working under a ridiculously low minimum wage allowed by SAG AFTRA, our union for "Ultra Low Budget" projects. The purpose our union had in creating this niche was to encourage young producers to get a chance at creating new film and TV projects which prohibitive budgets would not otherwise allow. I don't think that their intention was to allow 9 years of slogging away for minimum-allowed wage with no residuals. Always the optimist, our leader Gregory Martin has assured us that with the sale of the series to Australia there is hope on the horizon.

Am I as optimistic after all these years? I'm not so sure. Meanwhile, I occupy myself with other pursuits including that which you now read. A visual and most positive reminder that all was not lost. The two Emmys I received now displayed (not very discreetly) on my boat; are always a good talking point when conversations sag

Elena, my dear and precise wife, just reminded me that I have neglected to mention in this not-quite-tome my enjoyable time on the very popular and long running sit-com. *Facts of Life*. I played Blair Warner's father. Lisa Whelchel, the actress who played the preppy and wealthy Blair, is a smart and talented woman, and a very devout Christian. I found her to be absolutely delightful and was invited to functions as a cast member for years.

When I used to travel more frequently to New York, my favorite bar on the Eastside was usually full of airline flight attendants who lived nearby. When I would enter, almost invariably, they would, as a chorus, break out in unison the theme song from *Facts of Life*!

It's strange, but at that time I was completely unaware of the show's popularity; I was so busy in New York and LA on and off stage, that I didn't really absorb the impact the show was making and what a positive force it was in young women's lives. My daughters were both of that age then, so I was, more or less, living this life of a father both in front of and behind the camera.

I still get reminded quite often at airports from fondly remembering fans - just how impressive those stories were for impressionable teenage girls.

CHAPTER 27

A Sidebar With Willy

1982. I was back in Hollywood doing all sorts of Nighttime TV shows...probably too many. What was the justification for it, for going that route instead of holding out for more classy feature films? Kids, bills...Yeah, only the distant ringing of that warning bell of my own design: "If you're gonna be an artist nuthin' will stop ya...if you ain't, almost anything will!"

In fact, I met, on a studio lot, the rightfully adored director, Sidney Pollack, with whom I had worked so enjoyably on *Electric Horseman*, This was some three years since that filming, a wonderfully creative experience in which I befriended Willy Nelson, including a ride in my rental car into the far reaches of the desert...this after a party at which he played and sang for the cast and crew!

Slightly hazy, we discussed music and Eastern disciplines - his term (ha!) - most enjoyably until I realized that we'd become lost among the scant few Juniper trees on the Nevada desert. "Yonder is the glow of lights!" (at a considerable distance) says I. Continuing optimistically, I elaborated, "Probably Vegas". "Possibly Reno", chimed the laconic Willy. Another swig of Tequila and then we decided, during this vastly interesting, elevated conversation, to venture toward those lights lying invitingly on the horizon.

On set (his first film) he was rehearsing a scene, and casually added the line which went something like, "Let's go on down and get us a couple of Keno gals who can suck the chrome off a trailer hitch." Pollack, ever willing to invent, improvise, create anew, said "What did you just say?" Willy didn't remember...He had just "spun it off". Sidney listened to the tape of the rehearsal and said, "It's in! In the picture, he meant...and it was. One of the most memorable lines in that film.

I worked once more, with Willy many years later on an episode of *Dr Quinn Medicine Woman*. I played a Western judge; he, an accused man...Loved seeing him again. He has admirably helped farmers with tons

178

of his own money when they were in great need; a deeply caring, enduring talent...a fine, "Country Man".

A couple of years after *Electric Horseman*, as said, I ran into Sidney Pollack on the Warner Brothers lot, He said quite casually, and meant as a compliment, "I see you on TV in EVERYTHING!" I, sensing more information was to be gleaned, said, "Is that good or bad?" He, getting the point, replied, 'Well, not so good for feature film...overexposure maybe?" Prophetic that.

CHAPTER 28

A Life Changing, Challenging Time

Sometime during the year 1982, I received a call from a guy who had been badly wounded in Viet Nam who was starting an organization called *The Handicapped Scuba Association*. They were without money and had arranged to be represented on a TV prize show to win money.

Jim Getacre, that Veteran, called me as a scuba instructor and quasi celebrity, and asked if I would participate. I did, We did a prize winning game show, they got money, I joined the HSA and helped in the formation and first classes for disabled scuba divers. I made friends, learned a lot about disabilities, psychological, physical and survival, and kept on with it. Denise Dowd, my classmate (I finished the HSA Instructor course when I had time a bit later), was a lovely, young, smart, dedicated instructor. A physical therapist by profession, she has to this day been teaching disabled divers constantly. I admire Denise as much as any person that ever donned a mask and fins.

A few years later I was making money on *Santa Barbara* and got my boat captain's license and restored an old 52-foot Huckins, designed by the guy who had drawn up the first Patrol Torpedo boat, the PTs of WW-2 fame (John F. Kennedy's PT 109 among others). My 1947 Huckins looked exactly like a PT boat.; chariot bridge, et al. I bought it in New York, a near wreck, and shipped it to California, where, in Channel Islands Oxnard, many skilled guys and I spent almost 6 months restoring it, including cold molding (meaning an epoxy soaked and wood planking job) the entire bottom. We installed a mast and boom with which to lift disabled divers into and out of the water.

Those who were on that boat in 1984, and more from later years, are still my friends. Once a year, that same gal, whom I call "The Mother Theresa of Disabled Diving", Denise Dowd, throws a party for all our old chums with whom we shared so many adventures.

Beyond all other sentiments one TRUSTS - as you have to when either being or accompanying a disabled diver. A couple of stories - this afternoon! - to illustrate that point:

Before the stories I should explain that these days disabled divers are referred to as those engaged in "adaptive diving". It's a recently conceived courtesy I admire and really try to use; because, indeed, many divers with physical and or mental challenges are not literally disabled.

On our first trip on the *Bagarre*, our restored 1947 Huckins, a super eager paraplegic diver, Terry Luxemberg, one of the original H.S.A. trained divers, was a participant. Halfway home from the pristine island of Anacapa, the closest of the off-shore Channel Islands of Southern California, smoke was seen seeping thickly through the hatch of the engine room. On a Huckins the engines are aft (back). I, as captain, instructed everyone to don lifejackets, and then quickly, with fire extinguisher in hand, went aft, slightly popped the engine room hatch. Smoke bellowed upwards into my face...but there were no flames evident.

Holding my breath, I peered with flashlight at the grey/black fog below. I shut down the engine and the smoke disappeared. When it eventually cleared, I saw, at a cramped distance, a gaping hole in the exhaust system. Too big to fit into the tight space, I was at a loss as to what to do.

Terry quickly offered, "Lemme in there, my legs are smaller," which indeed they were, but his body and upper arm strength were the strongest on the boat. He nimbly went below, snaked himself alongside the burst pipe and called for a patch of some sort...Always the innovators, we found a large tin can, cut it flat and with some spare hose clamps strung together, sealed sort of, the hole. With very little smoke emitting from that point on, we got to home port...saved by a "disabled" person...pointing out the ridiculousness in that term!

I was a part of the training of a number of quadriplegic scuba divers. Almost to a person they, when witnessing my initial training regimens with Amy Alexander, opined that she was probably too injured for this sport.

I did not feel so...

Amy is a tall young woman who was a competition swimmer before being injured in a car accident. "She still has the MIND of an athlete," I argued. "That ability can give you good judgement about the use of your body...so we'll see."

We saw, she conquered.

At that same Anacapa Island we, she and I, dove eventually down to over 50 feet. That day (and I'm not making this up), for some reason never explained, we saw more marine life than I had - or have ever - seen! Yes, they all came to visit Amy...small harmless sharks (harmless by species, not size), rays, numbers of sea lions, young and old, the lot...an amazing assortment.

The singular astonishing result was, Amy, who could BARELY move her hands and head on land COULD, at 55 feet of (17 meters) of depth - ten feet short of three atmospheres of pressure, move her arms forward and back doing a gentle breaststroke! Explanation? Much less gravity at that depth.

I looked into her eyes....when one is accompanying a quadriplegic, one looks in their eyes as much as one can. Through the glass lens of her mask, at almost 60 feet below the surface...did I see a look of ecstasy?...perhaps. When we surfaced and I removed her mask, she said, "Oh, Nicky, you know I'm not religious, but I think I've just seen God at least three times."

When we formed a not-for-profit corporation in order to organize and record our work. We called it, appropriately, *Challenges Foundation*. Our two other officers, those of Vice President and Treasurer, were "challenged" diver buddies. Steve Cortwright, a triple amputee from birth and Sarkis Dirmijian, who had polio when a child, which limited his leg strength. They both proved invaluable.

When asked sometime later for a quote about diving to be put on the website, Steve wrote, not a glib push for the foundation, but a most touching tribute. To paraphrase, he wrote, *All my life I've been told what I can't do. Scuba diving, which most people never experience, has shown me what I CAN do.* And indeed it did. Steve overcame his "disability" and has risen to become a computer executive with a leading web services provider.

Many rewarding times followed at *Challenges Foundation*. We once decorated a Christmas tree with shells UNDERWATER...at 40 feet. Pictures, with me as a ridiculous Santa Claus, are included in this book. When diving I used to peel the rock scallops off the reef and then briefly removing the diver's regulators (breathing apparatus) would place the newly peeled scallops in the diver's waiting mouth! Their eyes expressed astonished delight. Afterwards, when surfacing, I said, "Them's the freshest sushi you'll ever eat!" laughs followed...a lotta laughs, some tears of joy...wonderful night dives when artificial light surprises marine life and provides much deeper, richer colors.

We taught and transported challenged divers on *Bagarre* the mini PT boat and *Outrageous*, a 65 foot Burger which we restored, and then a beautiful 58 foot boat I renamed *The Western Star* (its previous name was *Omnipotent Crocodile*).

Western Star, after a poem by Stephen Vincent Benét, is an epic poem about Americans trekking westward, as my family had, from the Virginia of 1681 to Tennessee, and on to "Calif-orn-ay-aaa". One visitor quietly asked why I had named the boat, *Western Star*, and when I explained why, he said, "What a tribute, I'm Stephen Benét grandson!"

I restored that boat at great expense, providing, ultimately, a "head" (bathroom in nautical lingo) with shower into which a wheelchair could roll with ease, an elevator, again able to fit a wheelchair, leading to the upper deck whereupon most of the party could be enjoyed. And party we did.

The years I spent providing the boats and sharing the teaching of challenged divers were the most touching, constantly rewarding years of my life. Perhaps my acting career, limited at the time to *Santa Barbara*, suffered, but the rewards to my soul were incalculable.

New scuba instructor, NAUI 3911, PADI 5400, 1974

Physically challenged scuba divers about to embark on the Western Star

With my son, Ian, who loved accompanying
us with the physically challenged divers

*Decorating underwater Christmas tree at 17 meters
down with disabled divers*

Teaching scuba to beauties in my pool, West Hollywood, 1979

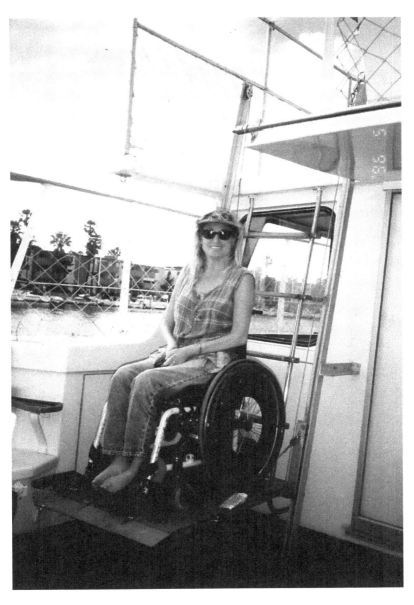

Great pal and "challenged" scuba diver, Julie Perez

At the wheel of my restored 1924 Yawl,
Emerald, on which we took wounded veterans

Cast photo, The Bay, Internet series

With the ever sparkling, ever generous Elizabeth Taylor, 1982

As dad of Lisa Whelchel on Facts of Life

With adored Gregory Peck in MacArthur, 1976

As Lt. Col. Sid Huff, MacArthur, 1976

*With my pal from Electric Horseman, Willie Nelson,
during filming for Dr Quinn Medicine Woman*

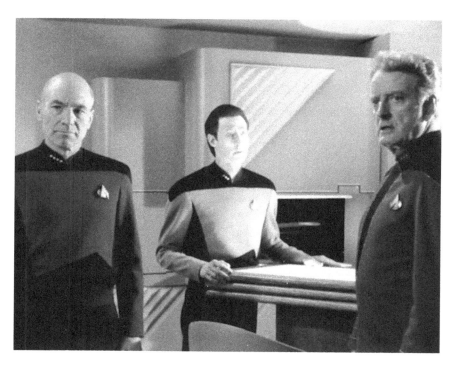

Killing the Android's daughter as Earth Admiral, Star Trek the Next Generation

*As George Bernard Shaw in Mr Shaw Goes to Hollywood,
Hollywood Laguna Playhouse, 2006*

Robert Redford, super guy, super creative, and I in All the President's Men

Santa Barbara cast photo

With my daughter, Dinneen, at her high school graduation

With my daughter, Candace, at her high school graduation

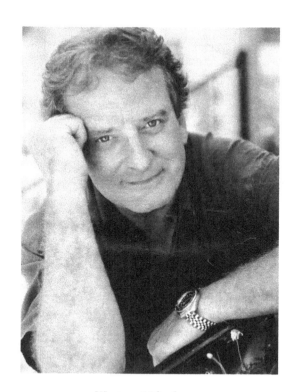

Westport Playhouse

Wedding photo with Elena, 2014

My unfinished dream house, Anguilla, 1993

Stephen Collins, Ned Beatty and yours truly,
All the President's Men 30th Anniversary Reunion

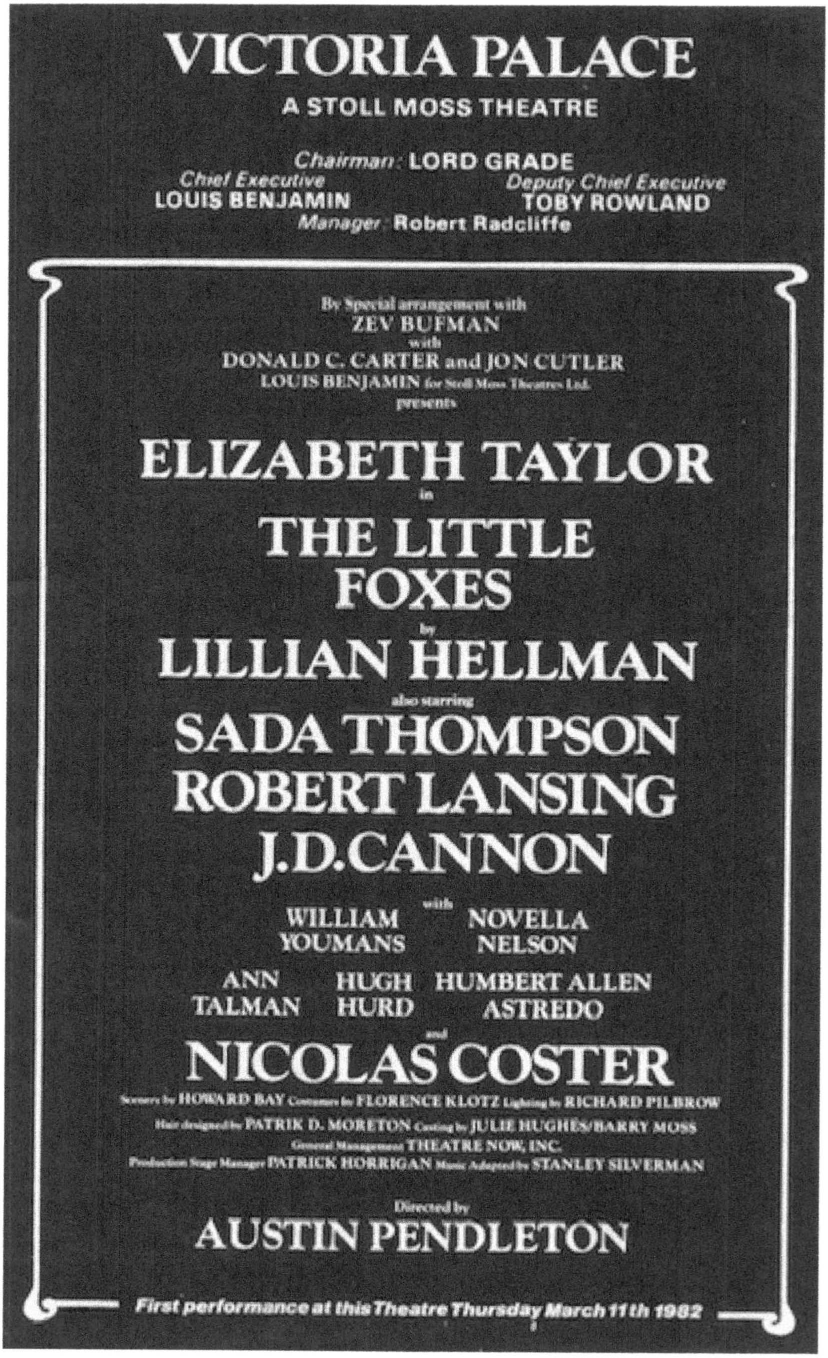

Poster from Little Foxes, 1982

CHAPTER 29

Anguilla Mon

In 1988, I visited everyone's dream of an island in the tropics. The Leeward Islands were one of the first island groups discovered in the Americas. The Spanish, Danes, pirates, French and eventually British captured the slender isle of Anguilla. It is now a British protectorate, but wonderfully independent.

George Milman, an attorney and a very bright and jovial buddy, was doing some business there and raved so much about the damn place, I got on a plane and went there with him.

Two tribes of bygone days partly remain in that area.

There are still strong strains of Arawak, the original settlers, thousands of years ago, and the Caribs, warriors and cannibals who invaded Anguilla and did more than a bit of damage satisfying their robust appetites. Not much remains of Amerindian culture or clear racial differences. Today the Anguillians are people of color, many shades, some light eyed, some not...a handsome island people. The Brits occupied the island until a peaceful revolution in the 70s.

I met the daughter of the "George Washington of Anguilla", one Roy Webster, who, it is said, led the revolution with a pitchfork in his hand while the British paratroops descended with their canopies exposed, as it were. Resolved peacefully, Roy was charged with something and his son in law, Scott Hauser, told me Roy hid out in "the bush" for years, until pardoned...the laughable "bush", being a flat island filled with low lying "bushes" and one hill...obviously, sympathetic islanders protected the elusive revolutionary during those years,

I wandered along all the beaches, which in 1988 were just beginning to be developed. The white sand softly gave between my toes on the mostly empty beach. The warmth of crystals of coral sand bordered by those light blue seas welcoming me...calling me...a gift and a curse. Little did I know of the expense and frustration to come.

West End, at yes, the Western tip of the island, was intriguing. A famous commercial director and then filmmaker named Bob Bean had built a superb house on the beach next to a private cove. Thai tiles adorned the roof, lovely gardens and pools made it a mixed cultural wonder. I visited with Bob, with whom I had done at least one television commercial during my New York career. From his terrace I could see the private cove with 2½ acres of land upon which somebody had started constructing a hotel which had gone belly up along the way, leaving strange concrete partly finished walls and a WW-2 bunker-like feeling. It stood there waiting for some really sharp, young guy to come along to rescue it from this ghastly sleep and build a dream house. Just in the middle of the cove was a large rock of coral, standing some 50 feet high, underneath, and alongside of which frolicked hundreds of fish...

"Shadow Rock" became the name of my home in the Islands.

The land title was still held by an Englishman who was a nasty chap...we'll leave it at that. To be charitable, perhaps the inevitability of his trajectory of going broke, approaching old age and just being another Englishman wandering the islands was a prospect unappealing.

I managed to acquire the land and structure, such as it was, for around 400 thousand US Dollars. The largest piece of land on the coast ever acquired by a foreigner. The most charming touch still remaining, was a gazebo out on the point of the cove. A gazebo done in British Colonial style, which stood ready to be companioned by an extraordinary house!

I envisioned a one story many bedroomed house in the style of the Spanish haciendas of my youth, with every bedroom opening out onto a veranda facing the sea. The house stood on a cliff. One walked down a stairway to the cove and out to the gazebo. I had planned another house for guests, a pool, and a tennis court. The government liked the idea, for when I was not there the idea was to rent it to the wealthy as did my next-door neighbor. His going price, even in the early 90s, was for a rumored 25k a week! The government got a room tax for rentals, so this would be a cash cow indeed.

I engaged a well-known British-cum-Anguillian engineer to help me design and construct my island hacienda. All went well at first. I shipped, he built. Time and money were absorbed by the project.

At one point, the wife of that same Brit engineer questioned, as had apparently others of the white-Brit clique, my being so friendly with the native Anguillians. I replied, "It's their country."

Yes, I was friendly - whites, blacks, whites married to blacks, Anguillians, all. I was invited by the very good tile man to his house. He climbed a tree and brought down fresh coconuts, they cooked fish outdoors. I was their guest, including the formidable, super friendly Jackie Ripple, who owns a wonderful restaurant and who is also very active in helping victims of the recent terrible hurricane.

Another, a sculptor, sold me at very little cost, a beautiful sculpture of a cormorant, a bird with a long neck and extended beak which was carved out of a solid piece of driftwood. My only remaining palpable memory of Anguilla, that cormorant stands majestic on the bridge of my boat in Marina Del Rey, California.

Strangely, a large bird, which I've been told is not a cormorant but perhaps a heron, a cousin with an equally long neck, comes to my boat dock late at night... My wife Elena and I live on a boat. I talk to the heron in some strange bird-like tongue. The bird stays for a bit and then, on huge wings, it flies off into the night...but not before leaving his calling card, a pile of white dung on the dock...Yes, I am the only one on the dock to whom he leaves this greeting...Each morning I hose off the remains of my nocturnal visitor's nautical dinner. Postscript as of this editing, my talky, squawkie companion has flown off to God knows where. He was a bit old, a bit tattered, I do hope peace was found.

By 1993 the house was finally almost complete. I'd had a frightful row about the paint job of the interior which was many shades of cream to beige and smartly done, but not what I had ordered. I wanted simple cream, as that was all the budget I had left.

The job was fantastically expensive.

I brought my daughters to the opening of Shadow Rock. My youngest, Dinneen, touched something in the bathroom of the new house, engineered by this shall be nameless arrogant Brit and was promptly ELECTROCUTED! Yup, had to take her to the island clinic. She was shocked, but not burnt seriously.

Dinneen, unlike the rest of us, stayed on, having met the gorgeous son of an Israeli-cum Anguillian, who had the best wine cellar from which I have ever tasted. I tasted, not the whole cellar, but some awfully redolent and tasty ones. One bottle of pre-WW-2 promised, an ancient 1937 Lafitte, was a disappointment, it was thick and I have yet to decide what it tasted like.

Shortly thereafter, prophetically, I chose to sell my paradisiacal home as my then wife Beth could not see the sense of flying 12 hours from Southern California to the Caribbean, and, more importantly, our losing my primary source of income, my last soap opera for years and years, *As The World Turns*.

I had been re-hired on ATWT. After playing Eileen (Lisa) Fulton's 2nd husband 30 years before that. Eileen was most gracious and seemed to enjoy gettin' together after decades. This time I was Eduardo Grimaldi, Maltese by nationality, entrepreneur by nature, lover by temperament (ha!). I ended up playing opposite the great Brit actress, Claire Bloom...Yeah, Claire Bloom on an American soap! She was wonderful and we became friends; two stage actors acting our asses off, and she with far broader roles in film than I, hit it off immediately.

I must say that the sensitive directors on that show keenly assisted in our efforts to make magic. One stagehand, after observing an intimate scene I had just finished with Claire, said, "Man, it's like watching a real good movie" I think dear Claire went off to the Greek Islands after that....her Anguilla.

That lasted until 1993. I had promised the local government that a large guest house and pool would be constructed, but with the loss of hundreds of thousands in income, I put it up for sale. It sold quickly to a billionaire who made nails or something. I never met him. He seemed very nice on the telephone. He even bought the 19th Century French armoire I had shipped from California along with the genuine planters chairs I had found in South LA. After the sale, neither broker nor bankers told me that I would lose the difference in Eastern Caribbean dollar exchange and U.S. Dollars. I was paid in dollars, but by the time it went through Anguillian banks, it was diminished considerably. This on top of other losses.

I cried into my beer and left my beloved Anguilla.

One week later, the meanest hurricane in years swept over, actually staying over Anguilla for days. The destruction was enormous. I felt sad for the guy who had bought Shadow Rock. Gone was the roof and the hurricane shutters, and then, knowing that I had sold the place, mysterious raiders in the night made off with all the fittings and furnishings.

Years, many years later, my oldest daughter, the always generous Candace, offered to take me there. She, adoring it, had actually been many times since. I said, "Sure, why not". She said, "You're not going to get all morose, are you?" I said, "Nah, that was then." And so, it was.

We went. We stayed at some elegant hotel on the beach which had not been there when I had almost called Anguilla my home. I went to visit Bob Bean, my former neighbor. He, as usual, was most welcoming, as if fifteen years had not passed. I did ask, as I glanced at the high wall now separating the two properties, "What's the ol' place worth these days?" "You don't wanna know", was his reply. "Aw, come on" says I. "Well, he did put a million-dollar hurricane roof on it after that storm, and several more buildings." He faltered. "You really wanna know?" "Yup," glancing at Candace, I said, "I won't get all morose" I laughed, Candace laughed, he said, "It's on the market for 45 million dollars...U.S."

Did I cough or cliché-like spit take my drink out in astonishment? Nah, not I, for of course, "That was then!"

There are nights when finances press on my brain, prohibiting sleep, or the bulkheads groaning in my not so big boat seem confining, or a chill wind penetrates the glass and wood barriers on that boat, that I think of Anguilla, its turquoise waters and pink sand and I do ponder the lilting reggae-like rhythms of "Coulda, woulda, should; coulda, would, shoulda; coulda, woulda, shoulda…"

Lots of Fun in Paradise
Photo by George Milman

CHAPTER 30

Russia, Belarus, ahh, the Borders

I met, got to know and some years ago married a Russian gal, Elena Borodulina, whom I met on Facebook. She had watched *Santa Barbara* as a teenager. An unlikely match but so far, she has put up with her ancient husband. She is a proud, very giving, intelligent woman. We've made trips "back home" and have had marvelous times visiting with her childhood friends at their modest "dacha" a few hours outside of Moscow. Last year, we tracked farther and visited Belarus together. An easy, pleasant drive to the border ended our visit there or so I thought.

The highway IN was unguarded at the Belorussian border. In going back there was a slight difference...they had a border check but NO passport control! They had never seen the necessity as Russians could freely travel from one country to the other. But an American! Ah, ha! Nobody seemed anti-American, just curious, and insistent that we follow the law, in this case to go through a passport control station.

Slight catch...there was no passport control station within 500 kilometers! My dear host without a blink of his humorous eyes, said in his excellent English, "OK buddy, we drive!" Now I was embarrassed...Should I have checked before coming and found out that a visa was necessary for a foreigner - other than Russian - to cross into Belarus? Yes, I bloody well should have.

With multiple well-meant apologies spewing from my mouth we set out on a peculiar and circuitous trip to the passport control center near the Russian town of Veselovka, to the border stop called "Three Sisters" because it borders three countries, Ukraine, Russia and Belarus. My whimsy took over as we stopped. I had done the play *The Three Sisters*, at the Guthrie Theatre in Minneapolis the opening season. I wondered to my host, always the humorist, if any in this area yearned to go to Moscow as had all the sisters in the Chekhovian play.

***

The insect was frustrated. On the screen window of the police station, he or she was climbing repeatedly up to the top of an opening, which, being a screen, was in fact not really open, and then the insect would drop to the bottom of the frame again and again. The screen allowed the air and light to penetrate the little box of an office, but not provide freedom. He (for this story we'll make him a guy) could feel the clean air of Belarus beyond and through the screen, but it was unavailable to him...How, how, could it be felt on the underbelly of the wasp...the teardrop belly of the wasp, but not allowing the freedom to buzz away into the nearby green woods? Vlad, I called him, occasionally confronted another insect on the same futile journey, but there was no battle. The enormity in comparison of the large, long wasp was too much for the still logical smaller insect trapped on that same screen, both limited by the same intelligence, which kept each transfixed by the fresh flow of air and the seductive light filtering through.

And so, they kept up their separate but energy draining struggle... Freedom, oh, freedom, where are you? You are offered me by all signs in my vocabulary but oh, that last, unexplained barrier...How do you say screen in Insect Belorussian?

I wondered that as I sat there in the Belarus border police station. I watched Vlad and his struggles well into the second hour while the guard typed my confession, the endless page upon page of legalese about how I had failed to obtain a visa to cross the border from Russia, where I had been staying, to Belarus where I had gone to visit...

Easy, my host in Belarus had driven us, his Russian wife, Elena, my Russian wife, and me, across to Belarus in an American GMC SUV! On a slick wide highway, we sped with no border stop...GOING to Belarus. Coming back, my host, Sergei, who had never driven a foreigner across the border, much less an American, was most surprised and embarrassed with all the fuss that ensued upon our return.

So, two innocent Belorussians, my Russian wife and their American actor guest headed back to Russia after an extremely pleasant weekend in the county, real country...Lake swimming in a public lake for free, for the people! No charge, even for parking...a small resort with log cabins one can rent cheaply for the day, paddle boats...all for the people...Do I sound like a Socialist? Ha! Perhaps a little. Certainly appreciative.

His dacha had been built by himself, his uncle and others. It was simple and straightforward; good, two storied, clean construction with indoor bathrooms and plenty of room for guests. Many surrounding dachas were quaint log houses, built decades ago, their natural wood sides darkened to a stained brown with age. Some reminded me more of Caribbean cottages, with bright blue, yellow trim, or green, red, and again yellow...lots of color. Our host's ancestors came from Belarus....He took me to an abandoned mansion, a huge country house which was built in 1840 or so. The great house upon the hill sat reflecting its former glory; scarred walls and empty windows shorn of their fancy sills and frames by long ago scavengers. The house had been turned into a school...for decades after the Bolsheviks took over...Then, since independence from Russia, it has been abandoned. The estimate to restore, around 500 thousand U.S. dollars.

One hopes the lace, silk and velvet clad teenagers of THAT household had not been executed by the revengeful ex-serfs and downtrodden.

The good guy, Sergey, entertained us at his version of a barbecue, shashlik as it's called...lots of fish and chicken in a backyard concoction which looks like a 19th century steam engine boiler on its side, with a tall smoke stack...a bit of a joke as the smoke bellows out the open front, ignoring the slim stack. It was inspired by an English boiler drawing and a clever uncle had built it, using the furnace and welding tools at the plant in which he worked.

Sergey's wife, Katia, was thoughtful beyond expectation. Their kids who stayed with Grandmama for the summer - blonde little girls 4 and 7. The 4-year-old, vastly curious and equally humorous, a born entertainer...the 7-year-old, a budding gymnast, practiced constantly on a set of parallel bars in the backyard. She had golden, silken ringlets which cascaded almost to her shoulders; a wry, sometimes wistful smile which along with her curiosity, was most entrancing.

Lastly or firstly, came Alexander, their 16-year-old son. His mother kindly warned me that he was extremely shy, to the point he would probably retire from view.

Ah ha! A challenge to the aging American.

I have already written about my exploits on the oceans with our disabled buddies under the banner of *Challenges Foundation*. Well, Alexander was no challenge. Upon meeting he gave a warm and patient smile as I struggled with a limited greeting in Russian. He responded in much better English than my Russian.

We played football, shot a pellet rifle, about which I, from my army experience, was able to give him a few tips about marksmanship. He responded with growing affection...at weekends end, we were in fact buddies. Perhaps he will come someday to visit, depending on the visa restrictions, of course. Always the visa restrictions. In Russia it's a crime to speak against authority. I speak nothing of Russian politics while there. I explain I am a guest in their country and would prefer not to be rude. I do say that as an American patriot, I believe in the United States Constitution and all its guarantees. Freedom of speech, the press and assembly...and I leave it at that.

The border patrol that day had not ever even SEEN an American at that crossing...So I was sitting in the office of the police at the Belarus border....I hadn't even arrived 30 meters down the road at the Russian border guards yet. The insect and I had gotten to know each other. His energy seemed undaunted. My mind wandered...I thought of the brave Russians during the Great Patriotic War...persisting against impossible odds. But their challenge was not a screen keeping them by limited intelligence from simply turning around and flying out the open door. No, the brave Soviet troops, which at that time included Belarus, struggled against the Nazi invaders. I wondered what confidence the Germans must have had. In the summer of 1941, when Hitler betrayed the Russians and invaded their homeland, it was a well-trained, well-armed, well clothed, confident army who had just crushed almost all of Europe and left the British army in tatters at Dunkirk.

We were to visit a site the next day where the partisans held out against the invaders for years. In the deep, thick forests of pine and what we call birch trees, they constructed underground caves, hideouts which are now superbly reconstructed in the forests replete with beds made of small branches upon which they slept in temperatures which reached 35 below fahrenheit. This was all not far from the border where I had languished. It was not really boring to me, not really to the insect. He never gave up on his quest for freedom.

Ahhh, Kafka!

The border police were uniformly polite...formal, but polite. There was even a young woman who attempted to suppress a nice wide smile...the repression was unsuccessful when she realized I had been on the number one TV show in Russia during the time when she was a child, *Santa Barbara*!

There I was, my imagination running wild as to my fate...It started like a 50s movie: "Stop! Your papers please!" and then the hours of questioning about my reasons for breaking the law. There were a couple of huge differences, though, from the 50s movie I imagined: 1. The guards were not huge apes with stern Slavic jaws from Hollywood casting or squat, nasty commissars with iron spectacles. 2. They, in fact, were all young and quite attractive. The commander, the guy with the big star on his epaulettes, looked a lot like Michel Fassbender!

All did not change drastically with the new found realization that I had been "Lionel" on *Santa Barbara*...The formal insistence on protocol was followed. Perhaps their hands were left a little more relaxed and further from their pistols with the gained knowledge of this famous Yankee being on their parent's favorite show.

There wasn't, I should add, even a tinge of corruption evident, as in the sly suggestion that if I paid the fine there, it would be less. NO! I was instructed to send, by mail, the small fine. When all was finished, I did get a really pleasant sendoff, replete with selfies taken on cell phones of the visiting Americansky TV guy.

The Russian border guards were a little more casual...my passport tattered by wearing it sometimes in wet clothes from the beach and that sort of thing was scrutinized...the Chief Russian border officer was convinced for a while that it had been tampered with...but gradually relaxed. Did *Santa Barbara* have anything to do with it? I'll never know.

Did Vlad the wasp, ever make it off the screen to freedom? Or perhaps some earnest policeman fearing a fierce stinging, simply swatted him to the ground with a casual swing of my completed confession....I dunno. Perhaps Kafka would have been amused if not entranced.

Athens, not Greece

The University of Georgia. How did a guy with no degree from an academic institution spend 14 years there as first an Adjunct Professor, afterwards and now as Visiting Lecturer?

Beth's mother, a Southern gentile girl from Athens Georgia, married a handsome army captain at the end of World War Two. He was a dentist and Jewish. She converted and even long after his death she remained a faithful member of the Children of Israel congregation in Athens. While visiting this glamorous lady, not THAT much older than I, she suggested I take a look at the University of Georgia just down the way.

The 18th Century Franklin College which became UGA, is a mix of stately antebellum homes which became fraternity/sorority houses and modern buildings from the Dean Rusk School of Journalism and so on. It also holds the Fine Arts building, a restored colonial brick structure in which lies the busy and productive Department of Theatre and Film Studies.

I wandered up the steps and as I did so, a young Professor approached and asked when talked to, whether I would like to meet the Head of the Department, Stanley Longman PHD. "Of course!" I went into Stanley's office and thus began a marvelous friendship that continues to this day.

My first encounter with students, faculty, and villagers, was my appearance onstage as Krapp in Samuel Beckett's *Krapp's Last Tape*, a one man show wherein he plays the tapes he has made of his life and great love. I loved it. It went well. As of this writing, I plan to drag that 1950's tape recorder out of storage and do a Covid safe video of the play and quell the curious who wonder if I might in my antiquity be too forgetful...Hmm, what was I talking about? (sorry, obvious follow-up joke)

Stanley eventually retired and the young professor who introduced us, David Saltz, PHD, became the Department Head. David, as well as being a director of enormous skill, acquired, with his team, a one-million-dollar

National Science Grant for the UGA Theatre Department! It was, I understand, for their work on stop-motion animation. Being a computer dummy, I am unable to understand fully the techniques involved in that area. I was, however, welcomed into that class to speak on movies - large budget and small - and other things that might interest these oh-so-fascinating students. For that and other classes, Dr. Saltz has put up with me ever since!

I come, usually once a year for a week at a time. Up to 9 classes a week! I love it, all of it. I augment the teaching of the Sanford Meisner and Lee Strasberg "Method" techniques, meaning I try not to interfere in the instructor's teachings but add flavor and of course stories and some exercises which might be educational. I actually studied with those long-gone teachers and so it lends a certain validity to those tidbits. All the professors have made me feel most welcome.

One of my favorite classes run by the excellent Professor George Contini, is "Queer Theatre" Yes! Actually, called that. I'm sure that having a gay son trying to be accepted as an actor has something to do with my interest in such a class. As long as I can remember, gay men with noticeably feminine mannerisms, lesbians with the corresponding masculine traits, were often made to feel helpless in realizing acting ambitions. George helps correct those misconceptions held by the actor. I believe I contributed a bit when that class first started.

I asked one young man what exactly he felt was the problem. He laughed and waved a limp wrist...the cliche sign of "gayness". I said, "Ok, let's talk about 'character', as in acting a character. You are now an African hunter with a spear in hand. An antelope is ahead, running across your path. Throw the spear and hit the antelope behind the shoulder! Do it!" He did it - in mime. "Now you're a quarterback. Throw the football and hit the tight end as he crosses in front of you...Do it!" He did. "That's character," I said.

Finding character is like a detective story. Investigation - in these cases of a hunter or an athlete's life - led to behavioral traits. Conversely, if it is to be an introverted intellectual, one must find the reasons for that needed emotional seclusion, the REASONS for that introversion; Family influences? Other environmental influences? Just an unexplained need since early childhood? When you can honestly feel those influences and behave like YOU in THAT situation, you've done your homework.

A class I introduced was "Auditions". When asking grad students including PHD candidates, what they were going to do after leaving UGA, almost all who were not going straight into education said, "audition!" I then asked casually, "Wanna show me how you audition?"

Several showed me how they came upon on stage, introduced themselves and proceeded to recite a classical or modern piece. Many, before reciting cleared their throat, "prepared" and proceeded to recite the material.

I usually start these individual sessions with the instruction...Prepare OFFSTAGE...hold that preparation like a drinking fountain with a ping pong ball floating lightly on top at low volume, then enter the stage not playing the character but holding, as it were, the ping pong ball floating ever so lightly in your inner being; introduce yourself, and then without hesitation, turn up the "prepared" water in the fountain so that the ball rests on a true geyser! and deliver your recitation without pause; you are in fact THERE without an obvious transition from you to character.

Another technique explored is the tendency, when doing a monologue, of not really having us believe the person (to whom you're addressing) is believably THERE. The actor has some vision of that person, but very often one can tell if it is an intellectual partial-reality, not really a full blown imaginative, almost palpable character.

I do an exercise which is basically an improvisation wherein I, sitting in the audience, ask questions during the monologue, forcing the actor to listen to his/her imagined partner. Then we go back to doing it without those questions and replies. I ask the actor to remember, to SEE that other person, pause to listen and even smell. This approach explored, usually helps the actor create a different kind of reality,

I could go on, but won't. Perhaps an acting book next? Possibly not. As long as I have something to share, and there are those fresh, vibrant students who take the time and have the interest to be there, I shall climb on a plane and then drive through verdant fields and piney woods to that citadel of learning, the University of Georgia. Meanwhile not a day goes by without cherishing the experiences and stimulus I receive from having "Georgia on my mind".

And, so, farewell for now: A longer memoir? Perhaps...on another afternoon. I have enjoyed and sometimes felt wistful and quite emotional in jotting down these memories. Is anything revealed that might be of worth? I dearly hope so. I do hope as well that some of the tales have entertained. To return to events which might and often have proven to be regretful, is I suppose, an essence of any kind of truth telling. I have enjoyed scraping the cobwebs away, putting fragments together, the telling of stories.

All these tales told are true...fiction is for another day.

My Boating Life

EMERALD STAR: A rebuilt Huckins 63 footer
(lived on this one for years as well)

EMERALD on her first trial after total refit

NIGHT MOVES: an original 50 foot Cigarette boat (My conceit I could not resist: 60 miles an hour, but much too much gasoline! My sensible wife at the time appealed to me to sell it (alas) and I got something slower...and diesel)

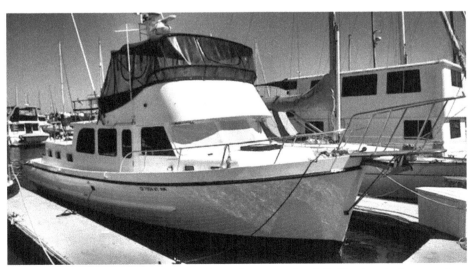

1968 rebuilt custom trawler, 47 footer by Jones-Goodell (lived on it for years)

30 foot Newport on which we took our first female wounded Veterans

EMERALD: Our most ambitious restoration, devoted to sailing wounded Veterans;
1924 William Pratt designed

*BAGARRE: The first boat I rebuilt for disabled scuba divers;
a gorgeous 1947 Huckins 50*

*OUTRAGEOUS: The largest, most expensive restoration I ever completed; a 65-foot
steel Burger*

Our latest restoration, a Uniflite 42 footer

Elena touching up our present home, a restored 1988 Bayliner 38 footer

*From soldier to sailor! My other career as a
Merchant Navy "Captain" (w/ Elena).*

With thanks to all who helped: Leading with the guidance and a startling amount of perceptive work from my editor and pal Eddie Aronoff, Producer, Writer, Teacher; without whom this memoir would still be an unrecorded series of nearly forgotten thoughts. I give much thanks to my wife, Elena for among other gifts, introducing me to Mother Russia, and to my two daughters, Dinneen and Candace, who, with their spirit, kept me enthused. And to my many, many friends and colleagues who contributed, I shall in time thank all personally.

CPSIA information can be obtained
at www.ICGtesting.com
Printed in the USA
LVHW040157260723
753507LV00020B/106/J